Grading the Teacher:
Memories from a few former students

"When I was in high school, I always felt like an outcast. Prom night was the best night of my high school career. The next school day, Marianne Love made a comment to the whole class about me and the 'dapper-looking young man' I was with at prom. For that moment, she set me above the rest. That is the memory I take with me for the rest of my life – the one day in high school that the ugly duckling was a princess, if only for a moment. I have Mrs. Love to thank for that and will always remember how she touched my life, how she made me feel special."

–Kathy (Wilhelm) Sauer, SHS Class of 1989
Sandpoint-area receiving clerk

"I had Miss Brown (later Mrs. Love) for first-period English during her first year of teaching. She didn't seem much older than I. I liked the class. I wasn't intimidated by her, but we also did not take advantage of her inexperience because of our respect for her."

–Mike Rogers, SHS Class of 1972
Sandpoint building contractor

"I used to walk into first-period English right before the bell rang because I spent every last minute in the halls chatting with my friends. Being in her last year of teaching, Mrs. Love remained extremely calm and collected when it came to telling me to zip it. I had a mild case of 'Chatty Katie,' as she used to say. One extremely vivid memory that I still smile about from junior English starts with Fritz Gibson. Our class was playing hangman on a Friday. It was Fritz's turn to go to the board. He jumped out of his seat and hurdled Mrs. Love's desk. We all expected her to be upset, but she calmly asked him to choose a letter so the next person could go. After a brief silence, the whole class burst into laughter."

–Katrina Rogers, SHS Class of 2003
University of Idaho interior design major and
daughter of Mike Rogers, quoted above

"I have fond memories of three-ring binder band and the 'word of the day.' Molly O'Toole and I had to go to the front of the class to demonstrate 'demure.' What would be more torturous than to make two of the shyest people in class go through this? Well, it was great. I started crawling out of my shell because of this woman. Mrs. Love was the model I used to form my own confidence and enthusiasm – because she oozes these qualities."

–Amy (Gunter) Jahn, SHS Class of 1992
Owner of graphic design/advertising studio in Sandpoint

Lessons with Love

Tales of teaching and learning in a small-town high school

Marianne Love

Introducing William Love

KEOKEE COMPANY PUBLISHING
Incorporated

Sandpoint, Idaho

Keokee Co. Publishing, Inc.
P.O. Box 722
Sandpoint, Idaho 83864
www.keokeebooks.com

Cover painting by Cheryl Klein, Sandpoint High School Athletic/Activities director

Editing by Mary Brown, retired adjunct English professor, DuPont, Washington

First printing 2007
Printed in the United States of America

Publisher's Cataloging-in-Publication Data

Love, Marianne, 1947-
Lessons with love: tales of teaching and learning in a small-town high school /
by Marianne Love.
            p.   cm.
ISBN 978-1-879628-28-1
            1. Love, Marianne. 2. Teachers—personal narratives. 3. Sandpoint High
School—anecdotes.
I. Title.
373'.1092–dc21   2007

Also by Marianne Love
Pocket Girdles
Postcards from Potato(e)Land

To my two most favorite students ever: Willie and Annie,
>   for your patience and understanding when Mom always had school on her mind.

To my husband, Bill,
>   for your quiet but steady support.

To Jenny, a former student who has taught me and many others so much about living,
>   for your inspirational courage.

To all teachers,
>   for the universal classroom mission and the miracles you help inspire.

To all my students,
>   for enriching my life, helping me learn and providing me endless memories and smiles.

Contents

Foreword

      By former student Colin Moody .... *ix*

Introduction: Teacher Prep .... *xiii*

Chapter 1. Ponderettes and Pie – Not a Good Mix 1

Chapter 2. The Tuba Solo: A Class Night Meltdown 21

Chapter 3. Furniture Farm: The Tony Bottarini Story 33

Chapter 4. Stay Outa My House 53

Chapter 5. Get My Drift? 71

Chapter 6. Emmel's May Day Smiles 81

Chapter 7. Angela's Antics 97

Chapter 8. Labor of Love: A Teacher's Maternal Challenge

      By "Mom" Love 111

Chapter 9. Confessions of a Reborn Student

      By William Love 135

Chapter 10. You Are Now What You Were Then 147

Chapter 11. Stupid Teacher Tricks 157

Chapter 12. Hair Hut: Marianne's Fountain of Youth 171

Chapter 13. A Debt Owed 181

Chapter 14. Semester from Hell: A Learning Experience 189

Chapter 15. Ya Mean *She* Taught the Pope!!! 211

Chapter 16. Love's Top 10 Teaching Memories 225

Chapter 17. Epilogue 255

Foreword

By Colin Moody
One of Marianne Love's 4,500 students

A bout a month ago, "The Voice" interrupted my workday reverie. Not *a* voice – *The* Voice. "God, is that you?" I queried. No response. Ears buzzing, I listened intently from my office cubicle. There it was again – that distinctive, timbral voice. Then, in a flash of insight, I identified The Voice; I smiled, then panicked.

I smiled because The Voice was the incomparable Marianne Love; I panicked because hearing The Voice reminded me I had procrastinated on a writing assignment – namely, this foreword.

While not divine herself, in more than 30 years of teaching, Marianne succeeded at putting the fear of God in her English and journalism students at Sandpoint High School; at the same time, she demonstrated genuine interest in every student. I was privileged to be one of those students.

Being one of Marianne's students is a lifelong event: once a student, always a student. Granted, I no longer sit in one of 30 cheap desks with pastel plastic seats and graffiti cut into every surface. But every time I run into Marianne in the grocery store, get a friendly e-mail, or receive a phone call from her on my birthday, it's clear I'm still her student. And I'm not the only one – hundreds of students could share similar stories of Marianne's ongoing interest in them.

My first encounter with Marianne Love let me know right away that she was no ordinary teacher. It was September 6, 1988. A 15-year-old with Stan Smith tennis shoes, bleached jeans and spiked hair, I was pretty sure I was all that. So on the first day of fifth-period sophomore honors English, I sauntered into Marianne's classroom without fear or expectation. I couldn't have guessed it then, but my classmates and I were about to get "The Treatment."

On that day in 1988, our other teachers had smiled and chatted as we entered their rooms for the first time. But in Mrs. Love's domain (Room 4, conveniently near the bathroom), things were different. Marianne sat silent and motionless behind a desk covered with photos of former students, a knowing look – somewhat amused, somewhat stern – etched on her face.

The bell rang, but since we didn't hear any instructions from up front, we continued to chatter away. Then, after a few minutes, we suffered a startling recognition: *Mrs. Love was watching us.*

We fell silent as Marianne scanned the room, looking up and down the rows of desks, pausing just long enough on each person to be unnerving. With the chutzpah of youth, I resolved to stare right back, but when her gaze arrived at my desk I withered and quickly looked down at the smudged floor tiles.

For a full five minutes – which felt more like 50 – Marianne scrutinized the class. Then I heard The Voice for the first time. "All right," she intoned with authority, "this is sophomore honors English." So began my friendship with Marianne Love.

I learned and wrote more that year in sophomore English than I had in all my life. We read Shakespeare, diagrammed sentences, researched ancient Rome, memorized Greek word roots and wrote essays from the ground up. Marianne's was a tough and fun class.

Honors English wasn't just about English, however. Marianne committed every one of our birthdays to memory, and led the class in raucous renditions of "Happy Birthday." She bantered with us to engage us in the day's activities; she asked us how our weekends had been; and she seemed to know about all the activities of every student.

One class with Marianne was great, and I knew another class would be even better. It took some wrangling, but two years after that sophomore class, I had the good fortune again to be one of Marianne's students.

I was slated to be editor of the high school newspaper, the *Cedar Post*, and I knew Marianne, a former *Cedar Post* editor herself, was perfect for the job of adviser. So, the retiring adviser and I twisted her arm until she finally relented and took the reins.

Marianne brought her characteristic optimism and magic touch to the journalism program and our group of ragtag writers. She encouraged us, cajoled us, convinced us that we were good and called us to do even better. She edited our stories faithfully: If they were good, she would let us know; if they weren't, they would come back covered in blue-ink suggestions.

Characteristically, Marianne made sure we knew that life isn't all business. Over the course of the year, she hosted our entire newspaper staff at her house for dinner, offered comfort after a punk picked a fight with me in the hall, and joined the staff in laughing at the reactions of passersby to a strategically placed pile of imitation dog poop in the hall. It was a great year.

I'm no education expert, but it seems to me that Marianne's teaching career spans a seismic shift in education. At the beginning of her career, teachers were expected to be schoolmarms who wielded rulers as brutal instruments of discipline; by the end, teachers were more likely to be touchy-feely peaceniks who cared more about "feelings" than creating environments conducive to learning.

Marianne had the incredible knack of bringing the best of these worlds together. Her unwavering demand for excellence in herself and her students was perfectly paired with her care and concern for each person she taught.

On my mantelpiece, I have a fairly innocuous talisman – a Steno-brand reporter's notebook. Marianne gave it to me my junior year, inscribing it, "To Colin: Congratulations, *Cedar Post* editor. From Marianne Love, former *Cedar Post* editor." That's classic Marianne – thoughtful, practical, fun.

The book you hold in your hands is an extension of the incredible teaching career of Marianne Love. Over the years, Marianne has influenced thousands of students. Now, with this book, she has the opportunity to influence thousands more.

So stop the chatter! Eyes up front. You'll get The Treatment, but you'll survive. Just listen for The Voice – it's time for *Lessons with Love*.

Introduction: Teacher Prep

Almost every morning for nearly two years, I followed my older brothers out of the house, climbed atop a big wooden post at the end of our driveway and sat, watching, wishing and waiting. Each day as they would climb aboard the North Boyer school bus, I would yearn for the day when I'd be old enough to go up those metal steps myself, find my own shiny vinyl seat, and go to school.

Morning after morning, I imagined what it would be like sitting next to other neighborhood kids as we rode down Boyer Avenue from our farm just outside the city limits of Sandpoint, Idaho, to Lincoln Elementary School two miles away. The partially filled bus would stop several times after our house, to pick up the Bests, the Gunters, the Samuelsons, the Brooks, the Pursleys and the Barnharts before reaching Lincoln, where the younger kids would get off and run toward the two-story, red-and-gray brick schoolhouse across the street from Balch Lumber Company's sawmill. A few of the remaining students would wait to get off at Farmin Elementary in downtown, while the older kids stayed aboard until the bus reached the junior high or the brand-new high school on South Division.

My big day finally came. After breakfast, my mother first helped me button my print dress, adorned with frilly white ruffles. Then, one by one, she removed the skinny white rags from my auburn hair that she had so carefully set to enhance my natural curl. Having taken extra time to primp her firstborn daughter and making sure that Mike's and Kevin's new shirts were properly tucked into their corduroy pants, Mother beamed with pride as she handed us our lunch boxes, with peanut butter and jelly sandwiches and chocolate chip cookies wrapped in waxed paper. Then, she stood on the porch and watched us walk out the door.

I began the first leg of my 49-year educational journey with Mrs. Mabel Kinney and her red fingernails on that September day in 1953. Those pointy, polished nails not only impressed me on that first day of school, but they kept my classmates and me in line from that day forth. Mrs. Kinney knew the most effective pressure points on little kids' frames, and her well-groomed, razor-sharp nails could inspire immediate respect. We learned quickly not to invite a visit to our desk from Mrs. Kinney and her nails. Some of my classmates also learned not to wet their pants.

Besides getting acquainted with school-behavior boundaries, I learned my ABCs. I also learned to read from the "Dick and Jane" books. With my clumsy left hand, I practiced penmanship on wide pieces of paper with blue, solid lines and blue, hyphenated lines that guided the size of our letters. We wrote with yellow, No. 2 pencils. As Mrs. Kinney sat in the front of the room with flash cards, we did math drills. I'm sure we did our share of finger painting too.

I got in trouble after school one day with Mrs. Kinney. While waiting for our school bus, David Harney and I were playing at the blackboard with chalk and erasers. David took an eraser and put chalk dust on his nose. I laughed and laughed at his funny, pale-yellow nose. David also laughed. Hearing my giggling, Mrs. Kinney came into the room and spanked me.

"Don't you ever do that again!" she warned. The humiliation of what I deemed unfair punishment followed me through the rest of my education and into my own teaching career. In fact, that distant scene of after-school injustice still remains vivid in my mind. At the time, except for those intimidating fingernails, Mrs. Kinney's harsh discipline style was no different from most other teachers. Corporal punishment was expected. Yet, in spite of that painful experience, even at that early time in my life, I entertained thoughts of someday becoming a teacher.

My grade school years were spent with Mrs. Kinney and the other elderly, women teachers, who kept their authoritarian thumbs on us while filling our minds with knowledge. This occurred at a time when our sleepy, little town on the shores of Lake Pend Oreille, tucked between Washington and Montana, was little known, except maybe to relatives of the farmers and loggers who had settled in Sandpoint and the surrounding area during the first half of the 20th century.

Lumber and cedar-pole businesses reigned supreme in the region at the time. There was also a healthy agricultural industry, supported by the hundreds of small dairies and beef farms. The Farm-to-Market Road was east of town, and a livestock auction yard sat in the middle of a residential zone on the west side of town. A few blocks north, next to the pole yard, stood a thriving meat-packing plant. My mother and I often rode our horses from our farm to Jack's Lockers in northern Sandpoint to collect a few packages of frozen meat, and we took cream from our milk cow to the local creamery.

On First Avenue, Merwin's Hardware, Del's Family Shoe Store, Ben Franklin's, Chapman's Food Market, the Sandpoint and Bi Rite Drugs, Jennestad's and Larson's Clothing stores, and J.C. Penney's brought locals to town for regular, weekend shopping. During these visits, folks might grab a hamburger or hot dog at the Sandpoint Café or Pastime. A motel or two housed the occasional tourists who passed through town during the three months from Memorial Day to Labor Day. Most of these visitors crossed the yellow "Long Wagon" Bridge across Lake Pend Oreille en route to Canada or Montana, but their numbers quickly dwindled as soon as Sandpoint went into its winter hibernation.

Another newer bridge, with a cement base rather than those boards that went "clickedy-clack, clickedy-clack, clickedy-clack" as cars passed over them, replaced this structure in 1956. Still, Sandpoint remained fairly quiet and isolated as I eventually moved on from grade school to Sandpoint Junior High as a seventh-grader. The firm grasp of those Lincoln School teachers – all female except for our token male, Mr. Scheibe – loosened a bit during our next level of education. We now met six teachers a day – in my case, half men, half women.

Junior high also meant a step forward in independence for us 12-year-olds. We no longer had to loop our y's and g's, as in the Palmer method that our previous teachers had dictated, and if we wanted to write our cursive "backhand," we could. We could also leave campus and cross Pine Street to purchase nickel-and-dime candies, and pop or ice cream bars at the Whatnot Shop.

In spite of these liberties, our school staff still maintained near absolute control over our lives. All students, teachers and parents knew that Charlie Stidwell, our no-nonsense, much-loved principal, kept and used a paddle in his office. He closely inspected skirt length for girls and watched closely for low-hanging, beltless slacks on the boys. Every morning we listened to Mrs. Keiski, the secretary, read a Bible verse over the intercom. No one objected to that practice or to the discipline, although one day, in seventh-grade English, we all cringed when our teacher, Mrs. Weaver, broke a plastic ruler on Billy Freudenthal's head for some infraction of her classroom rules.

Teachers and parents collaborated in the supervision of the kids who had filtered into junior high from the town and country schools. We could count on teachers always letting our folks know if we weren't toeing the mark. I remember only one unforgettable exception to that policy, which occurred when some other seventh-grade choir students and I removed hundreds of nuts and bolts from the seats in our third-floor auditorium. This vandalism occurred during a slack period between our choir concerts. While we were supposedly studying and allowing Mrs. Meehan time to prepare for the next concert, several of us spent the hour on the floor doing our dirty work with the nuts and bolts. Unfortunately, Mrs. Meehan caught us one day when someone giggled too loudly.

Instead of telling our parents, Charlie Stidwell spent an intensive five minutes chastising us as Mrs. Meehan stared, horrified at the huge pile of nuts and bolts returned by scared seventh-grade girls, and sat waiting for a janitor to reinsert them into the metal chair housing. Face red and jawbones pulsating, Charlie informed us that we would each perform a good deed for the school, or we would be blacklisted from Honor Society. Since most of us were destined for the honor society, we wasted no time completing our good deeds and having them approved by the principal. Fortunately for us, our parents never heard from Charlie about our act of vandalism.

The outside world still remained distant to us, most of whom had rarely traveled anywhere beyond Spokane, the "big city" 75 miles west across the Washington border. I remember listening awestruck, to Bobbie Brown, a college student, tell us about her experiences in Europe. Mrs.

Parker, the much-loved high school teacher, accompanied Bobbie to the meeting as Bobbie stirred up our minds with visions of emulating her someday. That was a far-fetched dream at the time, for most of us were blue-collar kids, while Bobbie's father, Jim Brown, was the wealthy owner of one of the region's largest lumber companies. The Browns and the McFarlands, owners of a large pole company, were among the few that we had ever heard of going so far away.

Our traveling realities were limited to the annual spring honor society trip to Natatorium Park in Spokane or the choir contest in Coeur d'Alene, 40 miles away. Each person paid a dollar, brought a sack lunch and 50 cents for spending money and rode the well-chaperoned school bus. By junior high I had also become a full-fledged 4-H'er. That organization expanded my horizons to Moscow, home of the University of Idaho, which got me thinking about going to college. In our family, as in many others, there was no "if" used in discussions of our going to college, but "how?" presented the major challenge for a kid whose father earned a modest salary as a water filter operator for the City of Sandpoint. I would also be the third of the six children in our family to head off to a university. Fortunately, college was then still a long way off.

During junior high years, I was still considering becoming a teacher. Little did I realize it at the time, but I was storing away ideas of the qualities that made me respect my teachers. Handsome, young Jack Bloxom, fresh from college and beginning his first year, set a model for discipline that impressed me and even made me behave. His firm, kind, no-nonsense approach from day one, coupled with his enthusiasm for history, won respect for a man who would eventually coach winning college baseball teams, year after year after year. We still considered some teachers old meanies, but, for the most part, they were positive role models and gave us reasons to consider the education profession.

When I was a ninth-grader in 1961-62, anxious to head off to high school, a monumental event occurred that would open the doors to our small town. After a trip by snowcat to the top of a mountain northwest of Sandpoint, some enterprising businessmen agreed that it looked perfect for a ski hill. Within months, the town was abuzz with the news that we would, indeed, have such a ski area by the time the snow fell the following winter. As the road leading to the ski area was constructed, Sam Wormington came down from Kimberly, British Columbia, to manage the resort. Bobbie Brown's dad had a lot to do financially with the development of what became Schweitzer Ski Basin, just 11 miles from downtown Sandpoint. Other businessmen from North Idaho and the Spokane area shared in the vision, and families like ours even contributed by purchasing $10 shares of stock in the new resort.

Our little town would never be the same again. Gradually over the next few years, our quiet neighborhood, which had seldom seen an out-of-state car, suddenly became accustomed to brisk winter traffic, morning and night, as skiers from Canada and the Pacific Northwest wasted no time getting on and off the new ski mountain via North Boyer. Schweitzer became a popular winter playground, and its success planted the seed for more changes to our North Idaho community in the next few years. People were recognizing the area's recreational potential.

Meanwhile, I moved on to high school. Except for the eighth-graders, who had joined our numbers from Southside and Northside Elementary schools, we could almost count on one hand the new students from outside Sandpoint who joined our ranks through the high school years. I loved high school and this close-knit student body. I joined every club possible, went to games, yelled the loudest at pep assemblies and even earned the title of "Best School Spirit" my senior year. High school activities offered us a better opportunity to get to know some of our teachers on a more personal level. I was thrilled to have Mrs. Parker, who had been chosen as one of the nation's top 10 teachers by *Look* Magazine. Despite my talkative nature, some of my instructors still intimidated me with either a well-placed frown or a sharply worded comment. The day that Marian Ruyle sarcastically asked me if I wanted to teach the Latin class, I definitely shut up.

That was not the case in all our classes, however. My mouth ran so steadily in some classes that my cohorts started monitoring how many times the teachers who were poor disciplinarians asked me to be quiet. We were good kids normally, but we could smell the weak souls among the teaching ranks. The weaklings paid. In fact, we drove two teachers out of the classroom: one my sophomore year, another when we were seniors. One was an elderly woman who had come from a private school; we sophomore English students provided her first and last public school experience. The other, a 30-something man, made it almost through a year as our senior government teacher. His total ignorance at how to run a classroom eventually did him in, after the principal heard one-too-many times how the inmates were running the prison in Room 2. The impish, sometimes-rebellious adolescent in me delighted in helping torment these people, but I was also disgusted that our education was being shortchanged by their ineptitude.

Certainly, *I could do a better job*, I thought. My confidence in that belief had been bolstered by the numerous teaching and speaking situations that 4-H had provided. Whether it was organizing a demonstration or working as a junior leader with younger kids, I enjoyed the creativity and the challenge of keeping an audience. Furthermore, I had always enjoyed interacting with people and knew that whatever I did in life, my love for people would always play a significant role.

During high school, I kept a critical eye on the methods skillful teachers used to keep an easily distracted mind like mine on task. When instructors showed a genuine interest in me as a person, they earned my loyalty. When classroom limits were clearly defined and maintained, I respected them. When teachers knew their material and could convey a clear passion for what they had to offer, I paid attention. When I could see value in what I was learning, I appreciated my teachers. I liked being in their classes. In fact, I admired most of my teachers very much. A few, however, stood out because of their extra efforts in guiding me toward the path I would follow in my own career.

Mary Parker's dedication to English and the vocation of teaching, in general, inspired me. I fought hard at the beginning of my senior year to get into Mrs. Parker's class after learning it was not on my schedule. When informed that both of her "accelerated" classes conflicted with my yearbook and newspaper classes, I opted for one of her regular classes. Even though she gave me extra materials, I knew I was missing out on significant information offered in the advanced classes, but I didn't care. The person in front of the room always made all the difference for me, and I was prepared to exhaust all methods to have Mrs. Parker.

My efforts were rewarded many times over, simply by the caring example she set as an English teacher and as a Future Teachers of America adviser. We spent many hours in her house, making candy Christmas wreaths for fundraisers to finance our way to FTA state conventions. Mrs. Parker knew my family and knew that we had not experienced an easy start because of our alcoholic father, whom my mother had divorced when we were younger. She took the time during my brief encounters at her desk to inspire me about my future. After having her as a teacher, I knew exactly whom I aspired to emulate. *If I can be half the teacher Mary Parker is, I'll be happy,* I would tell myself.

In Bob Hamilton's case, journalism has permanently connected us as mentor and student. His impact in my life has remained so powerful that when my son became a journalist and started winning awards for his writing, Bob always topped my list of folks to tell. He pointed me down another path that fit nicely into my goal to be an educator. He singled me out, during my junior year, to tell me I had talent as a writer. Until that time, although an above-average student, I had been stumbling despite my intense desire to achieve something notable. I tried to draw like my artistic mother but never could complete anything beyond a hen scratch. My ever-patient 4-H leader, Eleanor Delamarter, tried to teach me to sew but to no avail. I had enrolled in seventh-grade choir because of my love for music, but I was tone deaf and couldn't carry a tune, especially when anyone dared harmonize in my midst. I lasted one week on the trumpet after the instructor told me my lips were better suited to a clarinet. Since my mother didn't want two clarinets in the house, and my older brother already had one, my band career went by the wayside. I almost flunked P.E. in the ninth grade because I couldn't stand on my hands and, later, because my poorly developed hand-eye coordination wouldn't permit me to hit the birdie over a badminton net.

So, the day when Mr. Hamilton passionately told me he wanted me to go to the spring journalism convention in Moscow, I responded excitedly, only then to tell him that I didn't have the money. He said he would supply the money, if necessary, and then explained why he wanted me to go. I have never forgotten hearing him assess my writing talent. I went home, told my mother, and she said they would *find* the money to send me to the convention. Later, Mr. Hamilton further bolstered my self-esteem by announcing that I would be the editor of the student paper my senior year. This man had bestowed on me the opportunity to prove myself, and because of my admiration for him coupled with his competitive spirit for journalistic excellence, I vowed not to let him down.

During my senior year, I sat in classes with five different teachers and worked one hour in the office as a counselor's aide to Paul Croy. My teachers ranged from the most inspiring to the worst I had encountered during my 12 years of education. While instrumental in driving one instructor away before year's end, I worked my heart out for all the rest. After making the decision to attend the University of Idaho rather than travel 2,000 miles to my mother's alma mater in Michigan, I applied for scholarships. On Class Day in May, I went to the stage twice to accept two small awards of financial aid for college. A $125 scholarship came from the *Sandpoint News Bulletin* for journalism; the other $100 from the local Chamber of Commerce supported my desire to major in education.

Taking responsibility had always been a highly regarded staple on our family values roster, so I accepted the responsibility and set my mind to finding a way to satisfy both scholarship donors and did, despite a few bumps along my academic road. During my four years at the University of Idaho, I transferred from the College of Letters and Sciences to the College of Education. That's where I discovered an English major with a journalism emphasis. My history minor resulted from a lifelong interest and from another teacher who stands out in my experience. His name was Dr. Barnes, and he was tough. I almost failed history of civilization as a not-so-dedicated student during my freshman year. In spite of the D minus, I signed up for another class from Dr. Barnes, who still reigns as the most eloquent, most thought-provoking instructor I ever had. By the time I graduated, I had taken five of my history classes with Mr. Barnes.

His dynamic style served as another model for me to follow.

Another college professor taught me compassion. By the time I was a senior, Schweitzer Ski Basin was well on its way toward becoming a popular, destination winter resort. More and more skiers from throughout the West and Canada were purchasing season passes, which meant additional part-time jobs. I worked weekends selling tickets and taking pictures of season-pass holders. One weekend I decided to go home to Sandpoint a day early, so I would have some time to relax and to finish reading a novel for a literature test scheduled for the day I skipped. The guilt of skipping that test ruined my weekend. I dreaded going back to Moscow and facing the instructor, an older gentleman who had been around the campus forever. His name was Professor Banks. Throughout the semester I had sat like a sponge in the back corner, taking it all in but never volunteering a word. Needless to say, I had not established a rapport with Professor Banks. Monday morning came, and I went to class. Professor Banks handed back the bluebook essay tests to everyone but me. Immediately after class, I nervously asked if I could talk with him. He invited me to follow him to his office. I sat down and told him the truth about why I had skipped the test. During my confession, I mentioned my job at Schweitzer.

"How's the snow at Schweitzer?" he asked, after listening quietly to my story.

I was stunned, especially as he continued questioning me about the ski hill and Sandpoint. Finally, he returned to the subject at hand, asking if I had started reading the next novel on the class list. When I said no, adding that I hadn't purchased it yet, he pulled out two dollars from his pocket and told me to go buy the novel. He also set up a time for me to make up the test and never uttered a cross word about my skipping the test. He must have sensed that I had already suffered enough self-imposed punishment over the weekend to have learned my lesson. That incident would later guide me through similar situations, whenever my own students made stupid choices and appeared genuinely remorseful afterward.

By the time I finished the first semester of my senior year and went home to Sandpoint to student teach, new influences in the community were beginning to affect some of our students, not always in positive ways. The drug scene had found its way from the faraway cities to remote North Idaho. What's more, Sandpoint's location on a highway leading directly to Canada made it a hot spot for drug runners to and from larger cities.

During that quarter, I observed a few kids in my classes who manifested the glazed-over, spaced-out effects of marijuana use, but they were still the exception rather than the rule. That was fortunate. My student-teaching experience with Ragnar Benson gave me a boost far beyond what any drug could ever do. Because of my own bad choices, my academic successes in college had been slow to materialize. In fact, it took me two years to figure out that study habits, attending class and taking good notes were the keys to earning grades higher than a C. I made up for lost time during my final two years, but my self-esteem had taken a considerable hit after so many mediocre grade reports.

So, when I walked into Room 5 at Sandpoint High School, scared to death of what those seniors could do to me, I was pleasantly surprised. Mr. Benson spent the first couple of weeks giving me pointers and suggesting a couple of units for me to prepare, including the Shakespearean play "Macbeth." I watched how he worked and how he organized his class hour, and I observed how different kids reacted to classroom situations. Finally, one day I administered a spelling test to all five classes. It felt good. After observing me the first hour and offering a few tips on how the procedure could work more smoothly, Mr. Benson left me on my own for the rest of the day.

Almost instantly, a new feeling of confidence powered me toward my next appearance. That came a week later as I began the "Macbeth" unit. The first hour did not go so well. My normally deep voice cracked and took on a high-pitched screechy tone. Within minutes, my presentation ended. We still had 45 minutes left. Dumbfounded as to what to do next, I left the room and ran to the faculty room, seeking Mr. Benson's suggestions on how to fill up the remainder of the class hour. He just chuckled and told me I would have to figure that out for myself. My students loved it. We got to know each other that day.

It didn't take me long to learn about timing and to learn that much more time is needed to go into preparation in order to fill up time in class. In spite of that initial glitch, and after realizing that I could also polish up my down-home style a bit, the nine weeks with those seniors flew by. They also proved to be some of the greatest esteem-builders of my life, convincing me that I was meant to be a teacher. The hours spent with those kids seemed like pure magic. The satisfaction of knowing that my efforts – unpolished as they were back then – had had a positive effect on dozens of high school students transcended any feeling of success I had ever experienced to that point in my life.

Mr. Benson was also proud. Day after day, he showered me with praise, assuring me that I was a natural. The word spread around the staff. Soon, someone suggested that I consider applying for Ruby Phelps' position, as she would be retiring in the spring. Mrs. Phelps taught sophomore English and advised the yearbook. Since I had just completed a course called "Supervising High School Publications, " this idea seemed like a perfect fit, not only for me but for the principal, Richard Sodorff, who had known me as a high school student and liked what he was hearing about my teaching abilities. The possibility of teaching in Sandpoint excited me. I had considered going across the border into Washington, partially because I could earn more money there but mainly because I never thought I would be lucky enough to land a job in my hometown.

I loved my hometown and endured a lot of pooh-poohing from classmates who wondered why anyone would ever want to stay in Sandpoint. Admittedly, at the time, it may not have appeared to be a cultural mecca that it's considered to be these days, but its beauty, with that huge lake and those mountains, its wholesome sense of community, its endless outdoor opportunities, and its caring, friendly people had long satisfied me. I often used to joke that I could be Sandpoint's walking Chamber of Commerce, because I loved the town so deeply and wanted everyone else to know what a special place it was. At that time, many of my contemporaries didn't exactly see it that way. *That's their problem*, I thought, wasting no time talking to the Superintendent Jack Jones and jumping through the necessary hoops to secure the teaching job. Fortunately, that process didn't involve much more than a friendly handshake from our assistant superintendent, Mike Lamanna.

So, when I graduated from the University of Idaho in May 1969, knowing that I had a high school teaching job in the fall, I thought my own educational journey had ended, at least for a while. I walked into my alma mater, set up shop in Room 4, hoping to make my mark by blending qualities I had observed exemplary teachers without whose influence I could never have progressed that far. I still hadn't developed a decent set of fingernails, though.

By the first week in September, after getting acquainted with my own sophomore English students, observing the obvious tension among the ranks of a hand-picked group of senior girls on the yearbook staff, and taking on the added job of a total novice advising the Ponderettes Drill Team, I realized my education was just beginning. I still had a lot to learn, definitely a truth that's pretty hard to comprehend when you're know-it-all, recent college graduate.

During the next 33 years, as our Sandpoint community gradually emerged from its cocoon, so did I. When I started teaching at my alma mater, the back-to-the-land free spirits were already moving in, especially from California. A real estate boom in the mid-1970s brought hundreds more transplants of varying interests and talents, looking for their 10 acres of heaven in the country or seeking to escape whatever urban woes had driven them from their former communities. The student population began to change, and for a time, the drug scene escalated, creating some challenging times in the classroom. Drug problems came in waves during my career. I never dealt with them well, but, with experience, I did learn to cope.

During those decades, our school population not only doubled from 600 to more than 1,200, but it also gradually developed numerous cliques – quite a contrast from the town-kid, country-kid makeup that I had known while growing up. Our North Idaho populace was mostly white with very few minority students. That inequity in racial diversity even caused us some bad national press for a number of years, when White

Supremacists centered many of their well-publicized activities in the Idaho Panhandle. Nonetheless, we began to develop a rich diversity of thought and style in our high school, with jocks, goody-two-shoes, the dirts or ropers, the Goths, the heavy-metals, the stoners, the nerds, the Jesus freaks, the scholars, the average kids, etc. In many cases, the clashes among these extremes fomented conflicts and even out-and-out fights in the halls or at school events. Masochistic as it may seem, I welcomed this diversity, as it presented an ideal setting to teach understanding of the oft-repeated expectation of common respect. Occasionally, in tough circumstances, I learned through my students to open my own mind and contemplate views far different from my own.

As I reflect on my career, I relish those years of hometown opportunity for my own awakening, as I got to know and, yes, sometimes even fear, my 4,500 students, each of whom contributed his or her unique ingredients to my current perspective on life. For example, whenever Russell Faux, who sat in my third-period, sophomore honors English class in 1969-70, raised his hand with a question, I cringed. He was brilliant. I was not. To my mind, back then, not knowing an answer was tantamount to sitting at the stocks waiting for the next barrage of rotten tomatoes. I wonder if Russell experienced a similar feeling when he faced his own first group of students at an Eastern private school. Almost 25 years later, when Matt Ginzton appeared in my honors class, I recognized a marked change in myself. Instead of fearing his supreme intelligence, I embraced it. When I started a graphic arts program with Macintosh computers that spring, I summoned Matt, who eventually earned his bachelor's and master's degrees in computer science from Stanford University. I happily encouraged him to help me teach my students the inner workings of computers and computer programs. I didn't know all the answers and even felt comfort in knowing that I didn't know. I figured, why not take advantage of this walking computer encyclopedia, even if he was a mere high school student?

The experiences of kids from the early 1970s in once-provincial Sandpoint differed in many ways from those of kids in the early 2000s who attended high school in the same small town. Sandpoint has been recognized for its eclectic cultural appeal by numerous national trendsetting media and by *Sunset Magazine* as the "West's Best Small Town." Thanks to my hometown's gradual emergence and to my classroom experiences, I've learned many lessons about teaching and about myself. One of those general lessons was present every time that I stepped into a classroom. My students' backgrounds, intelligence levels, beliefs, appearance, sophistication or lack thereof, mattered little as long as the classroom climate offered a few timeless basics. It doesn't matter whether the classroom is in a storage room at a run-down, older school or in a plush classroom teeming with technology. If the climate promotes civility, high expectations for individual learning efforts, integrity, spontaneity, flexibility, creativity, and, most importantly, healthy and frequent doses of mutually shared laughter in that room, the sky's the limit. Anything can happen. It did for me during a career that spanned blackboards to white boards and mimeograph machines to PCs, as I continually learned and taught my own lessons to gifted, average, struggling and difficult students. And, best yet, I did it all without ever needing bright, red fingernails.

Now that I'm retired, with time to reflect upon my career, I have no regrets. Having remained in Sandpoint, I can still enjoy the fruits of my labors almost every day. I don't have a lot of money, but my riches come in priceless nuggets nearly every time I go to the store, stroll the streets or attend a community event. Each hello, wave or visit from former students reminds me that I chose a noble profession that reaps everlasting value. Colin Moody, who was kind enough to write the Foreword to this book, is gifted with talent, intelligence and enough dynamic personality to succeed anywhere. Yet, Colin, a Rhodes Scholar finalist from Seattle Pacific University, chose to return to his hometown where he serves the young people of Sandpoint as a beloved coach, teacher and youth minister. His decision represents the ultimate reward that any teacher could ever experience. It also reinforces my belief that an educator's influence is both powerful and limitless. In short, my own teaching career represents a rich tapestry of lasting, personal memories – funny, serious, sad, crazy, incredible, sometimes disgusting, occasionally poignant but, most of all, satisfying.

Let me share some of those times with you through these stories in *Lessons with Love.*

1.

Ponderettes and Pies – Not a Good Mix

Seven years had passed since I had trudged daily up those three sets of stairs to the third floor of the majestic, old, red-and-white brick building on Euclid Avenue in Sandpoint. Opening one of the double doors and peeking inside, I could see that, once again, I had arrived early. Grabbing a chair at one of many wooden tables in the Sandpoint Junior High library, I sat down. It was an early September day in 1969 – my first as a Bonner County School District No. 82 employee.

While waiting for the new-teachers' orientation to begin, my thoughts drifted back to the time I had spent in this room full of books, where school librarian Mrs. Esther Weaver ruled the premises and kept hordes of wiggly teenyboppers under control during study hall hours. Six periods a day, four students sat in their assigned seats at opposite corners of each table, pretending to be eager young scholars, digesting knowledge from the texts before them. Not always had this ideal been the case, especially where I was concerned. Quite regularly, as a matter of fact, two of my seventh-grade classmates and I had found distractions in the form of an eighth-grader who sat at our table. Seems this girl had habit of picking her nose, and it seemed as if first-period study hall provided the perfect opportunity to harvest her daily crop – and eat it. Sitting there every day unavoidably aware of the busy index finger constantly digging deep within the nostril was not our idea of an appetizing way to begin our day. Furthermore, yelling out in Mrs. Weaver's pin-drop-silent classroom to "Stop that!" was not an option in those days.

Ten years later, I sat there chuckling over the time when we, in our 12-year-old callousness, thought we had finally found the perfect way to send the nose-picker a clear message to quit her disgusting habit. Before school, the group leader, who shall remain anonymous, had prepared a single Kleenex before school with a message scrawled in blue ink.

"This is a Kleenex. It is to be used for BLOWING the nose so that you do not need to PICK the nose," the note read. "Please use it!" Before class, we gathered at the table, unnoticed by Mrs. Weaver, where one member of the Anti-Nose-Picking Squad placed the message on the table where the offender sat. Nothing subtle about us. We headed out to the hallway, for our ploy was to avoid suspicion by planning our entrance back in to the room to occur *after* the offender had sat down at the study table. Arriving at our respective spots, we could see the Kleenex cradled in her hands. She was reading the note. We feigned innocent curiosity. As we sat down, she wadded up the tissue, walked to the wastebasket and returned to the table. By hour's end she had resumed her daily picking routine. Sadly, our plot had failed.

On this September day, that experience and many other junior high acts of mischief had me deep in thought, when suddenly, I felt a hand on my shoulder. Turning around, I looked into the blue eyes of my former high school principal and new boss, Dick Sodorff. Suddenly, I was fast forwarding from a time of carefree, youthful irresponsibility to a time that required adult sophistication and mature behavior. I was beginning my career as an English teacher at Sandpoint High School. I had signed on that spring after a successful student-teaching stint in Mr. Ragnar Benson's senior English classes. The experience had gone relatively problem-free, except for the day I had had to leave the room for a short time and announced, "I don't want to see anyone talking when I return."

The seniors took me at my word. Someone may have talked, but I couldn't see them because the entire class had turned their desks around to face the opposite wall. Forty years later, many of those students, now in their 50s, still beam while recounting their innocent prank. Aside from that, Mr. Benson had adequately oriented me. He sat through a few early classes to offer some pointers and then for nine weeks left me alone in the classroom to succeed or fail. I thrived on the atmosphere of not having to worry about someone peering over my shoulder at every move and my rookie mistakes. Instead of intimidating me as a micromanaging mentor would have, he let me flounder when I needed to figure out my own solutions. He always remained available, however, when I felt the need to seek advice. The student-teaching experience turned out to be a positive for all concerned. Mr. Benson got a break from the classroom. The students, including a married mother named Mrs. Becker, enjoyed some fun with their friendly, greenhorn college student, and I discovered, once and for all, that I was, indeed, cut out to be a teacher. It felt both natural and exhilarating to stand in front of a class and actually see kids genuinely enjoying what I had to offer. I felt completely at home.

This experience provided a much-needed boost to my wounded self-confidence after my college years, which had begun dismally and had ended with a feeling of genuine uncertainty about my ability to succeed.

Toward the end of my student-teaching experience, Mr. Sodorff called me into his office and told me that a senior staff member, Ruby Phelps, would be retiring in the spring. She taught sophomore English and advised the *Monticola* yearbook. Since my college major included journalism and advising high school publications, the position was a perfect fit for me.

"If you want the job, you can have it," he said. All I needed to do was to go down to the Central Office, meet Mike Lamanna, the assistant superintendent, and formalize my upcoming employment with the district. The best part of this whole chain of events was that I had bypassed the resume, letter-of-application process completely. My one-on-one interview consisted of walking into Lamanna's office on Main and Second in downtown Sandpoint, introducing myself, and telling him that Dick Sodorff had sent me. He said "Hello," pulled out the paperwork, gave me a pen and showed me where to sign on the dotted lines. It was official. I had a job.

"How would you like a new job?" Dick asked on that September day a few months later as my thoughts switched from nose-picking to a reminder of why I was sitting in my old study hall.

"Huh?" I groaned. "Don't I already have a job?"

"Well, yes, you do," he answered. "This is an additional assignment." My first lesson in "administrative dumping on the rookies" began.

"Whaddya mean?" I asked.

"Well, we need a drill team adviser, and we think you'd be perfect," he explained.

Dick Sodorff must have been either blind or desperate that day. I knew he had gone to San Francisco a while before that time to have eye surgery, but his vision couldn't be *that* bad. He had to have noticed that I had an ample body. My ample body could never hope to fit in even the largest of one of those petite white dresses that served as the Ponderettes' uniforms.

What kind of example could I be to all those skinny little things? I thought. To make matters worse, I had almost flunked the only physical education class that could even remotely prepare me for this job. While enrolled in folk dancing at the University of Idaho, my instructor had summoned me to stay after class the day we practiced the Greek dance known as the "Miserlu." Waiting patiently for every other student in the class to leave the gym, she finally glared at me through her dark-rimmed glasses and asked, "Are you really trying?"

"Well, yeah," I said, as an all-too-familiar feeling of embarrassment and humiliation overcame me. "It's just that ever since I was a little girl, I've never been coordinated. My head and my feet just don't do well together."

Obviously doubting my sincerity and acting as if my success in folk dancing could be a life-altering experience, the P.E. teacher instructed me to go back to my dorm and spend as much time as possible practicing in front of the mirror. If only this woman had seen me earn my white ribbons for substandard modeling at the Bonner County Fair Style Review, she would understand. At this moment, though, I knew better than to bring up that story.

"I'll do my best," I said, dutifully, before rushing out of the gym. I did practice when nobody was looking, but God must have had grace and beauty on back order when I came along. It just wasn't in the cards for me to satisfy this woman. Fortunately, half our grade was based on the written test. The lady couldn't give me an F, if I tried really hard. The effort worked; I received a P (pass) for folk dancing and, with great relief, I thought that phase of life would never come back to haunt me.

Well, we all learn throughout our lives – painfully so – never to say or think "never." As Dick Sodorff stood over me, I had a decision to make. If that situation were a card game, I would say he was holding a royal flush, while I, a lowly, brand-new teacher who still viewed my former principal as a keeper of my conscience, couldn't even muster up a joker to improve my hand. Without much further thought, I threw in the cards.

"Sure, that sounds like fun, but you've gotta know, I've had absolutely no experience at anything like that," I said. "Have you ever seen me dance?"

"Oh, you'll figure it out," he reassured me. "And you'll get $200 extra a year as an adviser."

Well, who could turn down a generous offer like that? After all, adding that bonus to my $5,700 salary was going to make me rich, by my standards in those days.

A few minutes later, Dick went on his way, satisfied that one more vital vacancy at Sandpoint High School had been filled. The new-teacher orientation began. My thoughts drifted again to the moments spent at these tables back in the seventh grade. Once again, my personal tables were turning. I wasn't sure at the moment, but I can say confidently now that I was about to serve my penance.

For the next nine years, I advised the Sandpoint High School Ponderettes, which had been a well-established drill team up until the year before I came along. If anyone had worse credentials for guiding this group, it must have been my predecessor, who lasted just one year. During my student-teaching tenure, I had heard numerous stories about her "inefficient" classroom methods, one of which involved students having a contest to see how many could sneak into her class, unlike the usual practice of sneaking out. In this constant quest to "remain" in Miss X's class, one senior, who had not exactly endeared himself to her, showed up in class one day with his blanket and pillow. He set up shop in the back of the classroom and proceeded to take a nap. Miss X wouldn't have it.

"All right, I've had enough of you," she said, pointing toward the door. "Get out of here."

He refused.

She mustered up enough bravery to give it one more try.

"Take your blanket and pillow and leave," she demanded. He stormed out of the room, leaving his pillow and blanket behind. The class was amazed at how easily he had succumbed to the wishes of the weak teacher.

Their amazement was short-lived, however. A few minutes later, the door flew open, and he reappeared with his face and neck dripping with liquid. In his hand, he held a book of matches.

All eyes watched as the teacher stood paralyzed, staring at the sight.

He held up the book of matches.

"All right!" he shouted, pointing at his face. "This is gasoline! If you don't let me stay in here, I'm going to light a match and burn to death right here in front of you."

Having no idea, the "gasoline" was really water, she obediently relented as he went back to his corner and his blanket. Apparently, she was the poster child for naivete, and she generally remained oblivious to any student manipulation. She definitely had book smarts but seemed to be missing all the other survival skills that help teachers succeed with high school kids. As a result, during her tenure, the Ponderettes were marching to whatever beat happened to be the most dominant on any given day. So, when I walked in that fall, introduced myself, and told the marching squad I would be working with them, it wasn't long before I was aware of some uphill challenges – not only learning about how drill teams functioned but also mastering some tough refereeing skills.

My steep learning curve involved a series of stunning discoveries – for me anyway. Those first few months with the Ponderettes required quick and necessary adjustments to my management skills. In fact, molding this group of young ladies into a well-disciplined unit capable of dazzling audiences of doting parents, supportive classmates or even cynical students from visiting schools during halftime shows proved to be one of the major challenges of my teaching career. My initiation into this teenage mindset, totally different from anything I'd ever known, was fraught with daily traumas. At first, I was amazed at how trivial matters often incited all-out yelling matches between feuding factions among the squad. As a person who had generally gotten along in just about any setting, I found myself in the uncomfortable position of stepping in, sometimes physically separating drill team members about to engage in an old-fashioned catfight.

Actually, that first year is a fog to me now, but I do remember a lot of yelling. I also remember a lot of character building, not only for me but also within the ranks. I did live through it, and I came out with new insights on how to create an atmosphere where in-fighting became more the exception than the rule. Meanwhile, I faked my way through knowing anything about the technical aspects of what the marchers were doing. My comfort zone lay in serving as advocate for the group, whenever the band instructor put up a fuss about the music or whenever I performed as a friendly mother hen in the locker room by happily helping out girls as they primped, adjusted accessories or practiced for the big halftime show. I also took great pride in building up their confidence with inspiring words before performances and handing out hugs when some of them, having missed a beat or two or three, returned to the locker room in tears.

The usual Ponderette reminder, "smile" served as the appropriate antidote when all else failed. It took time, but I eventually gained some knowledge about what worked and what didn't in coordinating music with marching. With help from supportive parents, I even gained a sense for creating costumes that fit whatever piece the Ponderettes had chosen for a performance. We learned the hard way one year that we probably would not choose ever again to use green Glad Bags for any further Christmas drills. The design included holes cut out for heads and arms and edges accented with red tape. The resulting performance, to "Jingle Bell Rock," was so disastrous, that its ugly review appeared in a controversial and much-publicized underground newspaper, along with the painful suggestion that the adviser, a "cow," should be led out to pasture.

That was one time when I seriously questioned my decision to follow a career in education. Dismal as the event was, it did have its silver lining. After much consternation, I chose to stay with the Ponderettes. We turned around the catastrophe, and all of us held our heads up high while producing much-improved performances for the rest of the year. After learning that some folks thought of me as a "cow," I even embarked on the mother of all diets, which dramatically changed my life for the better. Happily, a majority of the underground paper's staff members and I eventually became the best of friends; in fact, some even helped me with some later projects associated with drill team. Some of those friendships still exist today.

On another occasion, I watched as a group of young women experienced almost unbearable public embarrassment during a drill-gone-bad, only to knuckle down, unify for a common goal, and go on to wow crowded gymnasiums on several occasions and thousands of spectators at two major parades in the region. In this particular performance, the captains had chosen the popular disco piece "The Hustle" as their song. With no band music available, they used a tape recorder as the sound system for their creative routine. Big mistake. Ghetto blasters had not yet been perfected in the mid-'70s. That fact did not become apparent, however, until the large crowd sat in the bleachers, waiting for the performance to begin – the button was pushed and – *no sound!*

Well, if people had happened to be standing right next to the recorder, maybe they could have heard it, but not the Ponderettes. Crowd noise drowned out any hopes of the marchers hearing even a faint note. As I stood on the side opposite the tape recorder, I sensed that a good time was not going to be had by all, especially by the 28 nervous performers, standing in the gym wearing their T-shirts, shorts and baseball cap ensembles and holding plastic baseball bats for snappy hand motions. Thirty seconds seemed like hours as they stood there waiting, waiting, waiting to hear the music. The tape recorder technician, having cranked up the machine to the highest level, shrugged her shoulders and looked at Sue, the captain, with a helpless expression, indicating that volume was at its max. Sue's only option was to blow her whistle and get it over with. If this drill tested how well the girls had memorized their counts, they failed. Straight lines immediately disintegrated into ripples. Smiles faded quickly as the marchers floundered in limp lines around the gym, trying in vain to follow a beat that didn't exist. I stood watching – helpless – knowing dark times lurked ahead in the girls' locker room. The performance continued to sour, as frantic faces told the story of a domino effect that gradually determined the drill's destiny. One line off course meant the next segment would turn disastrous. While watching, I listened to another comment from directly in front of me that would resonate in my memory forever. I was standing behind some male students from the visiting school who were taking in every misdirected move.

"Golly, they're even shittier than our drill team," one kid, wearing a letter jacket, said to his buddy.

"Sure are," his friend agreed. I slowly eased backward toward a temporary escape route, taking me directly to the locker room.

Might as well face the music when they come flying in here to hide, I thought. There sure hadn't been any music out there in the gym, and my ability to think on my own feet wasn't doing so well at that moment either. What does one say to a group of girls who have just met with such public humiliation? A second later, the door flew open. Plastic baseball bats bounced off the floor, and torrents of tears cascaded down nearly every face as the girls charged through the door.

"You did your best," I lamely reassured them. "You stayed out there and finished it, despite the circumstances. You can all hold your heads up high." However, they weren't buying my sugarcoating, and, more than likely, they sensed that I really didn't believe what I was saying.

"Yeah, sure. We were awful. I don't ever want to face anyone," someone blurted, between sobs. "We're the laughingstock ... "

The moment demanded leadership. Both Sue and Marla, the co-captain, stuck with me, chiming in with their best possible spin on the catastrophe. Fortunately, both seniors, in their friendly but businesslike demeanors, had always earned great respect from their fellow Ponderettes. Our voices must have been convincing because, eventually, the last few demoralized marchers composed themselves and bravely hustled out the door, down the hallway and into the night – more than likely ready to cry themselves to sleep. We three stood there, looking at each other, shaking our heads and agreeing that we faced a monumental challenge: to convince the group to perform again. Then, the moment of supreme hypocrisy occurred, as we slinked out a side door, ran down the school hallway, and sneaked out a seldom-used door, so we would not have to face anyone sitting in the audience. Later, we agreed to go our separate ways, dig deep within our reserves and come up with a plan.

One of the many "longest weekends of my life" followed. Most working folks like long weekends, but in the teaching profession when disaster occurs on Friday, having all weekend to stew over the situation doesn't make for rest and relaxation. In those cases, Monday can't come soon enough for the teacher to attempt to fix the problem and move on with life. Nonetheless, Monday did eventually come, and at our morning drill team meeting, we all united toward a common goal. The plan was simple. The captains had come up with a catchy piece of music. We asked each individual to set a personal goal of putting forth additional effort to learn the drill and learn it well. We encouraged them to work harder than ever and to reclaim quickly the drill team's positive image by proudly performing the best drill of the year. Two weeks later, marching to "The Magnificent Seven," the Ponderettes proudly cast off the albatross of the "Hustle" disaster and continued on a course that once again made the word "smile" come naturally. They learned one of the monumental lessons of life: *From our lowest moments can spring our greatest triumphs.*

From that day forth, the Ponderettes and I shared many smiles, and as time went on, fewer and fewer tears. By the mid '70s, the group worked almost year-round, preparing for three- to five-minute halftime shows and eventually taking on the additional adventure of marching in regional parades. To do this, we not only had to work hard on rehearsing for performances, but we also had to engage in another perennial activity that comes with teaching: fundraisers. We launched our share of raffles and bake sales. Local businesses also donated money to sponsor individual members, and each girl paid dues to belong to the organization. One time we even sold Rex, a multipurpose cleaner, but soon washed our hands of that project, when the cost of the bottles going home with each member exceeded the amount that came in.

We also made a lot of money each spring by sponsoring the annual Drill Team Variety Show. The event consumed our lives during the month of March, as we scheduled auditions that were followed by several rehearsals, often lasting nearly until midnight, leading up to a two- or three-night run of shows. Heretofore anonymous students often found themselves elevated into instant school-wide stardom with performances ranging from Tom Evans miming the local 10 o'clock curfew siren to Mike Kohanek explosively break dancing, a souvenir of his California past.

One year, shortly after we had announced auditions, one of my fifth-period English students, Connie Stutzke, came up to my desk.

"I'd like to sign up for the Variety Show," she said.

"What are you going to do?" I asked.

"Sing," she answered. A notion of what it was going to be like suffering along with this quiet, shy soul haunted me for two days, for she certainly would get up to do her gig and freeze with stage fright.

She has no clue what she's getting into, I thought, *but I guess she'll have to find out.* I privately prayed that she would chicken out and save herself the pain of self-destructing before her peers. When audition night rolled around, there stood Connie, along with a horde of other hopefuls. One by one, they ascended to the stage, performed their acts and then joined the audience to watch the rest of the contestants. Connie took the stage. My heart sank.

Here goes, I thought, grimacing and not wanting to watch.

As she began to sing an Ann Murray country classic, her beautiful, surprisingly seasoned voice kept the entire audience spellbound. Along with the voice came a sense of poise not often seen in a high school kid. I sat there, both relieved and awestruck. In that instant, I had picked up another lesson that would guide me through many more years of teaching.

LESSON: Students can have far more fascinating dimensions than those we ever see in the classroom.

Because she always sat quietly and attentively in my class, seldom saying a word, I had grossly underestimated this young lady. In our classrooms, we often see just one side of our students, and we often fall into the trap of thinking that what we see represents their whole being. Not true. Connie and a host of others over the years astounded both their peers and their teachers by exploding onto the scene with their talents, turning into instant idols. Prior to the variety show, most students simply passed these kids off as just more anonymous faces in the crowd. Afterward, their names became household words in Sandpoint.

Sometimes, sheer lack of talent stole the show.

Case in point: Dressed in hunting garb, toting a brown paper bag, Jim Hubbard, who had once blown me away with his eloquent oral book report about James Michener's *Hawaii*, walked on stage to demonstrate his original duck call. His strategy involved the K.I.S.S. theory (Keep It Simple Stupid). After discussing the science behind getting the ducks to come, he blew up the bag, held it in his hand and then shocked the audience with his unique approach.

"Here duck. Here duck," calmly coming from Jim Hubbard's lips didn't exactly lure any quackers into the auditorium, but it brought down the house.

One year, the Drill Team Variety Show satirized beauty contests with its "Miss Ellaneous" pageant. This feature allowed the girls to demonstrate that their skills transcended far beyond just rhythmic pizzazz. With the ultimate goal of determining "Miss Ellaneous," more than a dozen contestants from the Ponderettes took to the SHS stage and kept the audience off guard, especially during the talent phase of the pageant. "Miss Adventure" wore hiking boots and scaled an 8-foot metal stepladder, while "Miss Spell" deftly displayed how to crucify even the simplest of three-letter words. "Miss Shapen" was a crowd favorite, not only because of her less-than-ladylike approach to gorging herself on a large and messy bowl of spaghetti and meatballs, but also because of her enhanced sound effects (provided backstage by more-than-willing males) while gulping down each bite and occasionally belching in preparation for the next untidy mouthful. Meanwhile, "Miss Alignment" demonstrated a strange gait. "Miss Quito" probably stole the show, however, while gliding stealthily across the stage with her 3-foot-long, cone-shaped nose in search of a blood-sucking feast. "Miss Matched" needed a better wardrobe,

"Miss Behavior" refused to follow the rules, and "Miss Fortune" tried to bribe the judges.

The most stunning candidate of all, however, was "Miss Ing." Whenever she took the stage, nothing happened, and when Miss Ing's escort brought her down the aisle, he seemed a bit lonely. In spite of her non-participation, she won the pageant, which made it nice for the Ponderettes' treasury because no money needed to be expended to purchase her prizes.

Though they involved some challenging coordination and many nights of late hours, the Variety Shows of the 1970s unified the student body. The event was so popular that one year, when a week's worth of late-March-mud-season vacation threatened to postpone the show, many kids, who would normally have been no-shows at school under the best of weather conditions, exhausted every means to maneuver the gooey roads, show up for practice, and ensure that the show would indeed go on.

With each year's performances attracting larger and larger audiences, we could always count on a nice lump sum expanding the treasury for our parade schedule and the early-fall football drills. In spite of this springtime bonanza, we still had to nickel and dime our way through the last few basketball games in February. It was one of my brilliant schemes to earn a few extra Ponderette bucks that nearly led to the demise of my teaching career.

"Why not have a pie-eating contest?" I thought. "We can involve the whole school and charge entry fees, and the girls can supply the pies to make more money." It was 1973. By this time, I had learned that Dick Sodorff may have been blind when he hired me to advise the Ponderettes, but his vision tended to be extremely acute whenever an untried idea came his way. I was still employing the youthful teaching mode of asking first before apologizing later. I'd also had enough experience to know that most pie-eating contests were notorious for turning messy. I knew that if we were going to attract representatives from the entire school, we would need to use the gymnasium, and it certainly would not be nice to get any pie on the precious basketball court. If we were going to get the blessing of the principal, my instincts told me I had better make darn sure that every potential cream-pie liability was covered *before* broaching the subject to Mr. Sodorff. Since I had never even come close to angelic stardom, turning devil's advocate in the planning process posed no problem.

OK, I thought. *We'll put out newspapers to cover a wide area where the pies are set up. Contestants will lie on their stomachs with hands behind their backs. Assistants will bring them the pies so that they'll never have to touch the pie with their hands.* Each homeroom would pay a fee and select a contestant to participate. Homeroom teachers would read the rules to their classes, so there could be no excuse for misunderstandings.

To emcee the event, I chose the most responsible student I knew at the time. His name was Kent Compton. In addition to being a good Presbyterian and playing a mean cello, Kent was a wholesome, happy extrovert. His warmth, enthusiasm and big smile could win over the most dedicated misanthrope. I had worked with Kent for three years as his English teacher and yearbook adviser, which had given me the opportunity to know this kid inside and out. He was popular among the student body, and his traits included intelligence, amiability, honesty, dependability, respect for others and a lot of other positive adjectives that look good on college application forms. Along with those came common sense. Or so I thought.

With the plan complete and knowing that Kent was my ticket to a successful event, my confidence level soared. Dick Sodorff could not turn me down when I proposed this meticulously-planned concept. The kids would love it. The winner would love the $25 gift certificate, which had been donated. We could pay some bills with the proceeds.

As usual, Dick wanted to hear every detail before giving me the nod. Question after question was met with a response that demonstrated impeccable forethought. I had done my homework this time. The pie-eating contest was a go. Homerooms were notified. Students signed up. When the day came for the event, cream pies began appearing all through the halls. The cooks allowed us to store them in the lunchroom. When the lunch bell rang, we wasted no time, clearing the east half of the gym to get set up for the big event. Some drill team members formed a large horseshoe pattern on the floor with newspapers and later set out one pie for each of the 40-plus contestants. Kent and I set up the sound system on the stage and reviewed the rules to make sure we hadn't overlooked any potential for disaster.

"Let's keep this under control," I said, aware that even Kent probably needed a reminder. Excitement reigned high. Contestants and assistants filed in.

"Find yourself a pie, and get down on the floor," my bombproof emcee instructed. With a short time left in the lunch break, we wasted no time herding people to their pies. After a quick welcome, Kent read the rules and reminded everyone that the pie needed to stay on the newspapers.

"Any contestant caught using his or her hands will be disqualified," he announced. There comes a moment in the planning of every project when all fears of disorganization dissipate, everything comes together, and it's obvious that this has turned out to be a winner. I beamed with pride while standing on the sidelines surveying the scene, where 40 male and female bodies of varying sizes and ages and from various cliques lay patiently in wait, eagerly anticipating their first mouthfuls of chocolate, banana or lemon-cream filling. Standing over the contestants, each assistant held a second pie. The event had attracted several hundred onlookers, including a large representation from the faculty who stood a safe distance away along the wall near the coaches' office.

Kent, my trusted student, stood on the stage, microphone in hand, masterfully setting the tone for the proceedings. This would be a lunch hour to remember. Once more, I was sure of the event's popular success, certain my fastidious planning would clearly prove to Dick Sodorff that he need not worry whenever I came up with a new idea at Sandpoint High School. I couldn't have been more pleased – until the "imp of the perverse" so often mentioned in Edgar Allen Poe's horror stories found its way into Bulldog Gym.

It all started innocently enough. Some say Anna Bricker started it. Others blame Bobby Hamilton Jr. The perpetrator, whoever it happened to be, lacked foresight for sure. Who would ever expect that rubbing an errant smidgen of meringue from one of the pies onto someone else's shirt sleeve would start such a chain reaction? Probably any veteran of a pie fight could imagine this, but the innocent soul who started it all was instantly forgotten in the mayhem that followed. Sixty seconds seemed like six hours as contestants and assistants alike began flinging pie in every direction. First, the flying slop was limited to a small portion of the gym near the girls' locker room. Within seconds, a barrage of chocolate, lemon cream and whipping cream bombs went airborne and landed on its human targets with military precision.

As Poe says, there is something about the imp of the perverse that transforms the most innocent of souls (whether teenager or teacher) into fiendish monsters. Although I never would have admitted it to Dick Sodorff at the time, I must confess now (in the safety of my retirement) to the mortal sin of flinging at least one handful of chocolate cream at my colleague, Ray Holt. I believe that offense occurred only *after* wiping off a glob of banana cream from my shoulder and turning around to spot his guilty, grinning countenance.

So much fun, happening so quickly. Within seconds, I came to my senses and remembered my early determination to make this thing work. The plan had not called for an all-out war in the gym.

"Stop it!" I started yelling. "Please, stop it."

Was anyone listening? Was I in a dream?

"I said STOP IT!" Once more, no response. I tried the physical approach, frantically grabbing hands ready to fling another glob of pie.

"Please stop!" My worst nightmare kept on. I felt invisible as I yelled and grabbed in vain, but pie continued hitting people. People were walking, running and sliding on pie filling. This fiasco was occurring no longer on the newspapers but on the precious gym floor. Occasionally, some targets ducked at the right time and the pies hit the pine walls along the sides of the gym.

Somewhere between terror and hysterical laughter, I looked to Kent for help. What I saw on his face and heard from his mouth suggested that my trusted ally in this important mission had turned into a lowdown teenage traitor. Kent had red hair. His face now matched his hair; his eyes were filled with tears – not from embarrassment or shyness but from glee. His hand hugged the mike while his brain directed his lips to deliver some encouraging commentary.

"Oh, I see teachers!" he announced with a tone strongly implying their availability as ideal victims. A large handful of chocolate landed and oozed down a student spectator's shirt.

"Hey, great hit!" This on-location melee had proved far more entertaining than the pie fight Kent had seen just a few weeks earlier on a TV show. Instant quarterbacks started aiming their creamy missiles toward a group of teachers standing near the coaches' office. As the teachers tried to escape, moving en masse toward the door, Dick Sodorff stepped out of the office and walked toward the stage with a stern expression suggesting an imminent confrontation. Behind him, a frenzied mass of pedagogic humanity squashed itself through the open door, seeking escape from the maniacal mischief that had spread throughout the gym.

The teachers were safe. Dick Sodorff was not.

As he made his way along the east wall, staring straight ahead toward Kent on stage, he was oblivious to an event witnessed by just about all spectators who weren't busily engaged in the pie fight. Approximately two feet above his head and slightly behind his peripheral vision, a complete chocolate pie went SPLAT against the wall.

"Oh, God, no," I gasped, while yanking a flinging offender by the shirt sleeve. I never really asked to be the drill team adviser, but at that moment in my young life, I had a strong desire to keep my teaching job at Sandpoint High School.

"OK, we'd better settle it down," I heard the frantic voice caution the crowd from the stage sound system. Kent had seen the pie narrowly miss Dick Sodorff's head. Kent was a smart young man, one who knew when an attitude adjustment was wise. His attitude adjusted instantaneously. "There's Mr. Sodorff. Everyone back to their stations – right now."

Years later, Kent remembered his moment of decision vividly.

"I realized he (Mr. Sodorff) wasn't very happy," he recalled. "Then I decided to show that discretion was the better part of valor and started pulling in the reins." By the time the principal reached the stage to have a word with my emcee, everyone else in the gym had come to the same realization. As fast as it had begun, the aerial show ceased. Some students were salvaging what was left of pies so that the actual eating could begin, while others were performing unsolicited acts of citizenship by canvassing the walls and floors in search of messes to clean up. The show did go on with a lot fewer contestants and some disqualified students joining the spectator contingent. When it was over, a senior, David Jones, had devoured nine pies to win the title. The bell rang for students to go to fourth-hour class. I had a few words with Kent, who contritely apologized for letting things get out of hand in the hilarity of the moment.

Certain that this giant indiscretion would land me on Dick Sodorff's hot seat, I gathered a few Ponderette volunteers. We spent most of my entire fourth-period prep hour, armed with wet paper towels, scouring the gym for every last drop of sticky substance that could serve as damning evidence to justify my dismissal as a teacher at Sandpoint High School.

Maybe this was a blessing in disguise, I rationalized to myself while frantically scrubbing up chocolate and squashed bananas. *He can't fire me from teaching English, but he could decide that I'm just too irresponsible to advise the drill team. That may not be a bad plan; after all, I had never asked for the job in the first place.*

My personal spin job, however, could not erase one gnawing factor that had driven me most of my life – my pride. It simply would not allow me to retreat in failure. So, when we were satisfied that we had done the best we could, I sent the girls on to class and made an office-avoiding detour to the faculty room. My aim was to put off the wrath of my boss as long as possible. Realizing the teachers' smoking and blowing-off-steam center was safe for the moment, I slipped inside the door, announcing that if Dick came in, I would be hiding in the women's bathroom, and that someone had better notify me once the coast was again clear. For about five minutes, the other teachers and I chatted about the debacle. Of course, they all thought it was funny. Even though the humorous dimensions of the whole incident were clear to me at the moment, I wasn't exactly in a position of savoring them with quite the delight of my colleagues. Right now, fear over my future employment drove my every thought.

My eyes darted to the door. Through the blurred window, I saw a tall figure. The doorknob turned. I leaped into action, maybe touching the floor twice before diving into the women's john. As I closed the bathroom door, I heard the other one open. Standing motionless like a statue, I listened as Dick's footsteps went past my enclosed cubicle and on into the faculty room. My confinement could last awhile, if he were planning to light up a cigarette. I could hear only muffled voices talking through the wall, making it hard to pinpoint his activities. I hoped that my colleagues would remember to alert me when he was gone. So, there I stood silently, looking at my dumb face in the mirror, which managed to smile even in the midst of this potentially darkest moment in my career.

This is really stupid, I thought, as the if-they-could-see-me-now feeling made me almost laugh out loud. My family would think nothing of this scene; after all, the bathroom had always served as the escape hatch, whenever anyone had stolen some bread or cookies and had to hightail it when our parents had suddenly entered the house. In fact, I had almost choked to death on a peanut butter sandwich years before, when my mother came in from the barn a bit too soon. At least, back in those days, there had been something to do while hiding out in the john. At this moment, the only pastime that seemed somewhat reasonable was to revive a childhood favorite – make monster faces in the mirror. Even that quirky idea didn't really thrill me at that moment. I just wanted out of there.

Suddenly, the fourth-period dismissal bell sounded. Dick Sodorff or no, I now had no choice but to get out of there and hurry to my classroom for fifth-period English. Knowing that the passing bell would signal a lot of traffic to and from the faculty room, I decided to go with the flow and slip out of the bathroom, make a quick exit and hurry down the hall to Room 4. Making a clean escape, I greeted my sophomores who were still buzzing about the noontime contest. In their eyes, the event ranked as a great success. In mine, it still could spell doom. After fifth period, I needed to take a quick potty break. While making my way to the faculty room through the mass of students, I spotted him. He was coming my way. Our eyes met.

"Oh, God, here it comes," I thought. Maintaining my composure and considering the ridiculous notion of knocking over a mass of teenagers in a frantic escape, I feigned calmness and kept walking. That familiar stoic stare on Dick's face gave no sign of what might transpire once we met. A moment later, it was over.

"Well, did ya get it all cleaned up?" he asked.

"Yeah, every drop," I responded.

"Good," he said and walked on down the hall.

He never said another word to me about the pie-eating contest. We put a few dollars in our treasury and went on with the winter basketball performances. The Ponderettes and I stayed together for nine years, and we created many good memories and long-lasting friendships. Finally, after I announced to my boss that I was pregnant with my second child, Annie, and begged to be released from my drill team responsibilities, he set me free.

I finally walked away from this unsolicited extra duty a wiser woman, determined never to organize a pie-eating contest again. I've kept that promise.

2.

The Tuba Solo: A Class Night Meltdown

I sat beneath a giant pine tree on the Best Western Edgewater Resort lawn. The sky was blue. Tanned, slim, well-fed, young and old – a healthy mix of beachcombers comingled in a hot July sun on this day in the mid-1990s. Small slabs of decorative bark poked the bare skin on the bottom of my legs, while tiny insects took turns scaling my sweaty neck. Bill and I had ridden a 3-mile shortcut from our rural home to the Sandpoint City Beach. Although it took some extra effort to maneuver our mountain bikes through the blistering heat, we had arrived in time to hear emcee Ginny (Robideaux) Jensen complete her speech about the Pend Oreille Arts Council and introduce the Western Washington Brass Ensemble. Informally clad in jeans and white shirts, the quintet seemed pleased to sit in the shade on this Sunday afternoon and toot their horns for an appreciative audience.

Two trumpets, one French horn, a trombone and a tuba made melodious sounds just a few feet away. Bill was in his glory. As a one-time music major and longtime tuba player, he lapped up every note from each of the instruments while the quintet, facing beautiful Lake Pend Oreille skirted by its magnificent Cabinet Mountains, played music from around the world. As a junior high choir flunk-out, I appreciated the talented performers. They made their music all look so easy. While the melodies wafted through the air, I found myself distracted by the passersby and the activities that always make an event like this memorable. There was the man who seemingly fell asleep in his comfortable lawn chair *before* the concert began. Wearing brown polyester trousers, loafers and a short-sleeved shirt, hair slicked back and jaw wide open, he remained oblivious to all outside stimuli. The elderly woman accompanying him serenely ignored his state as if it were a regular occurrence. I watched lovers coo at each other on their blankets in the shade of the big trees. A naked toddler with soft blond curls waddled through the obstacle course of diaper bag, lunch basket and the sun-baked bodies of grown-ups who had accompanied him to the beach.

As is customary for me, the observer, I couldn't completely focus on the music. I've always believed in taking in the total experience – the sights, sounds, and quirky little sideshows contributing to the overall event. In fact, as the performance progressed on this lazy summer afternoon, my mind took me back to fleeting images of another distraction-filled musical presentation, long buried in the depths of my memory. I attempted again to concentrate on the present.

For now, I was enjoying most of the music, but I was even more fascinated by the tuba player's pulsating stomach as she pumped wind through her shiny brass instrument. Instead of marveling at her musical talent, I theorized that playing this imposing instrument with its big brass bell might offer a perfect exercise for flattening the midriff. Mesmerized by the rhythm of her stomach muscles in constant motion, I could see that physical conditioning went along with tuba playing. It occurred to me that certainly several tuba practice sessions followed by a full-fledged concert could certainly be just as effective as a hundred sit-ups a day over a month's time.

Hmm, I thought to myself, maybe that big ol' tuba Bill brings home and practices every summer for the Fourth of July parade is good for something besides scaring the horses and half the neighborhood. I'll have to try a few blasts on it and see if it'll help me get rid of my kangaroo pouch. I had never really held a proper appreciation for tubas, even though my husband has played one for years as a high school and college musician. And when world-famous tuba player and teacher Harvey Phillips has come to town for the Festival at Sandpoint, Bill has managed a few visits with the master. So on this visit to the beach, he was transported.

As a snappy ragtime number held my husband's attention, my own mind drifted again to that spring day many years before when I had attended a public social event, where another brass player unwittingly created a tuba legend that would be repeated in the faculty room for years afterward at Sandpoint High School. Our school gym, which doubled as the auditorium, served as the setting. On this occasion, Bill was more than likely off at some trout stream catching the evening hatch. It was a warm May evening, and I was a bit uncomfortable because I had to wear a dress and nylons for two hours while sitting on display in front of the audience of senior scholarship hopefuls and their parents. As a presenter for the annual Class Night awards program, I kept sliding around on my hard, metal folding chair while squeezed elbow-to-elbow among the 50 other people on the school stage. We had all gathered that night to present dozens of scholarships, plaques and certificates to deserving high school seniors. I would be presenting engraved bracelets to my drill team captains and to the *Monticola* yearbook editors.

Class Night at Sandpoint High School had always been a dignified affair. Formality reigned as the senior class president – seated next to the podium and carefully cued by the counselor in charge – did the honors of introducing presenters from local sponsoring organizations. It was common for the SHS sound system to refuse to cooperate and for the class president, who had not been schooled in the importance of speaking *into* the mike, to contribute toward turning the program into an interminable experience.

Thus, after a few years of teaching and of presenting awards on Class Night, I had developed a few personal methods for mentally moving the show along. For example, I did my best to draw an early slot on the program. This strategy limited those dreaded moments of squirming, taking quick, nervous breaths, and thinking about the fastest route to the nearest bathroom to settle my nerves. Fortunately, for me, most of the other presenters had never thought of this tactic, so I always managed to charm the organizer into allowing me to get my part of the show over with quickly. Always careful to avoid eating before getting up and talking into a microphone to large groups of people, I entertained myself by thinking about how good the assorted treats would taste at the tea after the program. Back in those days, Eva Whitehead and her Pep Club girls always arranged for a spread of fresh-baked cookies and refreshing strawberry or peach-flavored punch for the Senior Tea.

Another perennial highlight of Class Night was the "Imogene Show." My dear friend and beloved faculty colleague, Imogene Davis, could always be counted on to offer a major production at the awards podium. By this time, her sentimental performances at Class Night ceremonies had become classic. All veterans among the stage presenters looked forward to Imogene's segment because they knew it was going to be a good show with lots of tears. "Imo," as we lovingly referred to her, taught the business classes, which were made up of mostly girls. During their years with Imogene, young teenaged women came into her class a bit rough around the edges and within a year or two, went out her door ready for the job market as polished young ladies and accomplished secretaries. Imogene taught them shorthand, transcription and general office skills. With help from local bank officers, she provided them firsthand experience at job interviews. She also brought in experts who taught them about color coordination and proper and respectable makeup for the professional office settings. And her "girls" always returned to visit Imogene in her classroom and to tell this year's crop how it was out there in the career world. Imogene had been my teacher for one semester during my busy junior year at Sandpoint High School. For years afterward, she had never really forgiven me for dropping her shorthand class at midyear. A busy academic schedule drove me to give up the shorthand ship, but I still had always enjoyed and admired the lady at the helm, and we became good friends when I joined the faculty.

Every year at Class Night, Imogene found delightful ways to make "her girls" feel like the most special people on earth. With her hair in a stylish bun atop her head and attired in an attractive dress and fancy, 3-inch high heels, Imo glided to the podium, flashed a big smile and began her 15-minute presentation.

"It's always a such a pleasure to tell you about my girls," she would begin. "They're so lovely and they've worked so hard, and I just hate to see them go ... " One by one, each young lady, dressed to the nines, following the example of their instructor, would come to the stage to receive her certificate or pin. One by one, Imogene with tears streaming down her cheeks, made her way down the lineup of young ladies, giving each a warm, loving hug.

Finally, one student would emerge from the pack carrying a dozen red roses or a beautifully wrapped gift. Stepping up to the mike and choking back tears, the appointed representative would first tell the audience about their wonderful teacher. Then, while handing over the gift, the speaker gave Imogene another hug, and both would shed more affectionate tears. The Imo gang would glide off the stage all smiles and obviously pleased with this year's podium performance. Then, the senior class president, looking both relieved and shell-shocked, would step up to the mike for the next introduction.

After Imogene's gig, my time spent sitting on the SHS stage usually flashed by quickly as I indulged in my favorite pastime, people watching. Class Night always offered a bonanza in this category. This particular night was no different. There was always the delight of looking out into the audience and checking out the similarities between seniors and their parents. Or, there would be the moment where I would suddenly spot a student's mom or dad and realize that this individual was that same person who always rang up my groceries at the M & J Food market or sold me a shovel at the CO-OP.

Now I know why Nancy looked so familiar, I would note to myself. *I see her mother almost every day. Now, I get the connection.* This would be a conversation starter the next time I came through the line toting a loaf of Wonder Bread or some Meow Mix cat food.

Class Night that year started off like all the others until the class president introduced a talented young tuba player who had chosen to do a solo. This young man was one of the outstanding musicians in the SHS band, so it seemed appropriate for him to show off his talents to his classmates and their parents. He stepped to the stage, set up his heavy-duty, black, metal music stand, and began the piece. This young musician was performing the first tuba solo I had ever heard. Even though my music appreciation skills were limited at the time, I concluded that tubas toot-ing all by themselves don't quite come across like pianos or harmonicas or even kazoos.

I was sure the young man was doing a wonderful job blowing out those notes, but my ability to judge the quality of his tone or the correct-ness of his timing was severely handicapped by the fact that many of the sounds flowing from his tuba struck me exactly like the sequence of those loud methane toot-toots I had frequently heard from my horses as they trotted across the green fields of summer. I had also heard similar sounds back in grade school and even occasionally during my teaching years, when some student would "cut the cheese" anonymously but never very quietly. For some warped reason, this performance reminded me of those funny moments. As the young man continued through his solo, I stared straight ahead, practicing muscle-control exercises around my cheeks and lips. It would not be polite to laugh, especially with 300 people gazing back at me from the audience. I looked at the ceiling. I stared at the floor. I studied my thumbnails. I read my palms. I did everything to avoid eye contact with anyone. The harder I tried to avoid laughing, the more the muscles around my lips lost control.

The tuba played on.

I rested my right elbow on my left hand and cupped my right hand and fingers over my mouth and jaw. Then, my stomach muscles started pulsating, much like that tuba lady's at the Edgewater. "Barbarosa" was turning into the funniest piece of music ever penned, and the solo seemed never ending. While I shifted in my seat, peripheral vision alerted me to potential trouble on my right. I could discern a familiar profile with a mop of gray hair. The boy's father, also a presenter, was sitting in the row behind me! I could feel him staring directly at me. My restraint weakened with this new awareness. The harder I tried to control my desire to laugh out loud, the more my body and mind fought back.

Suddenly, a minor disturbance to my left temporarily interrupted my concern. Escaping the gaze of the father, I shot a nervous glance toward the person next to me and observed quickly that, compared to this despi-cable soul, I was wearing a halo. Don Albertson, the biology teacher, had come to Class Night to present a special memorial scholarship. He was doubled over hugging his stomach. Tears were rolling down his cheeks.

Gee whiz, I thought. *It is a memorial award, but it's not that sad.* His body kept moving forward in the chair. I feared that he might fall on the floor.

"What's the matter with you?" I whispered out the side of my mouth. "Settle down!"

"I caaaan't help it," he sobbed. "It's so funny."

Hmm, I thought, *called that one wrong! I thought he was crying.* Don Albertson was crying all right, but his tears had nothing to do with anything sad. His body began to fold into a fetal position.

This is getting embarrassing, I thought. It became even worse when I looked across Don's back and observed Hud Nieman, presenter of the Nieman Music Award, glaring down at Don as if this biology instructor were the lowest life form on the science charts. It was obvious that Hud didn't think anything was funny. It was also obvious that Hud's respect for fine music far surpassed that of the unappreciative soul sitting next to him.

"Stop it!" I whispered out the side of my mouth, while maintaining a rigid position, with arms folded, eyes staring straight ahead at nothing in particular. "Behave yourself!"

"I'm sorry," Don responded. "I can't stop ... look at that spider."

"Huh!" I grunted. "Whaddya mean?" I was sure that Don had lost his mind.

"The spider," he repeated. "Look at it!"

"What spider?" I asked. "What are you talking about?"

Don's behavior was degenerating. The more I pressed him, the more he hugged his mid-riff. This man was just about ready for a visit from the white jackets.

"It's on the music stand," he explained. "Look at it. It's bouncing to the music ... it's so funny."

I looked toward the soloist. Sure enough, a large spider *was* dangling from the music stand. Sure enough, it was bouncing up and down in sync with the tuba blasts. Every time the young musician inhaled, the spider and its stringy web shot up toward the music stand. Every time the boy blew his loud notes, the arachnid, blessed with an acute sense of rhythm, slowly descended toward the floor like a yo-yo on a string. Never once did the spider break or miss a beat. I wondered at the moment if this was an added feature that the young performer had secretly choreographed into his act. But I didn't have time to wonder for long because a crazy man was sitting next to me. Pretty soon, people would be noticing his childish behavior, and pretty soon I would be behaving just as badly as Don. Past experiences with my mother ensured that.

Throughout my life, I've always had difficulty accompanying Mother to any cultural event requiring reasonably mature behavior. It's just not possible for the two of us to sit together in any audience without eventually becoming public objects of scorn. I could see that a similar phenomenon was unfolding while watching Don fight back the tears that night on the stage. I knew instantly that I should never have leaned his direction. His behavior had triggered the all-too-familiar Adult Attention Deficit Disorder (AADD). This time it was striking a pair of teachers who should have known better.

Was there a tuba soloist performing on the stage? Heck, I didn't know. All I could think about was Don and the other man sitting directly behind me and how I had better not fall into my usual laugh trap. I worked harder than ever to discipline myself and more diligently to discipline Don.

"Stop it!" I commanded once more like a seasoned ventriloquist.

"I can't," he chortled. Then during a mercifully momentary lapse, Don proceeded to whisper to me a familiar story, which explained why he was in such a state.

"Once I start I can't stop," he disclosed. "This always happens to my mother and me. We get started giggling, and we just can't stop."

Oh great! I thought. *Could we be related? How could this happen that we'd be stuck sitting together on the stage in front of 300 people during such a solemn occasion?* Thank God our mothers weren't around. Our behavior deteriorated as Don leaned over as if his appendix were about to burst. Hud Nieman continued to glare at Don. Tears started rolling down my face as I began to hug my stomach. Continuing to gaze into the audience as an escape did me no good. Every time my eyes landed on anyone, that person was looking right back at me. Apparently, our vain attempts to stifle the giggling were becoming obvious to more spectators than just Hud. With each individual audience sighting, however, I began to notice hints of delighted amusement. The person would make eye contact with me and within seconds, another pair of lips began to curl. A dangerous epidemic was spreading.

Oops, better not look at her any more, I instructed myself. *She'll make me laugh that much more.* Like dominoes, every time I would escape the gaze of one audience member and resume a state of semi-dignity, I would come eye-to-eye with another amused individual, and the cycle would begin anew. There seemed to be no escaping this primal urge to just get down on the floor, roll around, and giggle the whole insane scene out of my system. That was all that would satisfy my needs at this very moment. Don was beyond salvation. I wasn't far behind. Others in the audience were catching up.

Finally the most welcome sound in the world brought our insanity to an end. Applause. Lots of it. The young man had, at last, finished his solo. He stood with his tuba and bowed. The audience enthusiastically expressed its appreciation for the fine performance – of the tuba, I believe. Don and I seized the moment to regain our composure.

The instant the awards program ended, I bolted from the stage. My mission: to avoid the tuba player's father at all costs. It was going to be difficult because, as always, I had wanted to do some schmoozing with parents and students at the tea. I had a difficult time concentrating on the small talk with parents because, once again, my peripheral vision kept alerting me to the familiar image circulating among the crowd.

Oops, there he is again, I would observe silently, while congratulating a senior who had just won three scholarships. Upon seeing the dad coming my direction, my strategy was to appear intensely involved in the conversation – so involved that certainly this offended father would not walk up and chastise me in front of other parents for laughing at his son's performance. Certainly, he would wait for his moment. By taking a long time visiting with several families during the tea, I might just escape his wrath. While the tuba player's dad went to the punch table, I could slip out the back door and be free. That plan seemed to be working well, as I was able to chat with many of my students and their parents. So far, so good. I said good-bye to the last of the other parents and their scholarship winners and headed for the door. Just as I neared the edge of the crowd, a figure loomed between me and the door. The boy's father stood right in front of me. No place to run. No one else to run to. Was I doomed? We had met face-to-face! Easing forward, I summoned my get-out-of-this-fix survival skills.

"Hi, how are you?" I asked.

Before he could say anything, I jumped in and took control of the conversation.

"I loved your son's solo," I began. "He did such a good job. Did you see that spider on his music stand?"

I had caught the dad off guard.

"Uh no, what spider?" he asked.

"Oh, it was *so* funny," I continued. "There was a spider on his music stand, and it kept bouncing up and down to the rhythm of the tuba sounds. It looked like your son and the spider had practiced for hours for a song-and-dance duet. They were in perfect sync. I've never seen anything so unusual and so funny."

"Well, uh, no I didn't see it," the astonished man remarked.

"It was great," I said. "Tell him he did a wonderful job and that he ought to market that spider act."

Before the father had a chance to open his mouth, I scurried off, leaving him a bit dumbfounded. Certainly, he would eventually digest all this, realize just how funny that spider must have been, and wish to heck he had seen it himself instead of investing his energy in loathing that awful Marianne Love who laughed at his son. Out the door into the darkness, I ran for the safety and solitude of my car. As I stuck the key into the ignition, the giggle gates burst open. Laughter kept me wide awake later as I lay in bed reliving the scene.

In the years since the famous tuba solo, my dear friend Don and I have teased each other mercilessly every time another Class Night rolls around. Like clockwork, every year, idle moments in our respective classes during the month of May always seemed to revive the story. One of us would tell our students the tale of the tuba, and for a week afterward, the other would be answering the inquiring minds who wanted to know all about the famous spider solo.

Don retired in 1996 but not before I got him back for making me behave so badly 20 years earlier. It was an elaborate scheme, but it went off like clockwork. Hud Nieman participated, and another young tuba player did his part. Don attended Class Night – not as a presenter – but as a guest. He thought he was there to be honored as a retiring teacher. Well, he was. But in addition to that, he was honored as a great appreciator of tuba solos. Hud Nieman, a trombone man himself, and a man with a good sense of humor, stood before the group of seniors and their families and told of a special, one-time-only award that would go not to a graduating senior but instead to a true tuba aficionado.

"This award goes to a person who goes beyond the call of duty when it comes to tuba solos," Hud told the audience, adding that, at another Class Night 20 years before, Don had truly distinguished himself on stage as few other music connoisseurs had done.

While a surprised and amused Don walked up to accept his plaque, a rent-a-tuba player marched behind him, blasting oompahs all the way.

Tuba players throughout the world would have been proud. I was ecstatic. The moment brought much needed closure to a tuba performance that had alternately haunted and tickled me for two decades.

3.

Furniture Farm: The Tony Bottarini Story

"There's a gawd-awful mess out there in the barnyard, and I'm not going to clean it up!" I made this announcement to the family one morning after discovering a yellow couch and chair of questionable vintage, sitting about 10 feet from the machine shed. The sofa was surrounded by assorted scraps of white foam stuffing and accented with piles of horse apples. On closer inspection, I observed a host of chunks of upholstery randomly scattered throughout the entire barnyard. My husband, Bill, and son, Willie, had received instructions numerous times over a three-week period to get the couch and its matching chair out of the yard.

"We're not going to have that eyesore decorating our yard all summer," I announced. As usual, both remained passive and stoically ignored my squawkings. Prior to the barnyard discovery, the furniture had sat day after day next to the hazelnut tree in front of the bunkhouse, sharing yard space with the mixture of running and recently deceased lawnmowers. Since Willie had brought it home from the University of Idaho, his dorm-room furniture ensemble had absorbed several drenchings and collected a healthy share of willow stems blown in from blustery, late-spring thunderstorms.

"We can put it in the living room," my son had suggested after hauling it home, along with his books, clothes and broken-down mountain bike. "It'll look nice in there."

"I don't think so," I said.

"But, Mom, it will enhance the seating and the comfort of the living room," he insisted.

"I don't think so," I repeated.

"Come on, Mom," he pleaded.

"No, we will *not* have that furniture in the living room. It doesn't exactly match the other stuff," I insisted. "Besides, there's no room." In spite of my hard-nosed attitude, I could appreciate Willie's loyalty toward the couch and chair because our first furniture looked very much like his – just a different color. In fact, one day while standing over my son's pride and joy, I thought back to 1974, the year his father and I had married.

We furnished our rental house at my folks' upper farm with a $28 purchase from Cedar Street Used in Sandpoint. While inspecting Larry and Alvie Jeffres' roomful of offerings, the rhubarb-pink ensemble stood out as adequate furnishings to join Bill's homemade brick-and-board bookcase in the tiny living room where we would spend our first three years as husband and wife. The couch wasn't too comfortable, but it was long. In fact, at least five moderately skinny people could squeeze into it if necessary. And since its cloth upholstery was frayed in some spots, smooth in others, we didn't have to worry too much about any rough treatment it might get.

The matching square chair was a bit more appealing because its thick foam cushion offered much better comfort than any one spot on the couch. In fact, when searching for the perfect plop spot on the couch for watching TV, it was hard to determine much difference between the couch arms and its cushions. Just one experience, however, of sinking into that chair with its flat, wide arms, and you knew you had found heaven. You could ease clear down to where your chin met your knees and remain firmly planted for hours. With that kind of comfort, we had no problem overlooking the threadbare area that gradually began to ooze a cream-colored foam padding much like outpourings from a zit. At that time in our lives, comfort reigned over beauty. Of course, price considerations sealed the deal. We hauled the living room set home in our 1970 Ford pickup and slowly maneuvered each piece through the kitchen doorway and into the living room of our little "Love nest."

The two-piece ensemble functioned quite nicely for about six years.

One Christmas Bill took some extra cash and bought a glider rocker, while on another occasion I brought home an affordable, old-fashioned rocking chair from one of Ernie Belwood's Furniture Exchange sales. With those additions, we advanced several steps up the furniture evolution ladder. We decided to remove the Paleolithic pink chair with its ever-increasing foam explosion and turn it out to pasture.

The chair's pasture turned out to be the Sandpoint High School faculty room, which had, in recent years, gone coed. The teachers at my school had finally broken past the his/hers staff lounge, after someone had decided to tear down the wall down that had separated the men from the women ever since the school's opening in 1953. The extra space enabled us to do more planning in relative comfort during prep hours and other breaks from the classroom. Instead of a row of metal folding chairs lining the walls, we could actually have tables and maybe even a couch. Some teachers even donated to the cause by purchasing flowered contact paper for the wooden tables. I decided that we Loves could turn benefactor by donating our original chair to the cause. But, when Bill and I hauled it down to the school one weekend and deposited it in its new home, the reaction from a few faculty commentators was less than enthusiastic. Since the chair had been left anonymously, my colleagues spared no words in their disdain for the new addition to our mismatched assortment of tables, chairs and couches.

"Where the hell did that come from?" Bob, the special-ed teacher, asked. "Someone ought to haul it off to the dump." His comment was one of the nicer evaluations.

"Look at that hunk o' junk ... I'll bet it has fleas or maybe even lice crawling out of that big hole ... " These critics were ruthless in their assessment of the newest addition to the faculty room ensemble. My colleagues, always opinionated souls, had no appreciation for ugly ducklings. After silently absorbing their harangues, I felt confident that these malicious tongues could have done a number on any beauty-impaired fowl's self-esteem. They had certainly sent a rather vocal message to me that my generosity for the good of faculty comfort would not get the recognition it deserved. The chair sat in the room, fielding unkind comments all day long, but when the school day ended, I walked into the faculty room, only to see one of the harshest critics plopped in the chair with his knees rubbing his stubbly chin. As he sat there with a satisfied grin on his face, I wanted to walk over, grab his head and cram it down farther into that opening of oozing foam rubber.

What a hypocrite, I thought to myself. *See if he ever sits in that chair again.* The anonymous and clearly wounded furniture benefactor, I gathered up my stuff and drove home. After enough time had elapsed for all the other teachers to leave the school for the day, I drove back and went straight to the faculty room. It took some doing to maneuver the chair back through the door by myself, but as in past experiences, I followed the old where-there's-a-will, there's-a-way philosophy. I eventually pointed it down the cement hallway toward Room 4 where I taught five classes of English and yearbook students. Taking care not to leave scuffs on the hallway floor, I slowly pushed the big chair to its new home.

The next day, my students showed much more decency and sensitivity toward the new addition than my uncharitable "friends" in the faculty room had mustered. Of course, the fact that I prefaced the class hour with one of my customary mean-teacher warnings, "Say anything about that chair and you're dead," may have influenced any unwelcome critiques from the mouths of my English babes. Students in most classes just stared longingly at the chair for two or three days, but my sixth-period yearbook staffers embraced it quickly. Not the least bit shy and never confined to the usual regimentation of "Get in that desk and don't move 'til the bell rings," they could venture to whatever spot their little hearts desired once I finished my daily announcements. In fact, after the first day, two or three eager bodies daily jumped from their desks and raced to attach themselves like barnacles to the new addition – never the least bit concerned about any fleas, lice or mice that might inhabit the depths of the exploding cushion.

Eventually, all classes came to appreciate the chair – so much so that each hour had a waiting list for who got to sit in it. For several years afterward, I allowed the hourly chair to be occupied on a "first-come, first-served" basis. Whoever took the bold move at the beginning of the year and asked, "Can I sit in the big chair?" had the honors. They were asked to follow only one basic rule.

"Don't make faces at me or at the class while I'm lecturing," I announced. "You do and you'll sit in a regular desk." For the most part, that warning worked, with the exception of a young man named Mark Brown who became quite adept at smirking across the room to his buddy, Tim Kramer. I always knew that Mark had sent a clandestine message when Tim's normally deadpan face developed a slight grin. These distractions usually set me off enough to shoot my own unsubtle glare Mark's way. He valued his classroom comfort enough to cut the nonsense.

The chair eventually elevated in importance. Despite its ever-increasing worn-and-torn appearance, students began to refer to it as "the throne." Many thought of themselves as kings or queens as they sat apart from the masses with plenty of room to drape their notebooks while enjoying 55 minutes of escape from the institutional discomfort of the standard metal classroom desk.

Having the throne in my room surprisingly led me to one of the most meaningful experiences of my teaching career. One of its inhabitants took possession partway through his junior year and maintained control until early May of his senior year. His name was Tony Bottarini. A lanky, brown-haired young man with light skin and kind, green eyes, Tony deserved every moment he spent in the throne.

He had cancer.

I had known of Tony through St. Joseph's Catholic Church in Sandpoint, which his family and ours attended. When the family of five came to Mass, it was easy to see from his anemic, frail appearance that Tony had some affliction. From friends, I heard the stories about his cancer, of how he had been fighting it since the sixth grade in his native California. By the time Tony showed up in my junior English class in 1985, I already knew a lot about his courage and his determination to live every day the best he could. I knew a lot about this young man, but I really didn't know him as a person. The next two years with Tony taught me much about the strength of a challenged inner spirit, more than he learned from any English lesson I ever taught him. Yes, Tony deserved his spot on that disreputable, but much sought-after, throne. A column that I penned during his senior year in March 1986, for a local newspaper explains why:

It's letter-of-recommendation time again. Thus, the keys to my Royal manual (typewriter) have been flying lately with words of praise for several deserving seniors seeking scholarships or entrance to college. This letter, however, is unsolicited. It's about a young man planning to attend North Idaho College this fall as a part-time student.

The Sandpoint High School senior spends every morning in my room – sleeping. A vintage, pink stuffed chair sits just inside the door of Room 4. To some, it's known as "the throne." This guy walks in, plops down, sprawls out and slumbers off and on until the bell for first period sends him on his way.

He's a student in my third-period (senior) composition class. Seldom does he take a note. Furthermore, he's usually behind because he misses about a week of school each month. And the same apparent apathy that takes place before school seems again prevalent in my class – at least to those who don't know better. Like Rip Van Winkle, he seems to snooze away the day with no concern for the importance of his education. But – ask him a question. He will answer it – correctly. Also – make a mistake lecturing. He will catch the error and politely razz the teacher later. This young man gets my vote every day that he walks into school, donned in his black seaman's cap. I really don't mind his daily napping in my room.

His name is Tony Bottarini, and he has cancer. In fact, he has lived with the dreaded disease since the age of 11. It has taken his lower left leg, and more recently, it has snuffed off the use of his right arm. Tony walks with an artificial limb and now wears his right arm in a sling. He sleeps almost round the clock in order to be able to attend school each day. And there are times that the drowsiness takes over because of the pain medication he takes every four hours.

Nonetheless, Tony keeps at it. And because of that persistence, he reigns as a hero to many students and especially to the faculty at Sandpoint High School. In suffering from a deadly disease, Tony has shown many of us a thing or two about living.

I asked Tony a couple of weeks ago if I could feature him in my column, and he happily agreed to the idea. Thus, I set about concocting questions, carefully planning the right approach for this interview. No right approach was necessary because Tony made the experience a complete joy with his sense of humor and his readiness to tell his story.

After putting it off a while, I had finally decided the time was right. Tony skipped his fourth-period shop class, and we went to the counselors' office to talk. At the time, I was experiencing some discomfort from a headache, and Tony was having a difficult time getting comfortable himself because of a tumor the size of a Coke can which has been growing in his back. In addition, the growth on his right arm was hurting him considerably. As he maneuvered himself to a reclining position between two chairs, I thought about my insignificant headache, popped an aspirin, and went on with the interview.

Tony told me about how, in the sixth grade, he had been the epitome of what most students term "Joe Cool."

"I was self-centered, the best athlete in the school, and I was always the first picked for teams," he told me. This attitude and the course of his life changed one day when the Mill Valley, Calif., native noticed a lump on his left knee. His doctor thought it was just a bruise and sent him on his way, saying that if it didn't disappear within two weeks, to come back.

Tony was back in two weeks with an enlarged lump. After X-rays, other doctors were called in, and the group decided that it was a bone tumor. Talk of biopsies, amputation, cancer and death took over.

"Most of it wasn't in my vocabulary," Tony noted. "What it meant did not hit me right away. The biopsy indicated I had cancer ... the day after that, I had my leg amputated about an inch above the knee ... three weeks went by and I got my first leg."

From that point on, Tony's life has been one of adjustment: learning to walk again, experiencing the continual nausea that comes with chemotherapy, missing weeks-on-end of school, watching other students participate in sports that he dearly loved, and facing the news that more cancer had found its way into his body.

Fortunately for his family, Tony's father had a Kaiser insurance policy, which has paid the limitless medical bills. The only major financial inconvenience has occurred since they moved to Sandpoint five years ago. Because the policy calls for care to be done in Kaiser hospitals, Tony's chemotherapy treatments have been administered at the nearest one in Portland. This has meant two days on the road and four days in the hospital every month.

While Tony continued to tell the story – about the tumor on his arm, the lesions in his lungs, the lump on his neck – I was amazed at his frankness, his matter-of-fact manner and his mature outlook. I attribute this to his experiences with the Center for Attitudinal Healing back home in California.

The center served as a setting for "kids to share experiences about death, life, sisters, brothers and general problems that occur in the home of a cancer patient." In fact, while associated with the program, Tony appeared on *Donahue* and *60 Minutes* to share the experience of his affliction with the public.

Besides the support he received from the center, Tony told me that his experience has enabled him "to learn about life quickly."

"It's growing up within a few months and comprehending things that usually take others years to learn. For example, you learn to appreciate life ... other people, and you learn to look at people's good sides rather than their bad side," Tony commented.

In fact, it is people that lure him to school each day – even when the pain is so intense he can hardly stand it.

"I don't really want to be in school because I only have so much time left," he said, "but I like the teachers and my friends." Tony's favorite friends at Sandpoint High School are Jon Stone, who has helped "me get in touch with myself," and Myra Evans who "was always there and helped me get over being depressed."

Tony's goal is graduation. "I want to graduate for the sake of my parents," says the young man, who makes every effort possible to get caught up with his work. "I wasn't supposed to live this long, so now graduation is important, because I want to attain the accomplishment for my parents, not for me."

He lives with his father and stepmother, Charlie and Elena, at their home in Wrenco, 10 miles west of Sandpoint. His older brother, Eric, is in the Navy, and his sister, Tonya, is an eighth-grader at Stidwell Junior High School.

His room is termed "an orderly pigsty," partly because it's not completed yet. At home, Tony is the instigator of his share of devilishness, and he reported that he grumbles continually while completing his nightly chore of putting the dishes away.

Back at school, Tony's courage is the talk of the SHS faculty room. All agree that he puts forth more effort and contributes more than many students who are physically healthy. He perseveres to get it completed eventually.

And he's not above a practical joke in class either. One day in wood shop, with the teacher's knowledge, Tony had the class convinced that he was piercing a metal hook into his leg. The class watched in horror as he poked the hook through his jeans. Some grimaced dramatically when they could even hear the sound effects. Most, however, were unaware that the leg was his artificial limb.

He connived a plan with this reporter (also senior class adviser) to arrive late at the prom this May 3. His date, Tracey Delyea, (just friends, of course) is from Coeur d'Alene. Tony will drive to Coeur d'Alene that afternoon and get spiffed up at her house. She will do the driving thereafter because he'll be on his pain medication.

First, it'll be a nice dinner, and then they'll drop in on her prom for a while. Next, they'll make the trip north to finish off the evening at the SHS prom. "She will stay with my family that night and I'll probably take her out to breakfast and back to Coeur d'Alene Sunday," Tony explained.

Having had Tony as a student for the past two years and having interviewed him, I am totally impressed. This young man has left a permanent mark on my life.

In closing this letter of recommendation, I am not trying to convince anyone to give him a scholarship, a job or a special break.

Instead, I recommend that by being acquainted with this young man, readers will find strength in their weaknesses, joy in their unhappiness, and satisfaction in learning from an individual who truly knows how to make the best out of every moment of life.

The column appeared in the *North Idaho Sunday* on Easter 1986, and many readers expressed their appreciation for seeing it on that particular day because of its illustration of how one strong young man chose to approach a daunting challenge. Shortly after its publication, I sent the piece to Steve Symms, one of Idaho's U.S. senators at the time, requesting that he pass it along to President Reagan in hopes that he might honor Tony with a personal letter. With the hectic pace of spring months at Sandpoint High, I never thought much about that gesture again. When spring vacation ended and we had returned to finish off the last eight weeks of school, Tony did not appear in his chair. I soon learned that his family had taken him to Arizona to receive therapy from a Navajo healer. Traditional medical procedures were ineffective, and the family's hope now lay in the powers of this man's herbs and prayers. We didn't see Tony for several weeks, but one day I walked into the classroom, and there he sat. He had lost weight, his arm was in a sling, but his color seemed better. He had come home to catch up with school and get set for the upcoming prom.

Little did Tony know that the prom committee had plans for him, too. One day the seniors came to me and asked if they could borrow the ugly chair on decorating day and return it to my room the following Monday. As always, the air around the school was electric as seniors made their elaborate plans for the biggest night of their young lives. Ballots for prom king and queen came out on Friday and were counted. The results remained a well-guarded secret. As the dance drew nearer, Tony beamed with enthusiasm while telling me all the details about his two upcoming proms. It was obvious he had put aside any health concerns in favor of what we all knew would probably be the most exciting night of his life – ever.

I attended the affair as a single that year, without my husband, Bill. He had never cared much for dances, especially because he didn't know how to dance very well, and my coordination hadn't improved much since the college days of nearly flunking folk dancing. My role was senior class adviser, but I had another aim in attending this prom: Tony's happiness. I wanted to see him in his tuxedo, meet his date, and see what the prom committee had done with the chair. I wasn't disappointed.

Like the gym, the chair had experienced complete transformation. Fabric surgery had been performed; it had undergone a complete "chair-lift." Now covered in white cloth with decorative trim, the "throne" was stunningly handsome, indeed, as was the young man in the white tuxedo who sat on its cushion. Tony was dashing and proud, to say the least. And Tracey, a tiny, down-to-earth, bubbly young lady, instantly won me over. I could immediately see why Tony had been so excited to show her off. It was also easy to see that she was a friend, true to the core and that she, the vibrant varsity mascot, was making sure this would be a magnificent experience for her buddy Tony.

Others had done their part, too. Not only did they decorate the chair especially for Tony's big evening at the prom, but the class had also voted nearly unanimously for him to reign over the evening as their prom king. As the royalty announcement was about to occur, a group of senior football players gathered around Tony and Tracey, who were seated together on the chair.

"The prom king for 1986 is – Tony Bottarini!" resounded throughout the gym. Students cheered and clapped as the football brigade lifted the chair, with Tony in it, and carried it to the center of the dance floor. In many cases, smiling eyes began to drip tears of joy as Tony's classmates, faculty members and parents celebrated what everyone knew in their hearts was an unforgettable moment. Shortly thereafter, Queen Denise

Nadeja joined Tony on the floor for the royalty dance. The moment was magical, not only for Tony but for everyone in the room. A young man's dream evening had suddenly turned into a heavenly experience. The seniors had spoken through their balloting and had lifted Tony's spirits beyond the stars.

"I can't believe it," he told me after the dance as he relaxed on his throne with the crimson prom king sash draped over his white tux. While the cleanup crew removed decorations and the few stragglers, who hadn't headed off to after-prom parties, hung around to collect souvenir decorations, it was rehash time for Tony. Almost in a daze, Tony grilled me about how in the world he had ever been elected prom king.

"Are you sure they didn't make a mistake?" he asked.

"No, Tony," I reassured him. "No mistake, you won fair and square." To witness this young man's genuine disbelief, followed with smile after smile as the reality of the evening's events all eventually sank in was an supremely satisfying experience. Tony sprawled in his throne with Tracey by his side and savored his version of Camelot. For a few shining moments, he forgot all pain, all misery, all hardship. This special evening belonged to Tony. He knew it. Those moments in his throne helped him seize it and enjoy a temporary escape from the inevitable and cruel fate that would result from his spreading cancer.

I didn't know when I said good-bye and wished him well that evening that my next meeting with Tony would occur 350 miles away a week later at another hastily planned and momentous event in his life. Like Cinderella, the throne would quickly revert to its original disheveled state, return to Room 4, never again to be occupied by King Tony.

Two days later I called the Bottarini residence to hear how the rest of the weekend had gone. I was stunned to learn that Elena, Tony's stepmother, who had driven thousands of miles chauffeuring him to treatments, was not there to answer the phone. She was at the hospital with Tony. Doctors had determined that his lungs had filled with fluid and more tumors, and he was being transferred to a Kaiser hospital in Portland. The tumor on his arm had continued to get worse; the arm would be removed. News of his condition traveled quickly around

Sandpoint High School. The prognosis was dismal. Tony's final dream was to receive his diploma. Was this dream possible?

By Tuesday, a plan was unfolding behind the scenes to ensure that Tony *would* graduate from Sandpoint High School. Jim Wilund had served as principal at Sandpoint High School for two years. Like the rest of us, he had watched Tony's bravery and marveled at his perseverance, for Tony made it to school as often as possible when so many healthy kids looked for every excuse to be elsewhere. A former University of Idaho Vandal football player, Jim occasionally put on a gruff exterior but always delighted in good teasing. He was a jock but also a classical pianist. Taught well by his parents, Ruby and Pat, some folks in town considered him a prince of a man. When Jim learned about Tony's setback, he went home that evening and shared the news with his wife, Raye. Immediately, Raye went into action. Why not coordinate a special graduation ceremony for Tony in his hospital room?

Within two days, all arrangements were made. The diploma company had been contacted. Tony's diploma would be sent in overnight mail to the hospital for Jim to pick up. The school secretary, Joni Sutton, genuinely touched like so many people, bought an airline ticket to Portland for Jim, while Dr. Forrest Bird, a world-famous inventor who lived in the area, donated money for a second ticket. I received a call one night from Raye Wilund, explaining the events that had so quickly unfolded.

"You're going, too," she said. "We've got an airline ticket for you. You'll fly over to Portland Friday morning and return that evening." Although caught off guard and prone to decline such an offer in favor of someone else, I offered no debate. Tony had inspired me so much for the past couple of years. I felt very close to this special young man and cherished our wonderful relationship. Tony had become my buddy. The opportunity to see him one more time and to take part in what we all knew would be a momentous event was a privilege.

I scurried around the next day so that I could leave early, early Friday morning. My feelings were mixed as I thought about how exciting it would be to watch Tony receive his diploma but how uncomfortable it would feel to see him lying in a hospital bed without his arm. The scene would definitely be a big switch from seeing him in the dapper white tuxedo on the fancy throne of a few nights before.

Arriving in Portland, Jim and I rented a car and drove straight to the hospital. We had barely four hours to spend with Tony and his family before catching the flight back home. At the hospital, Tony's diploma was waiting for us. As we began searching for his hospital room, my always-nervous stomach went into overdrive. The unknown, especially when it deals with the suffering of friends or family, makes me almost physically ill. In short, I find all the bathrooms. This experience was no different. I'm sure I stopped by two restrooms before we finally saw Charlie and Elena Bottarini standing in the hallway watching out for us. They welcomed us, met Jim for the first time and quietly updated us on Tony's condition. Jim reviewed his diploma-presenting plan with Charlie and Elena. The scheme included a carrot that we hoped would increase Tony's desire to keep going. Jim would present him the diploma with the idea that Tony would show up in two weeks to walk through graduation with his class-mates. Charlie and Elena thought the idea sounded just fine; they were thrilled that someone had gone to such lengths on their son's behalf. We walked into Tony's room, and I was immediately pleasantly surprised. Sitting up in bed, obviously eager to see us, he greeted us with a big smile. The fact that he was missing his arm did not make me feel nearly as uncomfortable as I had expected. He was wearing that familiar black hat, and his color was remarkable for a person that had endured such a trau-matic few days. I learned later that the sanguine skin tone was deceiving because he had just received a blood transfusion, which lends a decep-tively healthy look to a sick person's face.

We exchanged small talk. Then, Jim began the brief ceremony. Along with the diploma came a red-and-white tassel, which Elena attached to Tony's black cap. After a few words, Jim handed him the diploma with the stipulation that he would have to give it back for another presentation later that month. Tony grinned from ear to ear and promised that he would do his best. We visited for a while longer, enjoyed a quick lunch with Elena and Charlie and said our good-bye to Tony. That visit was the last time I ever saw him. To witness the obvious delight on his face and see his pride in that diploma was a moment Jim and I knew we must never forget. Charlie and Elena knew it, too, and Tony probably knew better than any of us that our visit and the ceremony had been a good idea.

Soon after our trip to Portland, Charlie, Elena and Tony left the hospital and returned to Arizona. Tony did not want to die in a hospital bed, so for the next two weeks, the family gathered at Joel and Janet Thalheimer's house in Phoenix. A family friend, Joel had played a crucial role in Tony's life, guiding him spiritually through the tough times. He would be guiding Tony to the end. During the next two weeks, Elena called to give me updates, which I passed on to Tony's friends and teachers.

One noon, while talking to students in my classroom, I was told I had an important phone call in the faculty room. My heart sank with the certainty that this could be the dreaded call – that Elena would be at the other end, telling me Tony had died. Walking down the hallway, I tried to prepare myself with hopes that I would have something intelligent to say when she broke the news. The faculty room emitted its usual low roar as teachers gabbed away the noon hour. Picking up the phone, I so wished that I could take this call in a more private place. I had a difficult time hearing the voice at the other end through the increasing volume of the chatter. In fact, I missed the name but was really relieved to determine that it was definitely *not* Elena.

"I'm sorry, " I said. "Can you repeat that again? I'm in a noisy room."

"My name is Nancy Theis," the warm voice at the other end announced. "I'm President Reagan's secretary, and I'm calling to see what you'd like me to do about this lovely letter." I *had* heard her correctly the first time, but I really had thought my ears were playing tricks with me. Once I realized this lady was for real, I attempted to shush the talk in hopes of hearing her better. The roar toned down a bit, but my colleagues continued their chatter as I asked the caller to repeat herself one more time.

" ... and what would you like me to do about this story?" she asked. "This is so touching. It's sitting here on my desk. I'm sorry I didn't get to it sooner ... I notice it was sent some time ago, but it just arrived in my office."

Still in shock, I admitted my surprise. "Let me pick myself off the floor first. I can't believe I'm talking to somebody like you."

Nancy made it easy. Her empathy also made it easy to understand why she had her job of contacting people under such situations. I later learned that Nancy Theis had been a reading teacher herself in California. After her hard work on President Reagan's campaign in the Bay Area, she had been rewarded with the position of director of presidential correspondence. She and her staff oversaw the millions of letters addressed to the President and decided how to respond to each. Her husband, Paul, had written speeches for President Gerald Ford, so the couple were seasoned players in big-time Republican politics.

"How can I contact Tony?" she asked. "How is he doing?"

I reported to her that Tony was in Arizona and that he had taken a downward turn.

"If you'll give me an address, I can get a letter out today," she said. "I'll send him a picture of the President too." We visited briefly after that, and the conversation ended. I hung up the phone and stood like a statue staring off into space.

"Well, who was it?" someone asked – recognizing that this was not just any call.

"It was President Reagan's secretary," I announced. "She called about Tony, and she's sending a letter from the President to him today." That exciting news dulled the roar. My colleagues were just as amazed as I that someone in that high position would just call a teacher at Sandpoint High. I headed off to class in a bit of a daze but thrilled to know that Tony would have his surprise. I hoped it would arrive in time!

That afternoon I rushed home and wasted no time calling Elena to tell her the news that Tony would soon hear from the President. We agreed to keep the news a surprise but at least she would know to look for something in the mail. During the conversation, I had a surprise of my own. After Elena and I had covered all the news, she said, "Just a minute."

"Hello, Mrs. Love," the weak voice said at the other end. It was Tony.

Never expecting to hear his voice again, I was stunned for a moment but regained my composure. We discussed how he was doing, and he wanted to know how things were going at Sandpoint High School. Once again, we talked about how he was going to have to get better and be back to the school by early next week for graduation. He promised he would do his best. I managed to fake a positive attitude throughout the conversation; then, we said our good byes. That bonus chat with Tony exceeded my expectations and even gave me a faint hope that maybe he would pull off one more trip to Sandpoint. He sounded pretty determined.

That trip was not to happen.

Two days later, his family gathered around him in the Arizona bedroom, prayed and said their good-byes. Elena later told me Tony had asked about me at the time. The letter from the President had not arrived, but Tony was told that it was on its way. He smiled.

Early the next morning, a Friday, I received a call at the school. It was Elena telling me that Tony had passed away. She told me that she wanted me to plan Tony's memorial service, that they would like it to be held at Sandpoint High School, and that they would like me to talk to the Catholic priest about the religious ceremony. This assignment, though daunting, was an honor and privilege for me. Elena told me they would be home as soon as possible but that they wanted me come up with the plan for a memorial service for the following Tuesday. Her only suggestion was that we encourage balloons instead of flowers.

Before thinking about any planning, I had one sad chore to complete: notifying the staff and students that Tony had died. I wrote up a simple announcement, no more than a paragraph, stating the available facts. It was first period when the announcement was made. For the rest of the day, what would have been a rather raucous Friday, with seniors wrapping up their last day, turned subdued and respectfully quiet. Until that day, the Class of 1986 had been notorious as one of the most difficult and rebellious groups SHS had ever seen. As senior class adviser, I had witnessed their disagreeable behavior firsthand. In fact, at one noontime class meeting, I literally had to out scream and physically separate some senior girls having a disagreement about an upcoming project. The day

Jim and I had flown to Portland, they had really distinguished themselves with the most publicly chronicled senior kegger ever held in the history of the school. What distinguished this particular beer party from any other was that instead of being held in some obscure mountain meadow, the kegger was held at a senior's house while his parents were gone. As usually happens, someone notified the cops, but for some reason, not too many of the partyers were too concerned. A few escaped by running into the woods, but by the time it was over, 74 seniors had been arrested. To add to the scandal, the following week, the local paper published the culprits' names in a banner story above the fold. Some students – athletes, scholars, leaders – had made the paper plenty of times before but never quite in that light. This was publicity they hadn't appreciated.

Two weeks later, when Tony's death was announced, this entire class of generally rowdy seniors grew up almost overnight. Lifelong enemies suddenly came together and became close friends. Their behavior, their sudden maturity and their seriousness showed that many had learned what is really important in life.

From Friday evening until the memorial service, many teachers, students, and parents worked nonstop to prepare a memorial fit for a king – a senior class prom king, that is. The flurry of activity included contacting people, preparing the programs, writing an obituary for the paper and the radio, and decorating. All was ready the day a procession of priests, altar servers and dignitaries filed into the gym, filled with about 700 mourners and at least as many colorful balloons, tied to folding chairs and swaying back and forth along the stage. During the service, several friends, including Joel Thalheimer and Tracey Delyea, shared poignant stories about their experiences with Tony. Because I was emotionally involved with Tony and his family, I had written a letter to Tony but asked a student to read it at the funeral rather than read it myself. The memorial service was both sad and upbeat. Tony would have wanted it that way.

When the program drew to a close, all attendees untied the balloons from the chairs, left the gym and walked to the grassy, central quad of the high school. Once the entire group had assembled on green grass beneath the deep blue spring sky, Tracey said a few final words of farewell to Tony and released her balloon. Soon after, like a flock of geese, several hundreds of other balloons followed its lead into the sky, as we all said good-bye to the young man who had touched so many of our lives. There were tears but also many smiles, as all eyes followed the balloons while they floated toward the heavens.

Tony made it to graduation – in spirit. Kari Saccomanno, ASB vice president and Tony's marching partner, entered the gym alone, carrying a single balloon. She sat next to an empty chair. When Tony's name was read during the diploma presentation, the gym erupted with enthusiastic applause. When the Class of 1986 walked out of Sandpoint High School gymnasium in their red-and-white caps and gowns for the last time together, instead of immediately running to meet family members, they gathered outside the school as Kari released a balloon to the cool night air. The students stood for a moment, watching as the single balloon slowly faded into the darkness. Then, they headed their separate ways – visibly touched by memories of a spirit that had united them and had taught them an invaluable lesson about the meaning of life.

It's been more than 20 years now since Tony's death. His memory, however, has probably affected more lives than those of his classmates, teachers, family and friends. When my friend Jim Wilund later became principal of Lewiston High School, Tony's picture hung in his office. Every time a tough, unruly student showed up, Jim pointed at the photo and told Tony's story. He told of the courage this young man showed in the midst of his illness, and he suggested that the troubled student think about Tony's story the next time he or she figured life had dealt them a bad hand. For several years, the Tony Bottarini Scholarship Award was given to Sandpoint High School seniors who had displayed some form of courage in tough times during their years as students. Recipients received a written summary of Tony's life and were asked to take a bit of him along their life journeys. A white-and-red, metal Bulldog outside the school crafted by Bill MacDonald's shop students bears Tony's name. A group of Jackie DeWitt's home economics students created a collage with his name, his picture and the poem written for his memorial service. The collage now hangs on the wall in the school office. His senior portrait sits on a windowsill in my living room.

Tony's throne continued to sit in my classroom for another four years, becoming even more disreputable in appearance but always maintaining its position of esteem. At least once during each school year, the students heard about the king who had once occupied that coveted spot and were always asked to demonstrate respect for the opportunity of sitting in his throne. When the new Sandpoint High School was opened in 1992, the throne mysteriously disappeared while furniture was transported from the old to the new. I never researched its disappearance; we were too busy dealing with the challenges of a brand-new school and a new principal.

Years later, the Love furniture farm once again donated a comfortable piece to my classroom. This time it was a purple pastel love seat, which headed to school after we bought new furniture to spruce up the house for our son's wedding. Cats at my mother's house, and later at ours, had shredded its four corners, so I took along a yellow bedspread to cover the damage. With its appearance, my classroom suddenly became a relaxing gathering place for both staff and students.

The "Love" seat also served as a great discipline tool for my English classes. Students had to earn the right to sit in it during class time. Each day a student's name was drawn. If the person had an impeccable behavior record, he or she could become the envy of peers and lounge in its comfort for the entire class hour. And as they had years before, the students sat in silence the day I told the Tony Bottarini story of courage and of his special throne.

4.

Stay Outa My House

'Twas the night after New Year's Eve and all through the Love house, most creatures were not stirring, but I, in my sweats, was watching TV. In fact, I hadn't even washed or combed my hair that day. The whole family had been pretty lazy since we had spent the previous, festive night welcoming in 1994 with some old friends, the Raiha family.

New Year's Eve is a big night at the Raihas. Rauno came to the United States from Finland in his teens. His wife, Margarete, immigrated to Washington, D.C., from Germany as a junior in high school. When the two eventually met, married and produced their three children Andy, Dan and Deanne, old-country traditions blended with their new American forms of celebration. The family followed a set, always enjoyable procedure every holiday, especially on Christmas and New Year's Eve. At Christmas time, it was the tall, skinny tree cut from the family property, brought to the house and embellished with strategically placed limbs cut from other trees. The Raihas also earned fame among friends throughout the community for their annual trays of assorted German Christmas cookies, each intricately formed, decorated and exquisitely wrapped in cellophane. Except for the year the dog ate most of our tray, Bill always stood a protective watch over the cookies, gradually selecting and removing his favorites from the assortment for himself.

A week later, each year, we usually attended the Raihas' New Year's Eve party, knowing we had a full evening of fun in store with ample and delectable fish trays, breads, salads, specialty imported liqueur-filled

German chocolates, and a variety of fine wines to suit each stage of the evening's activities. The amiable conversation, including a few quips from Rauno about "those Russians," always made for a convivial feast. After the smorgasbord, guests gathered with the Raiha family around the piano as Margarete accompanied our mostly off-key voices in traditional Christmas carols. Except for the few talented singers, most of us were pretty bad, but with the good wine and amiable camaraderie, who cared if "It Came upon a Midnight Clear" sounded like it really ought to go back to wherever it came from? As this special midnight drew clearly closer and the carolers resorted to more lip-synching than actual singing, we all gravitated to the kitchen where Rauno had an assortment of aluminum-cast bullets ready for meltdown. Once the big moment of the New Year arrived and we had finished off glasses of champagne, everyone took turns participating in the old German tradition of pouring molten lead into cold water. In each case, the marriage of lead and water created a unique, sometimes grotesque shape, destined to be interpreted as a symbol for what might lie ahead in the new year for that particular person. And at that late hour in the young year, we would come up with some pretty creative interpretations.

As the clock struck 2 a.m. on January 1, 1994, someone in the Love family suggested that it was probably time to go home. The hint was disregarded, for one more conversation would lead to another. I'm sure this enthusiastic early-morning chatting was the Raihas' method of making sure the wine had worn off and that all the guests were all fit to drive home from their charming home, nestled in the woods east of Sandpoint.

After saying what seemed like a hundred "good-byes" and many "thank yous" for the wonderful hospitality, we had finally arrived at our home at 3:30 a.m. After too-few hours of sleep, we all slouched around the house, doing little other than feeding the animals, stuffing ourselves while watching the New Year's Day parades and bowl games. Not long after dinner that evening, Bill and the kids filed off to bed. By 9:30 p.m. I'd decided to let whatever was on the tube lull me to sleep. Suddenly, as I was about to doze off, two bright headlights appeared at the end of our long driveway and began beaming their way toward the house.

"No way," I muttered to myself, jumping from the couch and racing down the hallway to the bathroom, instantly determining that these uninvited guests could come visiting some other time. I was *not* going to the door. It was hard to hear what was happening outside because of the TV, so I climbed into the bathtub, stood on the very narrow soap counters, grasped the ledge with one hand and, with the other, carefully slid open the tiny bathroom window in an attempt to figure out just who it was. Hearing some very familiar giggles, I became more determined than ever that this frumpy, exhausted hostess would not fling open the Love door. The prior year's high school newspaper editors, et al – much as I loved them – could go elsewhere and bug somebody else on this evening.

Ha!

They knocked and knocked.

Certainly they'll figure out that nobody's coming to the door, and they'll leave, I thought while precariously straddled across the tub, like a climber scaling Yosemite's Half Dome. Only I didn't have my rock climbing equipment for stability, and I hardly resembled a sculptured candidate fit for outdoor catalog stardom. For some reason, the toes on my right foot kept slipping from the soap tray, keeping me dangerously close to falling nearly a foot straight down into the tub. Though the odds of killing myself from a fiberglass face fall hardly came close to the dangers facing rock climbers, the embarrassment of later explaining why I was in the tub – in the dark – in my sweat clothes could permanently scar my reputation for reasonable sanity. The will to avoid such a circumstance kept every muscle in my toes, hands and arms focused on staying put.

After a minute or so, my concentration met with distraction when I heard the outside invaders leave the porch and start running around the back of the house.

"No!" I muttered along with a few other expletives. "They're *not* going away! Expletive! Expletive! Why don't they just get out of here?" The giggling and sprinting around the house continued. I heard them race past the bathroom window, heading back to the main entrance. Carefully but hardly gracefully, I extricated myself from the tub, dashed to the bedroom, and dove under the covers next to Bill who had entered into a comfortable, deep winter slumber.

"Those *Cedar Post* kids from last year are out there," I whispered. "They won't go away. Pretend you're asleep!" I'm sure Bill wondered why he needed instructions on pretending he was asleep when he *had been* asleep before my crash-landing beneath the covers.

The next sounds were the most unwelcome of all. *They* had entered the house. *They* were giggling uncontrollably. *They* seemed ubiquitous. *They* were in the living room. Then, some of them started down the hallway, squealing all the way.

"I can't believe this," I whispered to Bill. "Don't make a sound! They'll leave when they know we're asleep."

Ha!

Suddenly, we could hear the bedroom doorknob begin to turn. We could sense the presence of someone attempting to be quiet while pushing it open. Bill and I lay like corpses beneath the covers.

"Look – they're asleep," the invader observed.

My, *how astute*, I thought quietly. *Please get outa my house!*

The figure stood there for a moment, holding the door as her adrenaline-charged accomplices nearly pushed the leader into the bedroom while making lame attempts to stifle their snickers. I wondered: *If they'd come in this far, what was next?*

Finally, the door closed as they raced down the hallway to greet their buddies who were apparently up to other projects.

"They'll leave now," I whispered to Bill, not moving a muscle. "They've got to leave."

They didn't.

For the next few minutes, the muffled voices and occasional giggles kept us stranded, helpless hostages in our own bed. Miraculously, our son and daughter in the neighboring bedrooms continued to hibernate. Praying that Willie and Annie would not be aroused, I remained committed to one truth: Giving in, getting up and greeting them at this point was absolutely not an option. Entertaining uninvited company aimed on hanging out until long into the winter's night was the last item on my things-to-do list that night. I'm sure Bill agreed, but I knew better than to survey his thoughts at that moment. Feigning deep slumber seemed the only wise course of action.

The action in the living room continued for at least another 15 minutes. Inside our bedroom hideout, it seemed like hours. Finally, the noise subsided. Soon we detected the sound of a car motor running. Sitting up in bed, we watched the welcome sight of red taillights bouncing over the driveway potholes. Cautiously waiting to make sure they had indeed left the premises, I slowly tiptoed from the bedroom toward the living room. With the television still blaring, I surveyed the room. A series of Post-it notes partially blocked the football action on the picture tube. Looking further, I could see that yellow Post-its had added a new touch to our home decor.

"Do you always leave your TV running and your lights on when you go to bed?" one note inquired. Another expressed great disappointment that I was not able to visit with them. After reading all the "clever" messages, I knew I did not want to be caught off guard again, so I immediately switched off the TV and lights, locked the doors and hurried back to bed. After reassuring Bill that all was well, I dozed off to sleep.

I was at last entering Snoozeland. Suddenly, a noise outside interrupted my relaxed state. I sat up in time to spot headlights once again coming toward the house.

"No – no. Not again!" I wailed, once again waking Bill. "They're back!"

My patient husband had nothing to say. He just sat up in a dreamland stupor and looked into the darkness.

"I'm *not* getting up! What are they doing now? Why don't they go bother someone else?" I complained. Once again, we maintained quiet vigilance in our refuge beneath the covers. Once again, we heard the giggles and could sense active bodies moving around the house, but at least they could not come inside the house this time. After all, it was dark. The TV was off. The doors were locked. They were wise enough to stay outside, but apparently, they had returned to take care of some unfinished business. About five minutes later, the car once again departed, heading north.

"What have they done this time?" I groaned. Feeling another bedroom exit was now safe, I headed down the hallway and flipped on the porch light. The entire back porch was now adorned with toilet paper streamers. Stepping outside among the decorations, I looked further but could see no other new additions to our decor. Back to bed again.

"Well, this time they toilet-papered the porch," I reported to Bill, who was trying desperately to roll over and pretend this really wasn't happening. His main objective at this moment was sleep. I felt the same and soon fell off into never-never land temporarily.

If the third time is a charm, as they like to say, this visit might just inspire a call to the sheriff. This time, however, the invaders had four legs.

My slumber had once again rudely interrupted by what sounded like heavy pounding on the frozen ground outside the bedroom window. Eyeing the digital clock, I could see we would be experiencing another midnight in this young year, wide-awake. As the grogginess of my tired brain cleared, my senses zeroed into another fun project ahead. The pounding outside was coming from horse hooves – horse hooves definitely not in the barnyard where they belonged – but in the front yard, just outside the bedroom window.

"Oh goody," I announced. "That commotion from those kids must've scared the horses, and they've broken the fence down."

So, at 11:45 p.m., Bill and I arose from our beds to see for sure what was the matter. Bundled up with winter coats over our sweat pants and stumbling around in big barnyard boots, we spent the next few minutes rounding up our two friendly but impish Arabian geldings, Casey and Rambo. Now, anyone who has ever owned a horse will concur with just how easy it can be to convince the liberated critters to go back to bed when they're experiencing the arrogant delight of escaping their barnyard confinement.

Again, *Ha!*

With heads high in the air, noses pointing toward the sky, tails sticking straight up like feather dusters and displaying the proud, prancing gaits of the Royal Lippizans, loose horses love to play keep-away. And, it's even more fun to play this fun game in the dark. An irate human awakened from a winter slumber, having to don clumsy boots, heavy jacket and armed with a litany of nasty expletives seldom enjoys the fun while trying to entice the elusive equine escapees back to their corral.

In fact, if ever there had been a video camera in action while this human-versus-horse pursuit occurs, a new reality show could hit the markets. It could be called "The Near-Death Equine Experience." For some reason, every time I discover my horses have found an open gate or broken a board fence to take a trot down the driveway or leave their prints in the lawn and garden, I always hold out faint hope that they'll actually listen to me this time as I gently plead with them to go back to the barn.

Barnyard lesson: Just as I learned with students, years ago, kindness and a soft, soothing voice will not always work. These horses couldn't care less about listening to me, let alone honoring my polite request to behave. That's when the cursing begins.

Teaching lesson: The reader should note that the comparison between disciplining naughty horses and misbehaving students stops here. Although often strongly tempted over my 33-year teaching span, I can count on my index finger the number of times profanities fell from my lips to convince some adolescent human jerk to knock it off. With the exception of a few hard-core incorrigibles, who now more than likely have joined our nation's prison population, a moment of uncomfortable silence combined with the hate stare or the index finger firmly pointed toward the door usually sufficed.

To this day, however, hate stares and index fingers pointed toward the barnyard gate have never yet persuaded horses to return to their incarceration. Cursing – of the nature that the neighbors over at the place next door can hear it – along with a few strategically launched, often poorly aimed dog pans, pine cones, rocks, or sticks, have, on occasion, worked for me, but not without several laps around the house with horses and humans darting among the trees and through the garden. When all hope is lost that Rambo or Casey will obediently return home, we always give in and resort to the one and only sure bet – a rattling grain can and a hidden halter held tightly. A smart horse will recognize the sound of oats swishing within tin. A smart horse will also quickly key into the jingle of halter hardware, which is definitely not a welcome sound.

That's just what we did on that late winter night in 1994, and once more, Rambo and Casey wisely avoided punishment by responding to the grain can, allowing us to secure one of the errant pair with the halter as the other followed us obediently back to the barn. Making sure the gate to their escape route was secure, we headed back to the house.

We did eventually get some sleep that night, and those kids – we eventually identified them – did become responsible adults. I don't think any have gone to jail. One works as an award-winning Spokane *Spokesman-Review* reporter. Another uses her writing skills in various West Coast venues. Another helps nurture salmon at a hatchery in Alaska. The group also includes a social worker, a computer guru and a full-fledged veterinarian, who apparently redeemed herself enough to endorse the back cover of my first book, "Pocket Girdles." One young man even teaches high school journalism and English in an Oregon school. I cling to the perverse hope that maybe – just maybe – by now he has lost a little sleep because of his own late-night intruders.

• • •

That unwelcome New Year's visit marked the first time in a number of years that our home had served as a refuge for teens passing through that life stage where anyone else's home – even a teacher's – is more fun than where Mom and Dad live. The dearth of youthful visitors over the years came gradually and by design – my own. Early in my career as the yearbook and drill team adviser, I had welcomed such occasions and even felt somewhat flattered that kids liked to drop in to my home for a visit. During those days, the fact that they never seemed to know enough to go home until one or two in the morning didn't bother me. After all, I was single *and* young during some of those years, so it was nice to have the company. Besides, my youthful body and mind could recover pretty quickly from an abbreviated night's sleep. And, it had to bounce back frequently from all the energy expended in the planning, carrying out and aftermath of year-end picnics where champion eaters like Dick Ross or Wayne Sherwood stuffed away nearly a dozen hot dogs apiece. There were also the yearbook-signing parties or group hikes on North Idaho's beautiful backcountry trails.

Once Bill and I were married, our humble abodes continued as venues for kids to gather for such events. Most at-home activities were filled with food and quirky craziness. A couple of times we even hosted the Mud Olympics. This event occurred during late February or early March, when a walk across the barnyard could mean big trouble. This was a time when foot-deep mud would come alive, turn evil and suck the barn boot right off your foot. It all happened so quickly your bootless sock with foot inside was already submerged in the partially thawed muck. One year I determined that this was the perfect time to bring on the games.

The Olympics, which would pit Student Council against the Math Club or Leohono Honor Society, included such events as a spirited mud football contest, followed by the mud fling, the mud relay and the mud tug, which took place in our slimy garden spot with a mud consistency more like pudding than barnyard stew. The horses who inhabited the pasture were never quite sure of their role as spectators or participants.

I have photos to prove how down-and-dirty the action could get. For example, one shows ASB president Hoyt Bonar holding my willing son, Willie, who was grade school age at the time, by the feet and dipping him and his white blonde hair mop into a waiting pool of wet horse apples and mucky barnyard slop. The parade and medal ceremony occurred in our hay loft, with Bill playing the Olympic theme on his harmonica as the proud but filthy teenaged Olympians marched between the hay piles and received their respective awards. All participants also received strict instructions on exactly where they were to remove their soiled Olympic apparel before setting foot near the house for the potluck afterward. Boys had the tack room, while girls changed into clean clothes in the bunkhouse. Other educators, such as assistant principal Larry Jacobson, Spanish teacher Merriam Merriman and math teacher Rick Gehring and his wife, Ann, lent credibility to the event by actually showing up and participating.

While teaching senior English, I also hosted a spring picnic to honor Geoffrey Chaucer's "Canterbury Tales." Using the scavenger-hunt approach, my literature students began their pilgrimage by climbing the ladder to the hayloft to retrieve their first clue. Each clue, a short poem following a metrical tale rhyme scheme, directed the participants to the next spot either on our farm or somewhere in the neighborhood, where a group would pause long enough to read aloud their original tale of modern-day workers. Often, the most popular stories centered on whoever happened to be the school principal at the time. Fortunately for me, the lucky central character in the kids' literary creations was never in attendance. By the end of the pilgrimage, a couple of neutral judges (usually my colleagues) decided who had created the most clever tale. The lucky winners later dined on steak – not hamburgers or hot dogs – at the climactic eating fest.

These gatherings created vivid memories for kids and for me, and they usually went off without a hitch. A few times, however, the enterprising minds of a few teenagers looking for action led me to second-guess the wisdom of extending my hospitality toward my students.

Take the drill team picnic of 1976, for example. After a sumptuous feast of wieners, hamburgers, Nalley's chips and deli potato salad, we decided to take the girls on a hike up Greenhorn Mountain, home of the present-day Mickinnick Trail, behind our house. Once the group had arrived at an appropriate promontory for viewing of the valley and lake below, Bill would top off the night by playing nostalgic harmonica favorites like "Oh Susanna" or "Shenandoah." That first year that we had added the hike-harmonica segment to the evening schedule, the girls received my commentary on the points of interest in the forest as we made our way to the mountain. I pointed to the spot, for example, where I learned for sure I could never willingly kill anything. One time, I had pointed my pistol at what I thought was a grouse and couldn't pull the trigger. It turned out to be a stump. Then, there were the two weathered-but-intact wagon wheels partially hidden in a depression surrounded by needles, ferns, bushes and trees.

"These belong to my first grade teacher, Mrs. Kinney," I explained.

"She's lived here in the neighborhood forever. Must be they were left here when some pioneers came to Idaho. I wish I had these in my yard."

LESSON: Don't ever suggest your secret desires to students. The ol' phrase "you may just get what you ask for" happens more often than not – especially if teens feel a sense of loyalty.

A year later, the Ponderettes again gathered in late May at our tiny one bedroom rental house situated below Greenhorn Mountain. This year, for some reason, the mountain hike seemed to be just a popular precursor for expectation of the evening's events. Some Ponderettes just couldn't wait to get going. Stuffing down their hot dogs, Jacque and Sue seemed uncharacteristically anxious as they prompted the others to hurry up eating their dinner. Soon, two dozen well-fed troopers set off across knee-deep grass squealing as they stepped into the puddles left from the previous day's rain. As we reached the base of the mountain, the group began to splinter off into smaller groups, so when we arrived at Bill's concert site to await his annual harmonica performance, the fact that we had a few stragglers seemed like no big deal. With most of the girls seated on huge rock boulders or soft green moss, the show began. Several songs later and after enthusiastic applause for the outdoor musical treat, the May mosquitoes arrived for their blood-sucking smorgasbord, so we wasted no time heading back to the house.

"See ya there," I announced. "Be careful going downhill and don't trip. Stay away from the bears! We've seen moose in these woods, too!" That reminder usually got the slackers to speed up a bit. It was nearly dark by the time I arrived at the house in time to find the Ponderette revelers picking up their leftovers and heading for their cars. Exchanging pleasantries with the teens while enjoying the thought of another successful picnic, my mouth was too busy and my math skills were too tucked away to notice that not all the girls who headed up the mountain had returned to the house. Suddenly, as I waved good-bye to the last group to leave the house, I noticed an extra car still parked in the driveway. It was 9:30 p.m., almost dark.

"Where *are* they, and which ones are they?" I began to wonder out loud. "Bill, they haven't all come back!" Looking again at the car, I could see that it belonged to Sue, the drill team captain.

"Now, who was she hanging out with?" I asked as Bill and I stood outside our home, nervously wondering if someone had fallen over a cliff – and very quietly at that. We hadn't heard any screams or shrieks – but then again, we had all been talking so much and so loudly, how could we? Certainly someone would have noticed. I began deducing who would have been with Sue. Before any likely prospects had popped into my head, we heard a sound far off across the fields toward the mountain. We listened. A somewhat high-pitched "hee, hee" and playful little screams followed by obvious but muffled giggles broke the still night air. Wherever they were in the darkness, it had to be some distance from the house, and whatever they were up to sounded pretty suspicious.

"What are they doing out there?" I asked.

"Dunno," Bill said, shrugging his shoulders and turning toward the house, convinced by the gleeful sounds that his Boy Scout first aid wouldn't be needed tonight.

"Guess I'll go see what's going on," I said as he rounded the corner.

By now, it was pitch dark. Avoiding the puddles lurking in the tall grass would be impossible, so I accepted the notion that wet feet would be a part of this reconnaissance mission. As a country girl who had practiced faithfully over the years all the cunning strategies that I had watched and learned from the '50s TV Westerns, I also welcomed the notion that it would be fun to sneak up on these stragglers and catch 'em in the act. So, I crouched down and took careful, silent steps toward the sounds. There really was no need for my slinking because whatever their deed, it was obviously keeping them totally focused on the territory immediately around them.

"Oops! Gotta hold it tighter," an indistinguishable voice commanded. "Now, you grab this side, and I'll hold on here."

What the heck are they doing? I again asked myself while slowly lifting one leg and carefully, quietly advancing it one step closer to the action far across the field. Suddenly I heard a uniform outburst of giggles; something had obviously distracted their focus. Curiosity was distracting my concentrated effort to remain undetected, but again, they remained oblivious to all outside stimuli.

"OK, let's get moving," I heard the captain command her unknown lieutenant. I, too, followed her instructions and took a few more giant, hopefully indiscernible steps, one foot landing smack dab in the middle of a cold, wet rain puddle. I prayed that the sound of the splash would not carry across the evening air. My prayers were answered. They still had no idea of my presence as their grunts and groans became one giant cacophonous, shrieking outburst. The noise certainly announced to any critters of the night that unknown, two-legged monsters had invaded their hallowed ground. It also firmly implied that I wasn't going to like my impending discovery.

Deciding my attempts to scare the bejeebies out of them would go in vain, I sped up and yelled to them across the pasture.

"Hey, what's going on out here?"

"Uh-oh! She caught us!" one shrieked. "We're in trouble now!" Squeals and giggles echoed in the darkness.

My feet couldn't move fast enough for me to finally see for myself who was involved and why they hadn't returned to the house with the rest of the group. Suddenly, I was flopping flat on my face in the wet grass. This sudden mishap not only delayed discovery but once again revived the ever-present reminder of just why I had never tried out for drill team when I was these girls' age, and why I had questioned my principal Dick Sodorff's intelligence when he asked me to advise the group that first year of teaching. Pushing my wet, clumsy body upward, I took off again, intent on seeing the nefarious activity. One more obstacle, however, reminded me that it was dark – the barbwire fence, which I collided into with full force. I fell once more, this time partially pinned to the fence where the barbs had grabbed various parts of my apparel, refusing to let loose. Farm folks will tell you there is no graceful or easy way to remove oneself from a barbwire fence without ripping one's clothes or even body parts. Having a little extra bulk in the latter can complicate the situation further – and I had plenty of extra posterior to attract any barb looking for a place to dig into.

Since there's a definite dance that goes along with the effort to escape such a situation, getting stuck in the fence is the closest this clumsy body has ever come to performing the barbwire ballet. Fortunately, unlike some of my human friends, cows and horses have always had enough decency to refrain from commenting about my lack of grace and refinement as they've watched me perform the necessary escape steps. With the barb-laden wire one's unsolicited partner, the effort definitely calls for a slow dance. Fast dancing with barbwire nine times out of 10 results in disaster. To successfully loosen oneself from the grasp of this fiendish partner, one must keep feet in delicate balance and wiggle the torso ever so slowly. Maybe the barb will let go. If not, a few intricate arm motions are needed; one hand clutches the wire and the other contorts, attempting to reach the point of contact between the body and the barb. After carefully raising the wire and wiggling the torso a few more times, usually you can free yourself. But you have to be careful because those barbs know a good, meaty body when they see one, and just as one has succumbed to your escape tactics, another might just grab the seat of your pants. Using my long-practiced strategies gained from many similar predicaments, I eventually freed myself from the fence and sloshed onward through at least eight inches of water and grass. Even at up-close range, I could barely make out the two figures in the darkness, but by now I recognized the unknown voice. It belonged to Jacque, a junior member of the marching squad. Somehow her involvement in this great wagon wheel caper came as no surprise. After all, as a sophomore in my English class, she had recorded an entire Word Clues vocabulary lesson on the tips of her fingers – 25 definitions, roots, prefixes and all – in preparation for a Friday exam. She had forgotten, however, and raised her hand to ask a question before the test.

I had noticed. Jacque never did that again, but she always maintained her unique brand of creative devilishness. Though never anything serious, Jacque's creative pursuits to keep life interesting for herself and those around her usually succeeded. In spite of her occasional youthful indiscretions, Jacque's loyalty in my behalf endeared her to me from the get-go. I also appreciated her mother, Jan, a devoted drill team supporter whose sewing talents saved us many times. I admired Jacque's spunk and identified with her tendency (outside of drill team, of course) to walk to the beat of her own drummer – figuratively, that is. Therefore, it was difficult for me ever to get mad at her. Sue's involvement in this crime did surprise me. Up to this time, I had seen nothing but her maturity and no-nonsense leadership skills. Sue's senioritis must have finally gotten the best of her on this spring evening.

Now that I knew *who* the culprits were, I didn't have to spend any time trying to figure out what they were doing. They were crouched in the grass huddled over something they could not hide.

"Oh my god!" I intoned with articulation adequate for any creature within a mile radius to clearly understand. Sue and Jacque appeared ready to join me in prayer as they gripped different sections of one of Mrs. Kinney's rustic wagon wheels and knelt before me. I towered over them, totally stunned, not only with the nature of their crime but with the perseverance they had demonstrated in carrying it out. While on our hike to Bill's mountain concert, they had left the group shortly after we crawled through the fence on Mrs. Kinney's property. Somehow they had remembered for an entire year the precise spot in the bushes in those strange woods where I had pointed to the wheels. GPS devices weren't available to the general public at that time, so these two must have had X-ray vision or photographic memories. Even more amazing was that the petite young ladies had manhandled that heavy wagon wheel with its iron axle and rim across, over or under two barbwire fences and through a rutted pasture with knee-deep grass and, often, knee-deep water.

"We remembered how much you liked them," Sue announced. "We wanted you to have them. We've been planning this ever since last year."

Rather than chastising them, I couldn't help but marvel at their prowess and fortitude but most of all at their desire to do something nice for their drill team adviser. How could I get mad? Besides, Mrs. Kinney obviously hadn't used those wagon wheels for quite some time. Since she was living in a retirement home somewhere away from Sandpoint and hadn't been on her property for at least 10 years, I doubted she had even thought of them for several decades. *Better that someone who appreciated them should take over stewardship of the old relics*, I rationalized.

She'll never know, I thought to myself. *As long as they've moved it this far, might as well take it all the way. It's too far away from the woods to return it this time of the night.* A favorite discipline line in teaching circles suggests that "life is full of choices." Well, after all these rationalizations, I made a choice. The wagon wheel would move on to the Love house. I had served as a partner to this crime in progress.

We set out across the field. As we pushed and urged the wheel forward, it kept insisting on falling to one side or the other, pulling all of us with it. At one point, it landed on Sue's arm. Her watch broke. At another point, one wheel thief passed loud gas in the night air. Someone may have wet her pants. At several points, we just let the wheel tumble along its way, collapsed on our backs, looked at the stars and giggled our hearts out. Eventually, we maneuvered the pilfered artifact through one last barbwire fence, onto the lawn and up the ramp to a well-lit garage. I summoned Bill.

"Would you believe these girls?" I commented as he inspected the wheel. "This is what they were up to. Looks like we have a new addition to our yard art. But ya know we need the pair." The girls – wet, bedraggled, scratched and bruised – stood proud, admired the wheel and smiled at their achievement.

"We'll get the other one for you next year," Jacque promised. She kept her promise. The following year Sue went off to Idaho State University to learn to be a teacher, so Jacque recruited two other Ponderettes – her sister Jeri and her friend Mari Beth – to step up to the plate, eat their hot dogs, and later detour from the party to retrieve that second wheel. I now had a set, and Mrs. Kinney never seemed to mind. I stood prepared to return them if anyone ever complained, but I felt comfortable with the notion that one person's junk is another's treasure. Indeed, the set has had a place of honor, both at our first little home and later just outside my kitchen window of the home where we lived for nearly 30 years. Every year I paint the rims and hubs bright red, the same color as Mrs. Kinney's fingernail polish, and adorn the area around the wheels with flowers. In my mind, they serve as a reminder of my first-grade teacher and one of the many hysterical experiences of my own teaching career. If Mrs. Kinney were still alive, I think she would highly approve of the direction her set of abandoned wheels have rolled.

•••

Our Love home has served as headquarters for other invasions similar to the New Year's fiasco and the wagon-wheel caper. One day, three years before my retirement, as I lay snoozing on the couch just five feet from our huge living room windows, unknown culprits, equipped with Saran wrap and toilet paper, enjoyed a heyday just a few feet outside the windows. Arising the next morning, I found my Olds Cutlass completely enveloped with plastic wrap and a juicy, festering watermelon securely attached to the top. The lower 20 feet or so of every tree in the yard stood adorned with flowing ribbons of toilet tissue, as was the entire length of our driveway. The morning paper deliverers had to fling the day's editions into the driveway because both depositories had also been mummified with plastic wrap. The local supermarkets, Safeway, Yoke's or Harold's IGA, must have had a drain on their inventory for that project.

The IGA reminds me of the Seinfeld gang, a group who surprisingly graduated in 2003 in spite of their stalking activities. Prior to their graduation, they were Harold's IGA Cafe regulars, they shot videos in the local Wal-Mart, and while on their haunts, they also showed up at my house uninvited more times than I care to count. With the real Seinfeld television gang as their heroes, these harmless but annoying souls probably enjoyed the quirkiest high school years of any students I ever knew. During early morning hours they wired up televisions on people's decks. Then, they settled in and sat back to watch the tube as the inhabitants peered out their windows, curious about the group of strangers who had moved onto their porches overnight. While still in high school, they targeted a few teachers to torment playfully almost every night after school. Tired of telling them to go away, my sister Barbara, an English teacher, even resorted to locking her classroom door and hiding from view while correcting her papers. Repelled by Barbara's lack of after-school hospitality, they would show up in my room or lounge around the desk of Luera

Holt, the counseling secretary. I still haven't figured out what their absurd attraction to their teachers was, but some people considered them the SHS stalkers – harmless but still stalkers.

Even since my retirement, this crew has continued to come to my house unannounced to help themselves to the food, the couch or our indoor television set. Though not always prepared to be the hostess with the mostess, I've found their visits to be helpful for clutter elimination. They're very good about emptying the multitude of bags filled with stale potato chips, which perennially occupy our pantry. On their last visit during their holiday break, they even solved my problem of what to do with the stale Christmas cookies.

Once in 2002, while still teaching, I greeted them at 5 in the morning while walking out to get the morning papers. I learned later that many of their surprise appearances at my house at all hours of the day and night, with video camera in hand, were all part of a plot to create a good-bye video for my retirement. Their opus, which featured several scenes of me cussing my lawn mower, hiding my head under a sweatshirt, running my rototiller through the garden patch and providing plenty of posterior shots while escaping the stalking photographers, was shown to the entire student body as a special surprise for me.

The video was a thoughtful gesture from these boys at the end of my career as well as a stunning inspiration for me to cut back on the calories. In fact, I lost 40 pounds during my first year of retirement, thanks to daily reminders of scenes from that video. In its strange way, the production also epitomized the never-ending, always unpredictable moments that teachers can encounter 24 hours a day, seven days a week no matter how hard they try to escape. A teacher's home will not serve as a hideaway. The urchins will find you.

And, I also now know, thanks to the continuing unannounced visits from my crazy Seinfeld gang, that teacher duty does not stop with retirement. In most instances, that is also very nice to know.

5.

Get My Drift?

I can't imagine a teacher who has survived a career without a few "bodily function" classroom experiences. I'm also fairly confident that my elementary and middle school colleagues would probably have a slight edge in any storytelling competition dealing with flatulence, foul odors or free-running noses. Surely such experiences occur more frequently in prepubescent or adolescent circles where sophistication and self-control hardly rank high on the student list of "items I need to master for success in life."

On the contrary, I'm sure that set of primitive values motivates the actions of some of these youth, who rather enjoy that certain 15-minutes-of-fame distinction that follows their olfactory or auditory classroom performances. While I'll grant that such happenings are likely to occur at more frequent intervals in junior high or grade school than those we observe at the high school level, I believe that the more mature versions may also remain a bit more legendary.

Take, for example, a notorious event that seized the whole school by storm when I was a sophomore at Sandpoint High School. I would wager that mentioning this incident to just about any 50- or 60-somethings who attended school that day would elicit instant laughter. The notorious girls' bathroom sighting of a fecal deposit so large it could have been recorded in Guinness Book of World Records has been remembered by all for decades. The incident slowly drifted from people's conversation but never from the memories of all those who went, saw and gasped that day.

As a student, I had giggled over my share of similar incidents. That one did, however, rank historically far beyond the occasional, sudden embarrassing sound or aroma within the classroom that always sent anyone within the immediate territory into a fit of snickers followed by speculation of "Who dunnit?"

Once I began teaching, however, I knew my lifelong inclination to laugh myself into hysteria any time someone passed gas in my midst had to cease. I had crossed the line into teacherdom, and my behavior expectation bar suddenly rose significantly. I must use restraint. I must be a good example. I must pretend that such things just did not happen.

In one case I did not have to pretend. In fact, I had no idea until afterward – the next day, in fact. This occurred fairly early in my career when I advised the drill team. One afternoon, I knew something was afoul in my fifth-period English class when several students in the back corner near the window who were supposed to be working on a preposition assignment could not stop giggling.

"What's going on back there?" I finally barked.

"Nothing," one answered as they attempted to get back to their assignment.

A minute later, the muffled hysteria once again attracted my attention, this time summoning my infamous hate stare into action. Within seconds, the guilty students were once again searching for prepositional phrases. The bell rang soon after, and they were on their way out the door.

I thought no more of the incident until the following morning when a drill team member who sat in that back corner approached me at practice with an urgent look of distress.

"What's wrong?" I asked.

She summoned me away from the rest of the girls for a private conversation.

"Mrs. Love, Henry Doe farted yesterday in English, and everybody thinks I did it," she announced. "And that's all anyone talked about on the bus home last night." In this girl's case, the bus ride to her home was 15 miles. She had endured more than her share of jeers from her peers, and all she could do was sit and take it. Her insensitive tormenters refused to believe that she had truly been the victim of mistaken sound waves.

Obviously her concern jarred my early-morning blur into action. I thought for a moment and then asked, "What would you like me to do about it?"

"I don't know," she said. "Somehow, someone's got to let the class know that I didn't fart."

Though I wanted desperately to help the distraught young lady move past her embarrassing dilemma, I could fathom no graceful way to inform the class of their mistaken assumption. To do so would certainly make an embarrassing situation worse. All I could do was reassure her rather lamely that "This too shall pass." Years later, when her class gathered at the Cedar Street Bridge in Sandpoint for their 10-year reunion, I finally brought closure to the incident. Emboldened with a glass of wine and fully aware that most of the revelers had, no doubt, exceeded my few sips of courage, I announced to all concerned that I had an issue to clear up from years ago when a certain group had sat in my sophomore English class.

As one of the guest speakers, I knew that expectations were high for comments befitting specific memories about class members. I would do my homework, scanning the yearbook and jotting down a few anecdotes to dazzle the audience. I also felt comfortable that settling the issue once and for all that this young lady had not passed the gas in fifth-period English would bring down the house. It did. Fortunately for me, she was a great sport who had gained enough self-confidence over the years to find some humor about the situation that had temporarily marred her life years before.

As my own self-confidence as a teacher gradually reached a comfort level, I sometimes used such classroom incidents as teaching moments. Take the adverb-question-flatulence incident, for example.

This occurred in the same third-period honors English where I had already learned one of my many lessons about teaching. A young man named Jim Stoicheff Jr. had hidden my grade book in the file cabinet, thinking surely I would find it quickly – another assumption gone bad. But Jim's assumption was not as bad as the one I made after discovering that it had disappeared from my desk sometime during the morning classes. I relied on an old teacher tactic and just kept my mouth shut about the missing book, knowing full well that students' curiosity would be aroused, and they would talk. Well, they didn't. I spent the next four days frantically racking my brain and saying constant prayers to St. Anthony while searching everywhere for the book. Playing it cool, I never uttered a word to anyone about the incident. Only my family at home knew of my agony. Finally one day, deciding that all hope was lost, I made an announcement at the beginning of each morning class.

"I've been missing my grade book," I said. "If anyone has any knowledge about where it might be, please see me."

The first two periods passed with no results.

Within two seconds of the third-period summons for help, a hand went up.

"I thought you'd find it," said a sheepish Jim, the son of two local teacher friends. "I thought sure you'd know right where to look." He rose from his desk, walked over to the file cabinet, opened a drawer I seldom used, and pulled my grade book from the top of the pile inside. The expression on Jim's face indicated his uncomfortable embarrassment that the harmless prank had caused any problems. I was so relieved to see my grade book that I could not muster even an ounce of animosity toward him. Having the absent grade book back in my hands and observing Jim's remorse settled the score at that very moment. We both learned one of life's recurring lessons from that experience: Never assume. I also learned never to let my grade book out of my sight again.

Jim and the rest of his class always seemed to have a good time in class, but I'm betting none of them, including the offending culprit, ever forgot the lesson they helped teach themselves the day someone let loose with a "loud one" in class.

In this case, the lesson evolved because of its timing.

Class had just begun. I had finished my preliminary "word of the day," followed by the usual sentence mechanics exercise. We were studying adverbs that week. I began a quick review.

"What are the adverb questions?" I asked.

Within a split second, my query was punctuated, not by a question mark but by a rather loud, sharp fart. There was no question concerning this noise.

It was a fart. Period.

Again, I must remind the reader of my inherent weak restraint toward such happenings. My first reaction was to sit there and compose myself. I was determined to overcome my weakness. On this day, I would *not* laugh. I would *not* acknowledge what I had just heard. Using every muscle available, I held my lips in a locked position and looked past the sea of hopeful faces, straight ahead toward the back wall. I took a deep breath or two, preparing to move on as if nothing had happened. I could sense the collective attention directed my way. They waited eagerly for my reaction. I resolved to disappoint them. We *would* move on with adverbs, I vowed silently.

Unlocking my lips, I enunciated clearly.

"What are," my voice suddenly rising 85 octaves, "theadverbquestions???" I shrieked before collapsing head first into my desk submitting to a state of maniacal laughter. Tears rolled onto my presentation notes, causing the ink to spread across the page. My adverb notes were disintegrating into blue oblivion. The class was erupting into squeals and full-fledged belly laughs. I dared not look up.

"Get hold of yourself," my inner voice commanded. "You've lost it, you fool! Even if it *is* funny, *you* should not be laughing." I knew one unknown student was sitting in there, either very horrified or very proud. If the former, then I also knew I'd better straighten up. Once again, calling on all facial muscles to appear for duty, I took a deep breath, directed my face to behave, looked toward the class and attempted to begin again.

"OK, what are the adverb questions?" I asked with a sense of urgency not unlike a person racing to the bathroom.

"When?" a student shouted.

"Good," I said to myself, relieved that I had gotten past the self-destruction mode. That relief was short-lived.

A split second after "When?" a muffled but audible "Just now" came from an unknown voice among the students, followed by another explosion of glee.

"How?" another volunteer shouted, once the laughter died down.

"Out loud," an anonymous voice observed.

"Why?" another yelled.

"Had beans!" chirped an enthusiastic male voice.

"To what degree?

"Really loud!"

"Where?"

"In Room 4!"

The chorus of guffaws, squeals, haw, haw, haws would not die down. My classroom had transformed into an adolescent laughing factory. But, they knew the adverb questions!

It all happened so fast I sat speechless, transfixed in total awe. For once, in record time, the adverb questions had rolled off those tongues, like water over Niagara. How could I ever have designed a lesson plan to match this? Never. I was also pretty confident that the planets – er – sounds would never line up so perfectly again.

Nonetheless, I couldn't find any teacher handbook rules that stated anything about never telling the fart story again. So, from that point on, every year when we reviewed the parts of speech, I could always count on a captive audience while telling about the day the "loud one" right before the adverb questions "when, where, why, how and to what degree?" ignited my students and impressed all five questions into their brains for a long while.

Speaking of staying awhile, shortly after my return to teaching in 1998 after a semester away, I discovered one student's strategy for encouraging students' desire to leave the classroom before their designated time was up, i.e., the dismissal signal. The scene was third-period sophomore English in Portable Room 2. After walking away in 1997, saying I had quit and would never return to teaching again, my principal had convinced me to come back after another English teacher resigned in disgust at midyear.

My new assignment differed greatly from the honors English classes and high-energy, media-related classes I had taught for years. The schedule included three regular sophomore and two regular junior English classes. At the time, we had three English tracks: honors, regular and basic. My classroom was the second in a row of six portables behind the middle school, almost a five-minute walk from the high school. We were definitely out in the hinterlands. The location had its advantages and disadvantages. Besides the incessant telephone rings – calls from the office meant for our individual classrooms or one of the five others – we dealt with another daily irritation: no bells. Because of a tendency for someone among the six teachers to weaken and always let their students go early and parade past the windows on their way back to the main school, I discovered the first day that the end of every class hour would be a major pain.

Though not exactly motivated to listen to my every word or to happily jot down notes for 50 minutes, these kids were well-trained.

"Your assignment for tomorrow ... " I would begin announcing toward the end of the first period after introducing myself and giving an overview of "the rules." Before another word spilled from my lips, someone else's class had already spilled out a door to the north. The throng of kids with coats and backpacks marched past my window gleefully looking in at the poor saps who still sat there, having to listen to me. Without fail that first day, as soon as they spotted the leader of the departing herd outside trudging by, students in each class, five times a day, slammed their notebooks shut, put pens in backpacks and prepared for launch. Bodies squirmed. Heads leaned forward as if preparing for the starting blocks. Eyes fixated on the door.

" ... Write me a letter introducing yourself," I yelled over the commotion. Long before there was any need for me to put a period in my sentence, the last chargers were pushing their way through the door. In their minds, another first-period English class had ended for them, and they didn't need some stupid new teacher to tell them so.

I'm going to have to address that situation, I said to myself while reviewing the day. A new rule would begin the lesson first thing tomorrow. That was my first rather unsubtle hint, one of many to come during that semester, that the ol' authoritarian approach would have to be dusted off and re-instigated if I were to survive with these kids. After all, they had driven one teacher away. There *must* have been a reason.

"From now on, you will remain in your desks, your notebooks open and your pens in your hand while I give you the assignment," I emphatically announced. "I will dismiss you when I'm finished. In most cases, I'll make every effort to have this finished by the designated departure time, but if I'm still talking, you will still be expected to take notes."

All went well for a couple of days. Feeling a bit smug that my evil-eye, firm approach was working miracles with these kids, I attempted to move on with the business of education. About a week into the semester, other situations had reared their ugly heads, but the kids were still begrudgingly respecting the rule of staying put each hour until I shut up and dismissed them. Admittedly, it was difficult for them every time they saw another class from the north heading off to the school while they still sat. I wanted to say something to the teacher who had released them but knew better than to cause friction as the relatively new kid on the block in Portableville.

Finally, one student could stand it no longer. Let's just call him Beano. I don't know what combination of gastric bombshells he had stuffed into his gut the night before, but my acute nose detected, one day, that somewhere in my third-period English class sat a human methane tank that could damage an entire classroom of nasal passages within seconds.

Our rather spartan portables did not have great air circulation, so any smell that hit the air lingered for a long time. On this day, the human methane tank released the most ghastly odor ever known to man. No feet had ever smelled like that. No outdoor toilet. No Limburger cheese. No rotted contents in refrigerator baggies. No dead deer along the roadside. No skunk. Well, maybe it was a combination of all of the above. The odious smell attacked my nostrils within seconds of my hearing disgusted gasps and groans around the room as numerous sets of hands jerked toward faces to protect noses from inhaling the fumes. I couldn't open my mouth to utter another word about tomorrow's assignment. Someone ran and dragged open a window. The smell dominated every molecule of air in Portable 2.

"OK, you're excused," I shrieked. As the nearly asphyxiated herd shot out the door, I raced around the room to open windows and try to breathe some uncontaminated air. While sliding a corner window open, I could feel the presence of someone behind me. A student who sat in the far corner had stayed after the others to share some information.

"That was Beano," the mannerly informant said. "He does that all the time, usually at the end of the hour." My informant was NOT a tattler, goodie-two-shoes type. He had just thought the whole incident rather funny and was making a matter-of-fact statement, as if Beano's silent-but-deadlies merely came with the territory. Furthermore, this kid had to have a pretty strong constitution because he sat right behind Beano. A rare bird in those classes, he was more motivated to stay afterward to ask about the next day's assignment than he was to be a narc.

"Oh, really," I said, silently tucking away the notion that Beano's Bombs would need to be neutralized – and soon.

Apparently, Beano picked appropriate days to let loose because several days passed. At first, I figured he had sensed that this ol' gal meant business and that it was wise to control his olfactory assaults. I was wrong.

A couple of weeks later, I had just begun giving directions for the next day's assignment. I suddenly detected a stir in the back of the room. Within seconds, my nose told me why. Beano had launched another deadly internal missile. Its ammo was decimating every set of nostrils in the room. Several hopeful eyes shot Beano's direction. A satisfied smile grew across his face.

All right, I thought to myself, *here's your chance to nip this in the bud.* It would be a difficult few minutes, especially because I still needed to breathe to outsmart Beano.

Without inhaling, I issued instructions while pointing to four individual students situated near the windows.

"Open the windows," I ordered as the class sat in shock. Beano looked around with dismay. Knowing they had no choice if they wanted to breathe, each of the four stepped to the respective windows and slid them open. The room was silent, just like Beano's stink bomb.

Still doing everything possible to prevent the smell from entering my nostrils, I announced the rest of the assignment and then dismissed the class – all except Beano.

When the last student had left the room, I stood between Beano and the door.

"I know what you're up to, and I want it to stop," I announced, staring the young man straight in the eyes. "If you insist on doing that again, you will remain here after everybody leaves, and we'll talk about your problem."

His face turned a deep crimson. He had no comeback. He knew he had been nabbed.

"OK," he said, sheepishly.

"You can go now," I said. I watched him head out the door. When it shut behind him, my lips exploded into a huge grin, tears rolled from my eyes and I giggled all the way to the desk.

For once in my life, I had learned restraint in the face of a fart, and, fortunately – for my nose and 30 others in third-period English – so had Beano.

6.

Emmel's May Day Smiles

It started with a single yellow violet, firmly secured in a small plastic baggy full of water. The anonymous floral offering sat on my desk as I entered the room to begin second-period English on May 1, 1981. Its sweet simplicity touched me as I picked it up and displayed it before the class of sophomores.

"I don't know who did this," I announced, "but thank you." As I surveyed the room, one proud male face with twinkling eyes smiled back at me. I kept our secret and did not reveal his identity to the rest of the class. Later, I thanked him in the hallway for the May Day offering. He shrugged his shoulders with an "aw gosh" manner and went on his way.

A year later on May Day 1982, I boarded a bus at the Statler-Hilton Hotel in San Francisco and prepared for the long ride home to Sandpoint. I had accompanied the journalism students to a Journalism Education Association (JEA) National Convention. With many of them also serving on my yearbook staff, I thought it would be good to go along and take in some of the yearbook offerings. San Francisco sounded nice, too. Our mode of transportation to the convention would be the Silver Eagle, an older, red-and-white diesel bus purchased by the Sandpoint High Athletic Department and its community supporters for away games and other school activities.

Since Bob Hamilton, the journalism adviser, also coached basketball, he had clout with the powers-that-be who determined when and where the bus would go. In fact, his influence as the school's athletics historian netted our group the bus and three drivers, including the athletic director, Al Jacobson, and two Bulldog Bench members, Rod Thurlow and Bobby Moore. They all brought their wives. With three drivers, our trip to and from San Francisco with about 30 aspiring journalists moved almost non-stop except for occasional highway rest breaks. Following that schedule, the 1,000-mile trip to and from San Francisco clocked in at about 23 hours.

I was totally amazed early in our journey to learn that these well-seasoned drivers didn't even stop the bus to spell each other off. While cruising at 65 mph down the freeway, a switch-your-partner dance would ensue. Those were the days before relic buses, such as the Silver Eagle, featured the option of cruise control. The new driver would carefully maneuver behind the driver's seat on the left side, while his partner carefully held his foot on the gas and one hand on the steering while moving out of the seat to his right. Almost like magicians, one would let go and take a seat near the front of the bus while the other assumed driving duties.

With this much dedication toward seeing that we wasted no time getting down the road, I was surprised when, on the return trip, we actually stopped just outside San Francisco to visit a Golden Gate viewpoint looking back over the bay. After all, we had been on the road from the Hilton for a mere half hour, but the kids had been promised a few tourist stops for their good behavior. Everyone filed off the bus and strolled in their respective klatches to various parts of the park and admired the breathtaking view of San Francisco, where we had learned a little journalism and had thoroughly enjoyed getting to know this beautiful city.

We had gone up and down those hills, filled with awe while riding the streetcars. We had ridden escalators in big department stores like Macy's where I had endured giddy behavior from certain students. The anonymity of the moment while visiting the big, faraway city with their teacher drove favorites like Kari Daarstad and Jeralyn Lewis to tease me relentlessly in very public arenas. On this trip, they abandoned the usual moniker of "Emmel" (blend of "M" and "L") they had earlier attached to me in favor of "Mom." While headed down the escalator opposite my upward track, they delighted in pretending to be my slightly undisciplined progeny whose self-contrived version of ADD (Attention Deficit Disorder) was getting the best of them, as "Mom" tried in vain to shop and escape their presence.

"Mom, wait for us," one would yell. "We want to be with you, *Mom*." Then, thankfully, they would disappear from view as my escalator continued to ascend.

Ah, I'm rid of them, I thought, stepping off and quickly jogging to a far corner of the new floor in hopes of ditching my teenaged pursuers. Just as I would settle in to studying sale items, my concentration would be abruptly distracted.

"There she is! Oh, *Mom*, here we are! We missed you," Jeralyn would yell as she grabbed my arm from behind, embracing me wildly as if we had been separated for years. Within seconds, both young women were verbally and physically smothering me with a rapturous affection that would send even the most love-starved critter on a dead run. The store clerks displayed visible amazement with the passion of these teenaged overgrown kids who so loved their Mom. Though somewhat flattered with their wacky attention, I couldn't help feeling just a bit embarrassed with the melodramatic PDAs (public displays of affection). No matter the strategy, I seldom escaped these unruly, department-store scenes in the midst of the sophisticated air of this wonderful city. Somehow, its sophistication would not rub off on me nor my students.

But San Francisco's many quirky and alluring offerings on the shelves of its fascinating novelty shops – hardly available at the time in Sandpoint – meant entertaining times ahead for the teens during their stay in the hotel and especially when they returned home. Among the favorite purchases was the whoopee cushion selected by that very same, sweet young man who had left the yellow violet on my desk the year before. Within hours of reaching the city, Jeff Gustaveson, then a junior and a member of my yearbook staff, was already putting his purchase to good use in hotel elevators crammed with adrenaline-charged student journalists from all over the West. I hate to guess how many times he rode that elevator, but he always employed the same strategy:

Hide cushion in back pocket. Step inside. Stand at the back. Pull cushion from pocket. Place firmly behind back. Wait 'til elevator fills and door closes. Once the mass of crowded humanity begins its upward or downward journey, press cushion firmly. Once the crowded humanity starts looking around to see who did it, smile with definite expression of fulfilled pleasure. Watch how fast occupants leave elevator when door opens.

It was great fun for Jeff and for any in-the-know friends who accompanied him on his up-and-down shows. The cushion also helped pass time on this long bus ride home – as if a fake-fart cushion were even needed as bodies stuffed with chips, soda, sweets and other flatulence-inducing treats sat curled up in their seats for all those hours. The entire trip had meant a good time for all of us, including the bus drivers' wives who had shopped 'til they dropped during the three-day visit. So, on this beautiful May Day while walking back to the Silver Eagle and enjoying one more look at the city, many of us agreed we would have to come back some day. But now, we had to get home.

Taking my time moseying back to the bus, I admired the explosion of colorful California poppies and other wildflowers adorning the hillsides and deep green plots of lawn around the park. It would be a month or so before we would see such color in North Idaho, so I savored the scenes as long as possible before climbing up the steps and heading toward my seat. When I arrived to plop back down for the next leg of the journey, a large bouquet of those wildflowers awaited me. At first, I figured that someone else had inadvertently claimed my seat and left them there while chatting with friends in another part of the bus.

"Do these gorgeous flowers belong to anyone here?" I asked while holding up the bouquet. Nobody responded, so I yelled a little louder. "Whose flowers are these?" The bus was loaded by now. Still, nobody answered.

"Somebody must have picked these flowers. They're beautiful. Come and get 'em," I announced louder than before. No takers. Nobody seemed to know anything about them. Most kids just kept on chatting, oblivious of my persistent quest to find the owner.

"Well, I guess I'll just enjoy them myself then," I said, sitting down.

I relaxed for a moment admiring the bright, wine-colored poppies mixed with an assortment of yellow and deep blue wildflowers. Then, my detective skills kicked in. Today was May 1 – May Day – the flower-basket day. Last May Day someone left that yellow violet on my desk, *and* that someone was on the bus.

I whirled around, holding the bouquet and met eye to eye with the whoopee cushion technician, Jeff Gustaveson. Again, those green eyes twinkled – a satisfied smile gave him away. Again, I spared him any potential embarrassment and quietly mouthed a "thank you" amidst the din of chatter and giggles on the bus. The flowers wilted fairly quickly during our 23-hour trip home, but I cherished the thoughtfulness of this slightly impish student as we cruised through Northern California, Oregon, Washington and eventually across the Long Bridge spanning beautiful Lake Pend Oreille to Sandpoint.

Jeff Gustaveson came to my English class as a sophomore. I had met him a few years before when he was an aspiring junior-high actor helping with a local production. His mother worked as a local radio announcer at the time, and I had taught two older brothers, Dan and Darrell, and his sister, Tina. Teaching the fourth member of one family was definitely a novelty for me in 1980-81. I had been at Sandpoint High School for 11 years and had occasionally seen up to three siblings from one household, but teaching four Gustavesons was definitely launching into new territory in a career that eventually saw that number grow to eight when the Rust family came through our high school during the '80s and '90s.

This youngest Gustaveson found his way into my heart in that honors English class in spite of neglecting to turn in assignments – a malady I found over the years to be more common than rare – especially with young men. Jeff's assignment-challenged tendencies still baffled me at that point in my career, and as I had done with many before and many afterward, I coerced, cajoled and connived to get him to do his work – often fruitlessly. His appreciation for literature, his kind, polite manner and his delightful sense of humor sealed a friendship.

Because of this charm and because of my recognition of the latent talent that surely lay within this budding Renaissance man, I selected him to join the *Monticola* staff the following year. *Monticola* (pronounced mon-TI-kuh-la) is the name of our school yearbook. Someone in the long-ago past of Sandpoint High School history decided to name the annual after *Pinus monticolas*, the species of white pine that used to grow profusely throughout our North Idaho area. Other school publications like the *Cedar Post* newspaper and a creative writing magazine called *Timberline* followed the theme of our local North Idaho history so dominated by trees and mountains.

During Jeff's involvement on the yearbook staff, the class took to their hearts the beautiful, tree-covered mountains surrounding our town and lake. On weekends during fall months, the students often gathered at my house on Saturday mornings, loaded up in cars and headed to the mountains to hike Forest Service trails often leading to spectacular vistas. Armed with cameras, of course, Jeff and his other talented photographer friends like Rocky Kenworthy, Brett Converse, Kari and Jeralyn shot dozens of rolls of film, hoping to capture dramatic nature images for the yearbook's 240-plus pages. These hikes forged close relationships among the group and led to plenty of outdoor playfulness. Jeff and his buddies, for example, delighted in quietly disappearing part way through the hike and pioneering a route of their own so they could hunker down behind a log or boulder up the trail and surprise the rest of the group, coming from behind and rounding a corner. Whether it was on hikes or during the endless hours of yearbook production, this group of kids connected to form a magical chemistry during Jeff's first year on staff.

Though the yearbook work was demanding, Jeralyn, the editor, had a rare knack for maintaining a light and humorous tone as she delegated duties, making every staff member feel like his or her job was as important and as appreciated as anyone else's. In this comfortable atmosphere, good-natured teasing was a staple. Removing the front seat from Jeralyn's yellow suburban and hiding it somewhere around the school seemed to be among the favorites for the ever-creative boys. Jeralyn's exuberant, semi-disgusted reaction to their impish vandalism never disappointed them. Sometimes, however, she sabotaged their efforts by riding her motorcycle to school. They usually left that vehicle alone.

During the school year, a couple of weeks of down time always followed our intense deadlines. Every time a set of 40-or-so pages representing hours and hours of after-school and weekend work would finally land, neatly stacked in the mailing box bound for the yearbook company, we held a special ceremony to bid the project adieu.

Out would come a tube of bright red lipstick. Most staff members happily joined in the ritual of applying a healthy dose to their lips and then one by one – *smack* – they kissed the box, leaving the personal symbolic smooch of one more completed assignment. We always wondered what postal workers or the folks at the yearbook company thought when they first laid eyes on a mailer covered with 20 different sets of bright-red lip graphics.

During these down times after deadline pressure, the staff enjoyed spontaneous face-taping sessions where idle minds entertained themselves and the rest of the class with rolls of Scotch tape. The routine involved picking a victim and then taping up the face of this usually willing staff member. The object was to see just how wretchedly deformed the kid could look. When the job was finished, clicking cameras faithfully recorded the results.

During these idle times, students also discovered innovative uses for rubber cement. Using the applicator and spreading cement on the palm of the hand can result in any number of recreational toys. One of their favorite, crafted products took both perseverance and most of a class hour. Using nearly a full can of cement and following a continuous rolling and molding routine, they could build their own version of the famed Super Balls. Once the mass had been completed into a transparent sphere, a game of catch-the-bouncing-ball kept staff members occupied until the bell rang.

One student, who shall remain nameless, figured out how a tiny, rolled-up mass of rubber cement can be molded to resemble a nasal booger. She then felt the urge to put her yucky discovery to entertaining use. Before heading next door to math class, she planted the green mass firmly at the lower opening of one of her nostrils. Before the tardy bell rang – cement-booger implant in full view – she walked up to her teacher,

Cheryl Benjamin, with an urgent question about the algebra assignment. Cheryl did her best to answer and remain composed. Cheryl's visible efforts at restraint turned out quite satisfying for that student, who now teaches grade school and gets to witness the real deal on a daily basis with elementary kids during their perennial cold seasons.

Sometimes teasing among staff members backfired, as in the case when Jeff absconded with an academic progress memo from his junior English teacher Joy O'Donnell's desk. He filled it out as if he were Mrs. O'Donnell, supposedly concerned about Kari Daarstad's grades and general class attitude. Kari happened to be a 4.0 student and all-around leader, so Jeff felt confident that when Kari opened her mail and recognized Jeff's handwriting, she would certainly counter with the next practical joke and do a "gotcha" on Jeff. The best-laid plans this time went sadly awry.

"I know there were several choices to make about a person's 'progress' via filling in boxes or blanks," he recounted to me 20 years later. "Kind of the 'multiple choice' of report cards. I then proceeded to write some in anyway. Something along the lines of 'Kari is completely unprepared in class, has not been doing homework, is sassy and unruly, is falling asleep in class … signed by Joy O'Donnell.

"I, of course did that in my own handwriting," Jeff told me later, "for as you know, a practical joke is not as good unless the *jokee* suspects or knows who the *joker* is and the next round of practical jokes can then ensue. I addressed the envelope to Kari, sent it through the mail, and then waited gleefully for her reaction."

Needless to say, there was no "joy" among certain *Monticola* staffers, the teacher or Kari's parents when that happened. Kari's parents intercepted the note when they picked up their mail and spotted the letter from Sandpoint High School. Jeff learned a lesson or two about practical jokes during the aftermath of that trick.

During Jeff's senior year, the staff continued to suffer its ups and downs as additional conflicts unfolded among kids who knew each other like family. Maybe they knew each other too well.

LESSON: I saw similar situations over the years that helped me realize that teens – in even the best of circumstances – will not always get along, no matter what one does to intervene or referee. Their pride, their egos and their sensitivities often supersede good judgment at this time in their lives. And, most importantly, I often learned that no teen is immune from this possibility.

Over the years, I eventually learned that sometimes they can never get along, no matter how nice they are or how well-adjusted they may be as individuals. The key is recognizing this phenomenon with an understanding that regardless of their intelligence and apparent maturity (for their age), they're still young adults testing the waters. A good coach, teacher or adviser learns to work around these conflicts. Easier said than done in many situations.

As the central figure responsible for maintaining harmony among my staff members, I found myself emotionally drained often during the 1982-83 school year when the magic of the remarkable previous year had diminished with a change in staff chemistry. Besides advising the yearbook at the time, I also taught four English classes and coordinated a major school-wide fundraiser. My two children were 5 and 6 at the time, so there was plenty to do at home. As if that were not enough, in a weak moment, I agreed to teach a night class during second semester. It didn't sound too bad – three hours for one evening a week. I hadn't thought of all the time needed to prepare for three hours of teaching a brand-new class.

Needless to say, through a new predisposition toward severe insomnia triggered by constant worry of how to fit everything into my day and how to solve ongoing staff conflicts, I learned painfully that year that I was not a candidate for Superwoman. During the spring semester, after two consecutive school nights without one drop of sleep, I realized something had to give. That something turned out to be advising the *Monticola*. After a tearful visit with my principal, Tom Keough, the morning after the second sleepless night, I made up my mind to finish what had to be completed for the school year and then eliminate the activity that had provided me such creative stimulation, personal pride and ongoing challenges for 14 years. Every year since the beginning of my teaching career in 1969, we had taken the yearbook a few steps closer to a professional product. Together, with staff members, I had honed my own photography and darkroom skills. We had continually worked on perfecting our graphic design, and we strove every year to tell our school-year story a little better, in hopes that decades later, readers could gain a clear, well-reported history of those times at Sandpoint High. In that effort, I had met and worked with dozens of young people who would be considered a part of my extended family for the rest of my life. The 1982-83 school year, in spite of the occasional troubles, was no exception. Therefore, I faced an agonizing decision. Walking away from this significant dimension of my life was not going to be easy, but it had to happen. Like so many projects I've worked on over the years, the yearbook had slowly evolved into a second full-time job – and that job never stopped with the last school bell every year.

With the nighttime insomnia continuing to burden me emotionally and physically every day, I had to bite the bullet and make the decision to say good-bye to *Monticola* deadlines and all the fun that went with them. My own kids at home needed more of my time, and I needed some breathing room. Once the decision was made, I felt relieved, knowing that life would get easier. This knowledge freed me from enough stress to enjoy the rest of the school year. Life continued to get a little easier when the North Idaho College night class ended in April. I also decided not to do that again, even though the experience of teaching adults, who appreciated every tidbit I dished out to them regarding English language use, turned out to be one of the more satisfying segments of my career.

As April drew to a close, the fun times of the school year lay ahead – Prom, Class Night for seniors, the much-anticipated arrival of the *Monticola*. Staff members who hadn't gotten along so well during the school year were starting to realize that they would soon be parting. Their behavior toward one another began to improve as we anticipated the last few weeks of memories.

On May Day, Jeff Gustaveson once more presented me with a bouquet of flowers, starting the month off with a sweet reminder that through it all, working with young people in extracurricular activities can reveal the deep layers of some beautiful, budding souls. They may falter from time to time, and they may often test the patience of those around them in strange ways. Remaining constant in one's principles and working with these students for a common good, however, will usually win out. And within this young man, who loved to seize any opportunity to tease or to enjoy a good practical joke, someone had instilled a sincere sense of chivalry that could melt the most stone-cold heart. At times, his impish behavior had done a good chill job on my inner pump. After getting to know Jeff over our three-year teacher-student tenure, I became convinced of his incurable romanticism. Beneath that frivolous, fun-loving outer layer beat a sensitive, caring and giving heart.

When the yearbooks finally arrived, we left the school during *Monticola* hour and drove to my house. The entire staff gathered on the deck to break the seal of the first shipping box, grab copies and thumb through the pages. Occasionally, someone would break the total silence to announce a mistake or comment about an effective page layout. Overall, the kids were justifiably proud of their book, and I was proud of them for overcoming most of the challenges that had arisen throughout the year.

When May turned into June of 1983, the *Monticola* staff and their teacher left a successful yearbook program behind for someone else to guide. We all set off for new experiences. In my case, my goal was to spend more time with my family, get some sleep and reclaim my life outside of school, vowing never to face deadlines again.

LESSON: The well-worn cliché "Never say never" is true.

In the 1990s, I experienced another weak moment when my mentor, Bob Hamilton, retired as the school newspaper adviser. In response to requests to replace him, three times I vowed, "Never will I deal with kids and deadlines again." On the fourth, however, I waffled. Thinking about the exciting crop of young journalists with whom I would be working overpowered my discipline to resist.

Why not? I finally reasoned to myself and signed on to another of the most demanding jobs a teacher can do, especially at the time when staffs were converting to full-time computer layout and production. I rationalized that advising the newspaper would serve as a new challenge in my own pursuit of learning and that with my own kids coming through the high school, the newspaper activities might provide some good opportunities for us to spend more time together. I kept that job for seven years before the next "never" came along.

After commencement, 1983, Brett Converse headed off to the University of Idaho, where he earned a degree in engineering and eventually his doctorate from the University of California at Davis. He now works for a local engineering firm. Kari Daarstad pursued her photographic dreams to Montana State as a film major – following in the footsteps of her father Erik who spent his career as a documentary cinematographer, sometimes doing projects for *National Geographic*. After working as a production assistant on film projects for several years, she returned to Sandpoint to rear her family and to work as a photo manager at Coldwater Creek. Jeralyn Lewis had graduated the year before and made her mark as a student leader at Gonzaga University in Spokane, Wash., where, during her senior year, she served as student body president. Her career in public relations took her to Phoenix and Los Angeles. Like Kari, she eventually found her way home, earned her master's degree in counseling, married and started a family. She works for the school district as a part-time elementary counselor. Rocky Kenworthy majored in photography at Spokane Falls Community College. He and Jeff, who had spent some time at the University of Idaho, eventually set off one day in the late 1980s, with all their possessions in a tiny sports car, bound for adventure in the Big Apple. Jeff's little yellow MG convertible got them there, and they've operated out of New York ever since. Rocky's talents and persistence toward learning all he could about photography netted him some exciting gigs with *Time* and *Rolling Stone* magazines. In fact, he spent a couple of years assisting famous photographer Mark Seliger on *Rolling Stone* covers. He also jetted around the Mideast and Africa assisting with photographing the *Time* Men of the Year for 1993: Nelson Mandela, Yitzhak Rabin, Frederik Willem de Klerk and Yasser Arafat.

Meanwhile, in his day jobs, Jeff worked for banks and computer agencies. Pursuit of respective dreams with photography and acting has since taken both Rocky and Jeff around the country and on tours around the world. Over the past two decades, Jeff, who now goes by the single name, "Mercury," has performed in no fewer than 20 productions both on tour and in the New York area, many of them Shakespearean. He's played Odysseus, Oedipus, Oberon, Theseus and Marc Antony. He's also worked in film, on tour as a stagehand, production assistant, director, videographer, road manager and sound technician.

Regardless of what he was doing or where he happened to be, every May 1, he took the time to send or even deliver a bouquet of flowers to my home or my classroom. In a couple of cases, even in the midst of classroom lectures, this handsome, young hunk would show up inside the classroom, flowers in hand, walk to the front and, while 30 sets of curious teenage eyes watched, would present the bouquet to me. As quickly as he had entered, Jeff exited. Sometimes I saw him later, sometimes not.

"What was that all about?" a student would pipe up.

"That's all about thoughtfulness," I would answer. "It's May First, and he's been remembering me with flowers on May Day ever since 1981." For a few minutes, the lecture was tabled while I would launch off into who he was and how the tradition started. I would tell about Jeff and his friends and the good times we had on hikes and special occasions when I advised the yearbook. For several days, thereafter, I would walk into my empty classroom, smell the flowers and smile while thinking about how lucky I was to work with human beings like Mercury.

In 2001, no flowers arrived. My daughter, Annie, sent me a May Day basket that year, but I still felt a tinge of sadness that my annual connection with Jeff had apparently drawn to a close. I held out hope the following year that maybe there'd been a mix-up. May 1, 2002, passed with no word from Jeff. And the same occurred in 2003. Occasionally, I would receive a group e-mail about an address change for Mercury but still no word.

My touch of May Day sadness had nothing to do with the material aspect of an annual gift. Instead, the flowers had symbolized something much more significant – a tie with a dynamic young man and his friends who had added a significant dimension to my life. With each arrival of the flowers, their faces would pop up in a montage of images in my mind. A smiling Jeff resting on a boulder alongside a Forest Service trail in the Cabinet Mountains. Brett, Kari and Rocky basking in the sun on a remote dock overlooking the waters of Lake Pend Oreille. Jeralyn leading the *Monticola* crew through a forest of huge ancient cedars to remote Priest Lake, not far from the Canadian border. Together, we had climbed mountains and stood triumphantly on their peaks in awe of the gorgeous world below. Together, we had strived for perfection with yearbook dreams and talked for long hours about life and the future. Every year, the May Day flowers took me back to those times as if they were yesterday.

After three years of receiving no flowers, I finally faced the reality that as life marches on, our priorities change. It seemed selfish for me to expect the annual bouquet. Certainly, Jeff had more important things on his mind. Nonetheless, I missed the gesture and felt like something special had slipped away.

When May Day, 2004, came, I had gotten past the disappointment. Besides, my mind was consumed with a thousand details – announcing the annual 4-H horse-judging contest, getting home in time to watch the Kentucky Derby, packing for a nine-day road trip to California with my recently widowed mother and my three brothers. After watching underdog Smarty Jones from Philadelphia run away with the Derby, I pulled out my suitcase and began to pack. The dogs started barking. Someone in an unfamiliar car was coming down the driveway. The driver got out and handed me a beautiful bouquet.

"Who's this from?" I asked.

"Can't remember," she said.

"Oh, I know – I bet it's from my daughter – thank you," I said as she backed out of the driveway.

I walked back into the house and put the vase on the kitchen counter, lamenting the fact that with trip ahead, I would be missing these flowers at their best. I opened the unsigned card.

"Sorry I missed a few," the note read. "Have a nice May Day."

It needed no signature. I smiled while enjoying the sweet fragrance of the bouquet. That familiar feeling of silent satisfaction of so many May Day bouquets before soothed my stress of too much to do, too little time.

For some reason, this year Jeff had remembered again. His ol' teacher still mattered to this very special person who had traveled so many miles, gone through so many experiences and accomplished so much since that sunny morning back in May 1981, when the gift of his little yellow violet picked from the mountain behind his house had touched me so profoundly. Through it all, there remained a constancy of a lasting friendship between teacher and student. It made me very happy.

I immediately wanted to grab the phone, call him up and thank him for resuming his much appreciated tradition. Nobody answered at the number I called. I had also lost his most recent e-mail address. His thanks would have to wait until my return.

Once back to Idaho, I called his sister, Tina, who gave me his cell phone number and new e-mail address. Our first phone conversation lasted just minutes because he was working at the time. Later, I wrote him a long e-mail, catching up on events in my life of the past few years. I also told him about the plans to include him in my collection of teaching stories called "Lessons with Love." His written response touched on many of the great lessons that continue to unfold about the individuality of our students throughout our teaching careers. This is the letter Mercury wrote back:

Emmel,

I've done quite a bit since coming out here; doesn't seem like much to me though. I've enclosed three of my semi-current resumes that I use. They are self-evident as to whom they would be given. That is a nutshell for you to glean. They, of course, do not represent the other half of the life stories involved whilst furthering my life education.

You may wish to point out (to whomever) that some do not do well in formal academic settings. As you may recall, I flunked out of college after my first year. I have done many more things than listed in the resumes – all learned by doing. I have not taken any classes for anything of what I do, save some course work in film, as it is extremely difficult to break into the technical aspects of that field without some knowledge.

I highly regard travel as the most educational of all experiences. I have been to every state except Alaska (thanks to the national tours – part of the reason why I took them). I have been to every major city, innumerable larger towns, and seemingly every Podunk town and village in this country. All, many times. I think it's important that we see our own country.

I've traveled through Europe, more extensively southern and former eastern bloc countries. Have been through Mexico, Canada, and Australia, Trinidad, Tobago, etc. Alas, the list 'to visit' is always longer than the list of 'have visited.' I now own a motorcycle, purchased in California when I was out there last year for several months, and drove it back to NYC. Another lifelong dream of mine, a motorcycle.

Tell your audience that regardless of what you end up doing, you must try for your dreams, no matter how silly or what the cost or how many times you fail. If you do not, you will always, always wonder and regret. And believe me, the dreams will always change – and that's OK, too.

I am currently trying to get my s – together to start filming. Gee, how long have I been doing that? Quite some time, but I do get sidetracked quite easily. I have several short films that I've written that I need to get on celluloid. That is the current schedule. Of course, as you well know, the day-to-day living and surviving always bogs us down. Buck up little campers! Go forth and conquer!

I am glad you enjoy the flowers. I do as well. Every time I order them, I think of the first time. Running to the top of the mountain before school to pick those delicate little mountain lilies. They do not last overnight if picked the night before.

Now, how many comma splices, run-on sentences and partial sentences (ha! I forget what the English term is for them) do I have? I think I know where they are, and they are on purpose. Don't you love this language?

All my best,
Mercury

Yes, Mercury, I do love the language, but I beg to differ with you about that delicate little flower. Its beauty has lasted overnight and far beyond.

7.

Angela's Antics

In 2003, I began receiving digital photos of Cameron soon after his birth. With each mailing, his proud mother sent three or four photos to portray different reactions to Cameron's introduction to the world around him – on his dad's shoulder, taking a bath, sprawled out on the floor next to the family dog. A new batch of updates would arrive, and I would send his mom a note to ask how life's been treating her since she became a mommy. Must be she was busy in her new role because I didn't often hear back.

Actually, I'm surprised I heard from Angela at all. We did *not* part company as the best of friends when she walked out of my English classroom at Sandpoint High School for the last time as a high school sophomore. I doubt we even exchanged words, even though both of us probably had a few choice terms in mind to express our less-than-enthusiastic attitudes toward each other. Angela had pushed my buttons as many students had done over the years, but her antics stood out. She also taught me a very important lesson about teaching.

LESSON: Don't let classroom experiences or judgments cloud your thoughts about a student's future. You may be surprised.

I was surprised, and I'm glad.

My relationship with Angela Warren began in the fall of 1989, the same year I was fulfilling one of my life dreams, devoting after-school hours each day to writing feature stories for the *Spokesman-Review* newspaper. I had worked as a journalist off and on since graduating from the

University of Idaho in 1969. My stories and photographs appeared in the local weekly, the *Idaho Catholic Register* newspaper and the *Spokane Daily Chronicle*, which at the time was the afternoon daily. Like so many of its afternoon contemporaries nationwide, the *Chronicle* slowly faded away while the morning *Spokesman*, managed by the same owners, rose in stature as Spokane's sole regional daily.

For years, area correspondents from Sandpoint and surrounding communities with a flair for journalism had enjoyed lots of ink. With the transition toward the morning paper, however, the Cowles' organization dropped most of the correspondents in favor of full-fledged English/journalism graduates with master's degrees from schools like Cornell, the Universities of Missouri, Oregon, Montana, etc. Part-time journalists, like me, found it increasingly difficult to do any freelancing other than to provide story ideas. In fact, I worked for one year as a tipster earning $100 a month but would have preferred writing stories rather than merely suggesting them.

In the winter of 1989, however, a new opportunity arose. After expressing my interest in writing for the paper and receiving some tips from Shaun O'L. Higgins, the *Spokesman* director of sales and marketing, I made arrangements for a full-fledged interview with then-Managing Editor Chris Peck. I even bought a new teal dress with red accessories for the first and only job interview I've ever faced in my life. I vividly recall how nervously I said good-bye to Bill as he drove off to do some shopping. I then walked through the doors of the distinctive red brick *Spokesman* castle in downtown Spokane and rode the elevator to the executive floor to meet the managing editor. As I sat across a table from him explaining why I wanted to work for the paper, my words came with difficulty. After all, this was the big time for me. My body and mind knew it. Both seemed to be teaming up as I struggled with every phrase that left my lips. Chris Peck must not have noticed because after the grilling, he assured me that when an opportunity existed for some extra work in the North Idaho bureau, I would receive a call.

A few months later, I received that call. I got instructions to go to the local *Spokesman* office for a visit with a couple of editors and the

Sandpoint bureau reporter, Dean Miller. During this meeting, the trio told me what to expect in story assignments and with editing. They also reminded me about conflict of interest and my role as a journalist, suggesting that I needn't plan to write any letters to the editor and expect to have them printed. As Sandpoint bureau chief, Dean would be guiding me, and I would be working more as an intern than a contracted employee. My hours would be after school and on weekends; pay was based on the paper's freelance rates.

During that stint with the *Spokesman*, I soon discovered that I had *much* to learn as a writer. Until then, while working for other publications, I had always enjoyed almost a free ride from the editing department with little or no constructive criticism. My first encounter with Dave Newman changed that, however. Over the course of the year, through piercing criticism of my stories, he continually reduced my confidence and tested the very core of my mettle. When the first draft of a 45-inch story about my neighbor Betty Robinson, an 80-year-old who walked 3.5 miles every day, came back to me, I knew I had met my match. "Newman," as they called him, left two major comments: "Cut this down to 15 inches. Find a focus." Thanks to Dave Newman (sometimes for his ruthless and brutal approach to critical evaluations and even sometimes from his rare, caring guidance), I learned both humility and some valuable lessons about writing.

Working next to Dean Miller had its advantages. His purpose in my life at the time appeared to be to pick up the pieces and patch me back together every time Newman had sent me another bitter pill. A Cornell graduate and Vermont native, Dean Miller could cuss and gossip with the best of them. In fact, I've never met anyone before or since who could use the "F" word quite so frequently or so eloquently. Though usually intense about whatever issue he happened to be covering, Dean generously took time out to interpret and explain some of Newman's seemingly sadistic methods of torturing me into becoming a better journalist. Watching Dean Miller work and seeing the finished results of his journalistic efforts served as an education in itself – and the reason for my digression from Angela.

I later called upon Dean to help me introduce my students to a major interviewing/writing project that would both require their patience and reward them with the thrill of "having been published." At the time, a local writer/historian, Marylyn Cork, was coordinating the first major history book for Bonner County. Besides histories of local communities, organizations, churches and various municipal entities, the book would also feature family histories from throughout the county. I decided to involve my students, thanks to the suggestion of one of my teaching colleagues, Judy Hunt. She invited me and my students to participate in a social gathering where we could get acquainted with a group of elderly citizens. The project officially began in the late fall with an afternoon reception honoring longtime Sandpoint residents at the McFarland Inn, a local bed and breakfast. More than 50 honors students met, paired off, and visited with longtime area residents who had rich stories to tell about the lives they had spent in our community.

The tea resulted in some good matchups of students with community elders and with plans for a subsequent interview process at which the teens would spend more time asking questions and recording information to be crafted into a chronicle of each interviewee. In some cases, such as Angela's, the young historians selected a family member or a neighbor as their subject. She chose her next-door neighbor, Bob Nesbitt, whom I had known most of my life through 4-H and as our mailman. In spite of confidence that my students would eventually appreciate the lasting value of their interview projects, I had no idea at the time that this ongoing assignment would have such a profound impact in Angela's life. It would take a few years, a few patience-testing, one-on-one run-ins with this feisty young lady before I ever had a clue how much it meant to her.

Soon after my students had selected their partner for the history book project, Dean came to school one day and explained how to write a feature story. For the next few months, I continued to reinforce his suggestions while encouraging many students to hang in there and keep working toward the finished product. I knew these teens' passion for telling someone else's story didn't quite match up to mine. So, the cheerleader in me maintained a rah-rah approach until we finally reached the day for final drafts to appear.

I also had to do some quick thinking when a student named Justin raised his hand one day early in the project during the interview process. The deadline for their first installment of questions and answers was coming up soon, so I was explaining some note-taking methods to use while visiting their subjects.

"Look around the house when you first enter," I suggested. "Get a feel for the atmosphere. Zero in on details that contribute to that atmosphere – pictures on the wall, furniture style, pets roaming around the house … trinkets, etc. etc." In the midst of my explanation, Justin's hand shot up. One of my teaching idiosyncrasies – strange as it may sound – was to finish what I was saying before addressing questions. I knew myself too well and knew that if I stopped in the middle of my comments, I would get off task and forget half of my lesson plan. Time after time, I had emphatically reminded students to wait before putting up their hands. Must be that Justin had forgotten that day.

I kept talking. As his hand reached straight in the air, his eyes remained firmly fixed on me with such focus that my brain processes began to weaken from the distraction. Trying to maintain concentration, I talked on. Justin refused to give in. I tried looking toward another portion of the classroom, yet I could still feel that determined hand and those piercing eyes. I did my best to resist the overpowering temptation to yell out, "Justin, put yer hand down; I'm trying to talk!" Justin was just too nice a kid for me to do that.

Finally, I gave in, keeping my inner feelings in tow, and politely asked," Justin, do you have a question?"

"Yeah," he said, "I've got a problem with the person I'm supposed to interview." He had told me a few days before that his little ol' lady on Cedar Street wasn't feeling well, so I assumed he still hadn't been able to arrange a meeting with her.

"Is she still ill?" I asked.

"No," he responded.

"Well, then what's the problem?" I asked.

"She died," Justin announced. His revelation drew a few snickers from students, obviously not thinking ill will of the poor woman but realizing the irony of her choice to die rather than be interviewed by my student for the Bonner County history book.

How dare this lady! I thought to myself. "Well, you *do* have a problem. See me after class. I'll try to find you someone who's alive and planning to live long enough for you to do this assignment." Justin ended up interviewing my dad who did live another dozen years.

Weeks passed as first drafts were turned in, edited and returned for revision. By the time the students had rewritten their assignments at least three times, I knew enough to call it good. After all, readers would have to understand they were just high school sophomores, not Nobel Prize-winning authors. As with any challenge requiring more than a cursory effort, most students generally expressed satisfaction with the assignment, while some seemed happy to turn it in and forget about it. Still, others were actually vocal about how much they enjoyed the project – always careful to make sure none of their peers were listening as they admitted to me, "Gee, this was kinda fun." Then, we waited. The book was the first of its kind and required lots of volunteer effort, so the students would not see their final product until midway through their junior year. The 1990 school year continued on.

Involvement in the research assignment took up just a portion of Angela's energy during her year in my English class. Very intelligent and very social, Angela had presented a disciplinary challenge for me from the start. Not knowing her very well and having no red-flag alert from my sister, who had taught the same kids in ninth-grade English, I assigned Angela a back corner seat near several of her friends, whom I quickly learned also enjoyed chatting. Within days, I learned that I had made a strategic mistake in the fifth-period seating chart. I also figured out that Angela did not follow the mold of the usual obedient student who could be whipped into shape with one or two good hate stares or a few stern reminders of the class expectations.

Angela, whose SHS claim to fame came on the golf course, hung around with the class leaders. As a part of this group, she excelled academically and knew how to lead, especially in any class-versus-the-teacher situation. She learned quickly both the information in the textbooks *and* the best methods for getting under Mrs. Love's skin. The first time I chastised her, asking her to please pay attention, she brazenly ignored me and kept on chatting. Any time I countered with my deadly "hate stare," she could retaliate with a confident defiance that could jolt the most seasoned of disciplinarians. Angela feared nothing. I feared that this was gonna be a long year.

It was.

Cunning enough to irritate me daily but wise enough to avoid pushing her luck too far, Angela managed to stay in her corner seat for most of the year. Part of her success evolved from the fact that I knew that if she were any closer to the front, one of us might regret the possibilities. I also recognized in her attitude a bit of myself from long ago when I was a sophomore at Sandpoint High School sitting in the back corner. The only difference was that I had, at least, honed my ventriloquist skills, making the unsuspecting teacher think the guilty party sat just in front of me. One of my friends went to the office for mouthing off at the teacher after receiving reprimands for chatter originating from *my* mouth. Later, I could see firsthand why my teachers might have been a bit cranky with their classroom yakkers, and I felt really bad for my friend. I had also had enough experience, both personally and with other students, to know that with students like Angela (and me), a teacher must tread lightly to avoid having situations escalate. Finally, I rationalized that with time and patience maybe this, too, would pass.

I left her there for several months. We even created a tepid bond through our common association with admiration of Bob Nesbitt. As winter turned to spring and golf season, though, Angela became bolder, knowing she could escape my afternoon class for the spring tournaments. Such attitude often blooms with spring, when students can sense the end of another school year coming. In Angela's case, she knew her hours of having to behave for me were winding down. As April turned to May, her chatty tendencies increased, as she would talk out loud at will, with apparently no concern for the consequences.

The problem with spring is that with every ounce of student bravado comes an equal rise in the teacher stress meter. Behavior tolerated in

February seems intolerable in May – mainly because virtually all students embark on a gradual testing of the limits by not turning in work, not sitting where they belong, strolling into class late, staring out the window, mouthing off, etc. Multiplying each new behavior by 140 creates an obvious challenge. By fifth period on these spring days, the teacher's lid is about to erupt, much like Mount St. Helens did in May 1980. So, as preventative maintenance, veteran teachers who prefer to avoid spewing forth regrettable comments or actions tend to tighten the discipline. Thus, one day when Angela's antics seemed more overt than ever, I decided to move her.

"Angela, I'd like you to sit in this seat right here," I announced calmly, pointing to the desk in the front row directly in front of mine.

"Me?" she inquired, feigning total surprise. Surely I must mean Angela Rebella, who was in the same class. But Angela Rebella did not sit anywhere near Angela Warren, and the fact that my eyes were glued directly on her should have provided clue enough that I darn well meant her and nobody else.

What guilty student hasn't given it the old college try?

"Are you talking about me?" she asked once more.

"Yes," I said. "Right here."

"But I didn't do anything," she insisted.

I had taught long enough by now to not fall for that lame claim.

"This desk, right here," I repeated as the class quickly grew silent, knowing a standoff between Mrs. Love and her fifth-period nemesis was unfolding.

For some reason, Angela postponed the confrontation, disappointing her peers – but definitely not me. Slowly, emphatically slamming her books on top of each other, she stood up, sneered at me, marched forward with an air of arrogance, and slumped down in her new seat. Her classmate Jeff Bock had earned the same spot during my first-week seating chart strategy session and had since redeemed himself with good behavior and fine creative projects throughout the year. Among his best was a video created from the daily-words list called "Eggs in the Mist," produced, of course, by his Cracked Egg Productions. The entire class and I had all howled through the 15-minute movie as Jeff put all 20 medically related words to vivid, graphic use during a blood-and-guts, bad-dream scene. With this and other similar artistic creations, I had grown fond of him and felt confident that Mr. J.T. Bock could be trusted to sit in the back. We no longer required that close geographic connection where I could evil-eye him, if necessary, from a mere three feet away. But Angela definitely needed a few of my notorious hate stares. From now on, she and I would be on intimate terms. No longer would I have to yell over the heads of several students to get her attention. Or so I thought.

The first day of Angela's front-row seat incarceration went fairly well except for occasional glares. At least she remained quiet. At various times, I had looked up in time to catch her sneaking looks or motions to her friends at the back of the room, only to whirl around, face the front, resume her obedient behavior, and avoid my wrath. I considered this new arrangement pure heaven while happily going about my teaching without interruption. My period of bliss lasted but a couple of days. Angela was plotting new strategy. Day by day, these indiscretions became more frequent. Once again, I met with the frustration of having to stop talking while trying to explain an assignment to the class.

One day I had had enough of looking at the back of Angela's head.

"I don't want to see you turned around talking to your friends – ever," I warned her out loud. At the time, we were studying *Julius Caesar* from the sophomore literature anthology. The yellow textbook was huge and heavy.

Angela simply glared back, picked up her book from her desk, and held it up directly in front of her face. Wide open, the book created a wall between the two of us, completely shielding her expressions.

Rather than pressing the issue, I decided to let her sit there and hold it. Surely with 20 minutes left in the class hour, her hands and wrists would tire from propping it up so long. The bell rang. Angela's determination won out. She gathered up her materials and left the classroom. I sat, stunned in utter amazement at her stubbornness. But I eventually figured all would be forgotten, and tomorrow would be a new day.

Not so. As soon as she arrived in Room 4 and sat down, Angela's literature book went to its position in front of her face.

"She looks pretty stupid sitting there like that," I thought. "Let her look stupid. She'll never make it the entire hour." I had surely underestimated this young lady's will. Had the *Survivor* series been the rage at the time, I certainly would have suggested that Angela try out. Anyone who could hold a five-pound literature book in the same position for 55 minutes without faltering could definitely compete in some of the immunity challenges on the series.

When Angela left the room, all I could do was shake my head, wondering how long this behavior would last.

"Bet she's got some tired muscles," I later said to colleagues while sharing the classroom drama in the faculty room.

LESSON: Yes, teachers do gossip about such things in faculty rooms; it's their means of releasing the stress that builds up in a classroom. Discussing the situation with colleagues often yields insights into possible ways to solve the crisis. So, I would never apologize for blowing off steam outside of my classroom; in fact, it's probably saved a few students' lives.

The next day Angela resumed her pose – elbows on the desk, book six inches in the air, directly in front of her face. As we progressed through Caesar's assassination, I began to notice that she was initiating a new method to communicate to her friends at the back of the room. As much as she thought the book was hiding her rotating head, I could see the tip of it turn around. Surprisingly, I could also see the responses. Deciding to let nature take its course, I held out hope that those arms had to be really aching by now – but then, again, Angela was a star golfer. Maybe those arms were better conditioned than I thought. When the class hour ended, and Angela hadn't given in, I realized this situation had reached an impasse. I also realized that her dignity was at stake here. To give up in front of her friends would surely embarrass Angela, and knowing her, she would put up with her self-inflicted anguish every day for the rest of the year to avoid allowing that to happen. Someone had to end Angela's literature-book agony. That someone was going to have to be me.

On the fourth day, when she resumed her position, I decided to do Angela a favor by initiating a pre-"Love and Logic" choice. We teachers at Sandpoint High School had not yet been indoctrinated with Dr. Foster Cline's discipline approach, but many of us, through trial and error, already employed one of the major principles – offer them a choice and let them live with the consequences. I had also learned by that time that an in-your-ear approach with a misbehaving student when I was really going to say something stern usually netted the safest results, lest the kid would later tattle to parents and counselor that you had cruelly embarrassed them in front of the entire class. In this case, I doubted that I could have done anything to embarrass Angela more than she was already embarrassing herself each day, maintaining that obviously uncomfortable 55-minute-long, self-imposed routine.

Before the second bell rang, she had assumed her position. I assumed a position directly to her right, slightly kneeling with my nose just above her ear as she stared straight ahead.

"You have two choices," I uttered directly into her ear in a low, firm tone. "You can put that book down and act like a human being for the rest of the school year, or you can take it and your notebook, leave this class, and never return. It's your choice."

The lifeless stare continued for a few seconds. The book went to the desktop. Angela let go. I stood up, breathed a deep sigh of relief and returned to my desk. This standoff ended so quickly that I was amazed. Not wanting to show my relief and to keep it low-key, I sat down and started taking roll, never looking at Angela. The class hour went well. We tolerated each other until the end of the year. I was positive we had never communicate again and somewhat surprised when the student history book project came out the following winter, that she actually signed a copy I had left in the library. She even knew it belonged to me.

Angela moved on, continued her golf career and assumed a leadership role among the go-getters at SHS.

• • •

Six years after our sophomore English standoff, in early May, I received a phone call.

"Hello, could I speak with Marianne Love?" the male voice at the other end asked.

"This is she," I replied.

"Well, my name is Tom Callister, and I'm director of teacher education at Whitman College. I'm calling to let you know that you've been selected as one of two high school teachers to be honored during our commencement ceremony."

Surely there was a mix-up. Except for a few students who enrolled there over the years, I had never had any connection with Whitman College in Walla Walla, Washington, four hours away.

"There must be a mistake," I said. "I teach at Sandpoint High School. I've never even been on the Whitman campus."

"I know," he responded. "This is an award for high school teachers who have sent students to our school. Every spring we ask our seniors to nominate a teacher from their past who made a significant difference in their lives. From those nominations, we choose two and honor them with our graduating seniors."

It was starting to make sense, but now I was even more puzzled, especially because Dan Raiha, the only student who might have written such a nomination, had graduated the year before.

"But I don't know anyone who's a senior at Whitman this year," I protested.

"Yes, you do," the dean insisted.

"No, Dan Raiha graduated last year," I explained. "He couldn't have done this." I had worked closely with Dan Raiha for two years; he'd been my English student; I had been his adviser on the school paper. I had written several letters of recommendation for various scholarships and awards he sought and had gotten to know him well as a family friend, so it would come as no surprise if he had taken the opportunity to return the favor.

"He didn't," the dean informed me. "A young lady wrote the letter."

Now, I was really scratching my head, trying to think of a young lady I knew who had gone to Whitman. I knew that another of my favorites, Jenny Jacobson, had started out there, but she had transferred to the University of Idaho after two years.

"*Who* is this person?" I asked.

"Her name is Angela Warren," he answered.

The instant the words left his mouth, a loud laugh exploded from mine.

"ANGELA WARREN – no way!" I chuckled, still giggling.

"She said you'd do that," the dean announced.

"No – she would never do such a thing. We didn't get along so well," I told the dean. "I'm sure she hated me."

"She said you'd say that," the well-informed voice announced next.

"Why would she *ever* pick me for such a thing? Is this a joke?" I asked, beginning to wonder if this was really a prank call.

"Her letter says that you inspired her to go into history because of a project you had your students do during her sophomore year of high school," he explained.

"Oh well, we did spend a lot of time on a local history project," I told him. "Their work appeared in a book."

"Well, it must have had a profound effect on Angela," he said, "because she felt it truly made a difference in her life."

By this time, I sat holding the phone, awestruck and almost speechless. After all we had suffered at each other's expense during that turbulent year, Angela had apparently matured enough to separate personal differences from something of far more importance: actual learning – and learning that would steer her in a definite direction in her future.

This was a teaching moment – albeit delayed by six years. This was one for the books.

"Well, thank you," I said to the dean, still stunned. "What does this mean?"

"We're going to wine and dine you here at Whitman, and we want you and your spouse to be our guest for the weekend. You'll stay in a room at our historic Faculty Center, and you'll receive your award at commencement on May 18 with our seniors," he explained. "We're looking forward to meeting you."

"Well, thank you so much. I'm honored," I said. "I'm sure we'll be there." After discussing the other details and hanging up, I walked around in a daze for a few minutes, still incredulous that Angela Warren would be so magnanimous.

With two weeks to wait before going to Whitman, I wanted very much to call her. It was the busy month of May, though, and finding the time to run down her telephone number proved to be impossible. I finally decided we would talk when I arrived on campus. Besides, this meeting was going to be a moment where I would need to validate with a live body standing in front of me to assure me that she really had written a letter on my behalf.

The weekend came and passed. I felt like Cinderella from the moment we hit campus and were escorted to our suite on the upstairs level of the stately and historic Faculty Center. A huge basket of Washington goodies, complete with $100 cash sat on the dresser. On Sunday, the magical event seemed even more unbelievable as I learned that my marching partner for commencement was none other than U.S. Sen. Mark Hatfield, of Oregon, the main speaker. During the weekend's festivities, I saw Angela for the first time in four years and met her parents at a dinner with Whitman faculty in our honor. Her pleasure at pulling off this wonderful honor for me was evident as we all shared laughs about her antics with the literature book in sophomore English. She also reiterated to me and to the Whitman faculty what the dean had already told me.

"I majored in history," she said. "It was all because of that project in your class. I loved it so much that I knew I'd love studying history." After she graduated, Angela immersed herself in oral history projects at a little community where she lived on the West Coast. She has since worked for the American Red Cross in Bend, Oregon.

That weekend I learned a very important lesson from my former student, Angela Warren: Never underestimate the positive power a teacher can have with students, even in what may seem like the worst of situations. From that time on, as an educator, I enjoyed a renewed and even more passionate commitment to the significance of my chosen vocation.

Thank you, Angela. You were truly an *angel* in disguise!

8.

Labor of Love:
A Teacher's Maternal Challenge

By Mom Love

This is for all parents and teachers of boys. LESSON: Give young men time to mature. Prod them for results, but don't feel like a failure if your encouragement goes unheeded at the time. Some day they'll find a purpose and, in most cases, will make up for lost time and will generally succeed just fine in their lives. Many simply take a little longer than expected to see the importance of those reports, chapter questions and out-of-class essays. Many also will even confess years later that they wished they had worked harder as students.

This story is about boys and how I learned, through rearing and teaching my own son, to do all of the above. During the last few years of my teaching career, I frequently found myself reassuring parents of adolescent boys to remain patient. I often used my son as a prime example.

In fact, I learned much about teaching from my own two kids, William E. Love III and Ann Elizabeth Love. As they grew up, they taught me more than I ever absorbed from any education-methods manual. I especially learned through their example that every human being sets his or her own schedule and determines his or her individual goals. We, as parents or teachers, can influence the future of young people, but we should allow them to control the direction of their dreams. Often, if we push too hard, we may be infringing on their right to succeed or fail on their own terms. In some cases, our passionate parenting can even create bitter resentment or a major disappointment that could come back to haunt us. I have never forgotten the poster of the bird flying off into the sky with the brilliant observation: If you love something enough, set it free. It will eventually come back to you. Not the easiest lesson of love, for sure! But true.

Like most other parents, I traveled my share of rocky roads while rearing my children, but I'm very proud that both of them are doing what *they* want to do at this moment in their lives. As 20-somethings, they have definitely charted their own courses while working toward the overall goals that they have set for themselves. They've had fun in the process.

Unlike the norm of my era, both kids took six years to graduate from college. They each earned degrees from Boise State University where, as students, they teamed up for nearly two years to produce a weekly alternative music program for student radio called *Ten* 9. After Willie graduated, Annie headed off on her own as an exchange student to New Zealand where she spent nearly six months learning how to drive on the wrong side of the road and embracing the rich cultural mix of Maoris, British Isles-transplants and Asians.

Admittedly, during her formative years, I recognized the wisdom of the old bite-one's-tongue adage after painfully learning that offering advice that I deemed crucial did not, at times, seem equally as essential to Annie. Sometimes, I didn't bite soon enough. We've definitely had our moments, but I am proud that she has learned on her own to be self-reliant, capable and adventuresome. The latter quality has led to some great times for Bill and me.

Meanwhile, William E. Love III or "Big Man," as his father calls him, has often seemed to be late getting things done. In fact, he even got off to a late start in life – in more ways than one. Our first child was due March 31, 1977, when I was almost 30 years old and finally becoming a seasoned teacher. I remember so vividly the moment of sharing with a few select students that motherhood was just around the corner. At the time, my school schedule was demanding from the minute I walked through the door for early-morning drill team practice until I dropped into bed, sometimes after midnight. I realized that when motherhood did come, something in this schedule would have to give. So, about three months into my pregnancy, when the students were devising an elaborate new drill team project, sure to add to my already heavy load, I balked at the idea. They couldn't understand my out-of-character reluctance. Feeling the need to reassure them that I was not purposely obstructing their desires, I called three drill team leaders into our tiny school darkroom for a conference to explain. They were sworn to secrecy, but as a female, I knew that word would eventually get out to the masses and that no further explanations would be needed.

As Willie's ETA drew nearer, so did the baby showers. The faculty surprised me with cake and presents one day after school. My second-period English class had planned to do the same for my last scheduled day of school. Willie, however, did decide to get the process started early, so I missed the shower. The kids enjoyed the cake and laughed about "Theodus" soon adding to the population. In answer to their curiosity about possible names, Theodus seemed to be a class favorite.

We did go to the hospital on the afternoon of the due date, but since Willie's entrance took 15 hours, he has spent his life as an April fool, with his birthday just one day before his dad's. He has *not* spent his life as "Theodus," however. Bill chose to keep the family name of William Edgar going, so over the years he's answered to "Will," "William," "Willie," "Wilbur" and even an occasional Bill. As his mom, I'll always call him "Willie."

The limelight shone on Willie at a very young age, as his photo showed up on the front of the school newspaper. Tagged "Newest Bulldog," Willie's pressure to succeed started early on. Poor kid didn't have a chance with a teacher for a mother. Like a good teacher, I laid out clearly achievable goals and expectations for my little boy when the *Cedar Post* reporter asked what my hopes were for his future.

"He must be a fly fisherman and musician (like his dad), football star (like his uncles), and, of course, editor of the *Cedar Post* (like his mom)," I began. "I also expect him to be a super intellectual (like all family members, of course), a horse lover (like his aunts), a hiker (like his dad) and a long-distance runner (like his Uncle Kevin).

"Besides that, I want him to live a normal life," I added. I did have many other wishes for Willie, but I also knew how space plays a factor in newspapers. Besides appearing on the front page of the *Cedar Post*, Willie was probably exposed to an outside world faster than most infants. I took five weeks off from school after his birth, but he would often show up with me in his baby carrier at Sandpoint High School, while the drill team prepared for the big Apple Blossom Festival Parade in Wenatchee, Wash., early in May. An assortment of teenage "aunts" from the Ponderette squad fell in love with him immediately and delighted in holding him or passing him around to one another. Willie seemed to enjoy the attention.

As time went on, Willie grew from the baby mode into a handsome toddler with his characteristic Dutch Boy white locks nearly shielding his saucer-like brown eyes. He became a well-known figure while trotting alongside me around town. Those big eyes could melt anyone's heart. This early socialization, coupled with his size and his extroverted personality, turned out to be deceiving when he enrolled in first grade. Outwardly, he appeared like a little man with maturity beyond his age.

Like a typical proud parent, I was sure that my son would wow his teachers with his intellect and his sophistication. When the first parent conference with Mrs. Alma Riffle (a very much revered and inspiring first-grade teacher) came, I experienced a rude awakening.

"I have concerns about Willie," she began. "He's such a big boy I'd hate to hold him back … "

I was stunned.

Hold him back? Not my kid, I thought. I'm sure most of Mrs. Riffle's thorough explanation shot right past me as I tried feebly to maintain eye contact.

"Willie has problems reading out loud," she told me. Mrs. Riffle went on to explain that he seemed confused whenever he read aloud at his table. He seemed to jump around from line to line. Maybe it was nervousness, she told me. She also wondered if his hand-eye coordination may not have yet developed because, even while using his finger as a guide, he still had noticeable problems with his oral reading.

Talk about a lesson *for* Mrs. Love – this was it! How could my motherly instincts be so wrong in assessing the child so closely bonded to me?

Therein lies the lesson: No matter how extensive our training or experience, when it comes to our own children, our common sense can often take a nose dive. Familial love often clouds our views.

If parents could learn that lesson early on in a child's existence, I have a feeling there would be a lot less frustration in the child-rearing process. I'll be the first to admit that it took me a while, but this first shocker from Mrs. Riffle started me on my way. I realized during that conference that I might do well to temporarily pull in the reins of high expectations and let this kid mature at his own rate rather than following my preconceived pace. As the year went on, Willie did succeed at moving along successfully enough to proceed to the second grade. He performed as an above-average student in spite of his well-honed preference for being social rather than studious.

Willie's social skills in the fourth grade revealed another truth about kids.

LESSON: Learn to ask the right questions.

One day, while visiting his school for some reason other than a parent conference, I was sitting in the Farmin School library when Willie's class and his teacher, Mrs. Val Sawyer, came in to work on a research project. Once the students had settled in to their assignment, the teacher walked by the table where I sat. It seemed like an apt time for a quick, informal check on Willie's progress.

"How's Willie doing?" I asked.

"Oh, he's doing fine," she responded. "You *did* receive the notes, didn't you?"

I was dumbfounded. Had I been so busy that I had completely forgotten notes coming home from Mrs. Sawyer? Couldn't be.

"No, I don't recall any notes," I said.

"I've sent you two," she revealed. "I was wondering why I hadn't heard from you."

"And what might these notes concern?" I asked, with my eyes

suddenly focusing on Willie who was sending me big smiles across the room, apparently totally unaware of what his mom and teacher might be discussing.

"Oh, well," she said, arming herself with the diplomacy of a seasoned professional. "Willie seems to like being the class comedian. And sometimes that's a bit distracting."

"Oh-h-h-h," I said. "Very interesting. No, we've not received any notes, but we'll be sure to check with Willie to find out why. And if this behavior continues, give me a call."

I decided the best approach to this situation was to let Willie continue his state of ignorant bliss until his dad came home. This was surely a situation for both parents to address as a team. When Bill arrived, I told him about the visit to the school and then asked Willie to sit at kitchen table. We both sat down opposite him, and I began.

"Willie, when I was in the library today, I decided to ask Mrs. Sawyer how you were doing, and she asked me if I'd read the notes she'd sent home," I said. "The only problem is we've never seen any notes from Mrs. Sawyer. Do you have them?

"Yes," he said.

"Well, where are they?" I inquired.

"In my bag in my room," he answered.

The next revelation taught me to adopt a new perspective I had never dreamed existed.

"Well, why didn't you give them to us?" I continued.

"You never asked for them," he said in such matter-of-fact innocence that even the most callous of humans could never have retaliated.

We Love parents learned from that day forward a dramatic reinforcement of the rule my mother had reiterated throughout my childhood dusting-the-furniture days. Whenever I missed the legs and frames underneath, she would remind me that everything has more than one dimension. In this case, we learned to consider all possible perspectives before drawing conclusions. Willie also learned that evening that Mrs. Sawyer didn't appreciate his comedic distractions in the fourth-grade classroom. No more notes came home – to our knowledge, but we had learned to exercise our inquiring minds.

Willie's sixth-grade teacher was Donna Lang. I had actually worked with her during my student-teaching experience. In fact, she was a member of the class who turned their chairs around after I left the room for a minute and announced that I didn't want to see anyone talking. They followed instructions and all I saw was the backs of their heads upon my return. The experience turned out to be the first of many of lessons about literal interpretation. Speaking of moving chairs, Willie rose from comedian in fourth grade to a sixth-grade class leader who got results. Mrs. Lang tells it this way:

It's the first day of school and in our newly created classroom we have desks but no textbooks and only folding chairs from the kitchen next door. As we are discussing this, the superintendent pulls up in front and enters the building. I could tell something was afoot and tried to get the darlings to hush up and sit down, but under the leadership (?) of three of the six or so children, including William Love, who were the offspring of teachers in this district, all of my students stood and chimed, "Good morning, Mr. Humble," as he passed our door and started up the stairs.

He came back down and said, "Good morning. How is everything?"

To which they answered, "Good, if we had chairs."

He answered, "You have no chairs?"

They said, "No."

Then he said, "Other than that, how are things?"

To which they answered, "OK, if we had books."

He said, "You have no books?"

Of course, they answered, "No!"

After wishing us a good day, he continued up the stairs. Less than an hour later, a flatbed trailer showed up outside our windows with chairs and textbooks for each student.

Willie and his friends earned lifelong brownie points from Mrs. Lang for their assertiveness with that particular superintendent, who happened to be at the right place at the right time, when a school district-logistics nightmare called for some quick action.

While still in grade school, Willie joined the Cub Scouts along with a bunch of his other longtime friends. It seemed like a natural move since his father was an Eagle Scout and a very active scoutmaster for the local Kiwanis troop. Once again, I had no doubts that Willie would shine as he followed in Bill's footsteps. Then we attended the first Blue and Gold dinner at Sandpoint's Community Hall. Approximately 200 little guys in blue shirts, blue jeans and yellow neckerchiefs, most accompanied by a set of two parents and assorted siblings straggling along behind charged through the doors that night, mainly to run around with their groupies but also to snarf down a potluck meal and participate in a traditional scout ceremony. The highlight of the evening was the awards presentation signifying what were generally automatic achievements at different levels for the little scouts. As Bill, Willie, Annie and I sat at our table, the presenter read off name after name of young boys, signaling them to receive their certificates or pins. Halfway through the presentation when every other member of Willie's den had gone to accept an award, I began to worry. There's nothing more painful to a mother's heart than to witness her child being ignored, picked on or hurt. Well, the pain started as a dull ache.

"Certainly they'll call his name soon," I thought, while watching kid after kid trot to the front. "Maybe they're doing it by alphabetical order." We were getting down to the wire when I could stand it no more.

"Is Willie getting an award?" I finally whispered to Bill, taking extreme care that our little boy would not hear me.

"No," Bill said, staring straight ahead in his characteristic unemotional manner.

"Why not?" I asked.

Still with no change of expression and without looking to the left or right, he uttered the straight facts.

"Because he didn't do anything," he said.

I tried to control the sensation of being hit between the eyes with a rock. I tried to remain calm. I tried to avoid the realization and subsequent personal embarrassment that it was very possible our adorable little

William E. Love III, the son of Sandpoint's foremost scoutmaster, William E. Love Jr., would be the only Cub Scout among 200 little guys not to receive an award that night.

That moment in Community Hall, where many 4-H achievement nights were held, brought back the memory of an event hauntingly similar from my own past. As a 10-year-old, like Willie, I had joined 4-H, attended all the meetings, ate all refreshments, and did all the cooking and arts and crafts projects, but failed to complete what was most hated by kids but most crucial for adults – the *record book*. Mrs. Hudon would not sign my record book because I had not filled it out. My mother tried to convince Mrs. Hudon to sign my record book, but my leader refused. That meant I did not complete my first year of 4-H. It seemed perversely cruel to me at the time, but in later years the humiliation of my 10-year-old self-esteem surfaced, and (except for a couple of pathetic years as a college student) if I might be tempted to half-do anything, I dug in and finished the job.

Maybe – as painful as it seemed to me at this time, when Willie would go home from the Blue and Gold dinner without a certificate to proudly place in his scrapbook – just maybe he would benefit from the same lesson as I had learned decades before. Relying on that notion helped ease the maternal pain I felt for my little boy that night. He did continue with scouting and eventually earned a few achievement pins but never immersed himself in the organization to the degree that his dad had – after all, with 4-H, soccer, basketball and baseball, a little guy has to manage his time.

On the school scene, I would have to say his middle school years remain a blur for me. He made it through with no problems and, as a seventh-grader, got tapped to be as a Natural Helper by his classmates. The worst thing I remember about this time was the gentle, frequent nudging of his principal, Ron Hopkins, to persuade Willie not to wear his baseball cap inside the school. For years in our district, the debate over hats in the school occupied an inordinate amount of time among faculty and administrators. I couldn't have cared less, because over the years I had seen a lot worse and often much more offensive apparel show up at school.

To some, however, it was important to remind students of the old rule of gentlemanly courtesy that one removed one's hat when entering a building. Ron Hopkins always liked to remind Willie, but the two also enjoyed some good banter. Ron even presented Willie with a baseball cap at his Stidwell Junior High's eighth-grade graduation.

I was thrilled when my son finally arrived at the high school where he immediately helped me out by filling the void left by Jim Feldhausen's graduation as the *Cedar Post* "pop machine technician." That title meant loading the machines daily and taking the money to the school clerk. It also meant a free soda every day, so Willie was happy to perform the duties associated with the newspaper's major moneymaker.

Ninth grade and age 14 also meant drivers' training. I received a letter from a student of Willie's vintage recently, recalling good times in the automobile with teacher Ron Hunt and fellow ninth-grader Adam Long. Adam is two days older than Willie. He still claims to this day that he remembers Willie being brought into the newborn unit, where the two of them first discussed the meaning of life.

Well, part of their life also involved learning to put their foot on the brake every time they saw a stop sign. One of Willie's student driving partners, Donovan Libring, who is a Spanish translator living in France, once recounted to me the joy at watching the first person among their group to run a stop sign. He thought it was Willie. We were amazed to learn that Willie hadn't shared this achievement with us at the time.

"Why didn't you tell us about running that stop sign when you took drivers' training?" Bill asked him after I had mentioned Donovan's letter. Before Willie could respond, I jumped in with a reminder.

"Don't you remember, Bill? We never asked him," I quipped. "I thought you learned a long time ago that we were supposed to ask him about such things." Well, my comment turned out pretty lame because once Willie had the floor, he suggested that Donovan probably remembered it wrong.

"It was Adam," he said. "He had to get out, apologize to the stop sign and buy the rest of us ice cream." Hearing this, I wrote back to Donovan, who did concur he was mistaken and that Willie had, indeed, remembered the story correctly. Willie says he never did run a stop sign – during the class, that is. So, he had no trouble earning his driver's license and opening the door to drive the family's brown Ford pickup to school.

I couldn't wait for him to move on to his sophomore year when he would finally sit in my honors English class. I had already had the experience of teaching two younger sisters and a younger brother and had nothing to worry about as far as conflict of interest. They were all top students, and for them to earn anything less than an A in my class would have shocked even the most skeptical of detractors. I had worked overtime to dismiss any notion of favoritism extended toward my siblings. In fact, my efforts were so masterful in one case that more than half of my brother Jim's English classmates were shocked at the end of the year to learn that my brother sat in their class.

Now, with Willie in my English class, I faced some different challenges. There was no hiding the fact that we were related because all his classmates had known since the days of summer T-ball who Willie's parents were. In addition, he had not exactly performed as a top student, although he definitely had the tools by that time to tackle honors English. To put it lightly, Willie didn't always use his tools, including his pen. No automatic A's here. In September that year, I became acutely aware of his study habits when the first set of Greek Word Clues sentences came in and Willie's paper wasn't among them. While recording grades, I thumbed through the pile a second time that evening, figuring his must have stuck to another paper. No sign of his assignment.

"Where are your Word Clues sentences?" I yelled down the hallway.

"In my room," he said.

"Why didn't you turn them in?" I asked.

"I forgot," he said.

I *had* learned my lesson from Willie's days in Mrs. Sawyer's grade school class. I *had* asked. The only problem was I hadn't asked at the right time! Stupid me! I immediately made a mental note to ask Willie on mornings *before* an assignment was due if he had it with him when he went to school. Little did I know that even this strategy would prove fruitless as the year moved on.

By the time Willie arrived in my class, I had taught more than 20 years and had established a firm late-paper policy. This came after years of accepting piles of assignments at the last possible minute of the quarter, as if I didn't have enough to do. It took me a while to learn a staple among Foster Cline's "Love and Logic" rules: Take care of yourself first, and then you're much better equipped to take care of your students.

Finally, one year I devised my Late Paper Box, complete with instructions that any paper turned in after I had stapled those I had collected would go in this box. The most a student could receive for that assignment was 65 points. An F was better than a zero, I would tell them. I also assured them that the paper would be corrected only if I had time.

Usually, during the eighth week of each quarter, I would post a list of students' names, listing all assignments each student had missing. They had until the last hour of the last day of the quarter to get those assignments into the Late Paper Box. Every quarter Willie's name appeared on the missing-papers list; in his case, the number of missing assignments depended on how many Word Clues sentence assignments we had had that quarter – usually one or two. For some reason, Willie was not enthralled by composing 25 or 30 sentences, using the Latin or Greek words from our vocabulary study. In fact, I don't recall too many of his assignments appearing among the huge pile stuffed into the Late Paper Box. So, having had every opportunity to redeem himself, Willie remained quite content with his do-just-enough-to-get-by attitude. Usually he had enough grades to eke out a B minus for each quarter. It was exasperating, to say the least. It didn't matter how many times I came close to blowing my cork in mother-son discussions about this problem. Willie remained unaffected and contented. As his high school career continued, other teachers were discovering the same habits I had encountered. His main problem was that teachers generally loved him and gave him slack, figuring that certainly this personable and popular young man would get his act together and eventually turn in his work. On the average, at least once each quarter, a colleague would sidle up to me in the faculty room and quietly repeat words similar to what I had heard from someone else the previous quarter.

"Well, I was checking, and Willie's got a D in my class," the conversation would begin. "He's got a week to get some assignments in, and maybe he can get it back up to a B."

"Have you talked to him about this?" I would ask. "It doesn't do any good for me to say anything." Most of the time I would learn such a conversation hadn't taken place, and then I would assure them that Willie was on his own. "Go ahead and talk to him. He'll make the decision to turn it in or let it go."

Of course, I would mention the conversation to Willie but with little success. Each time, the teachers, at least, went away reassured, relieved that this parent was not going to threaten their careers if her son didn't make the honor roll.

In spite of his reluctance to turn in assignments, I still encouraged Willie to sign up for my journalism class his junior year. I figured it would be cool to have him along when the newspaper staff went on annual trips to national conventions. I secretly hoped he would like journalism, especially sports reporting, enough to pursue it as a career. Willie may not have performed well as a student, but ask him anything about sports, and he could fire off the answer in a split second. From the time he single-handedly played all positions on his own make-believe football team as a toddler, Willie has remained an enthusiastic student of sport. He knows teams, players and statistics, and he can intelligently discuss virtually all aspects of sport with the best of experts. His hero in his high school days was Michael Jordan. As a basketball player himself, Willie identified closely with Jordan's story of being an above-average but not great player who later found his niche. Deep down, I think Willie knew that about himself at the time because he also greatly admired David Letterman for similar reasons – an average guy develops into monumental success. If only everyone else had figured that out at the time, we may have saved ourselves a few moments of frustration.

Willie's journalistic achievement in high school was moderate. His writing skills were excellent, and he learned quickly how to put together a basic sports story. Meeting deadlines, however, was a struggle for him, but he would usually come through with the basketball story at the last moment, knowing that a blank space on the sports page in the newspaper could guarantee a mad mother at home.

Willie enjoyed participating on the staff, but his passions at the time leaned more toward earning a spot on the varsity basketball team and participating as a student leader. He met with great success at both during his senior year while serving as student body president and, after some initially tough times, earning the vote of his basketball teammates for "Most Inspirational Player." The Sandpoint High School varsity squad won only a few games that year. His coach, Jack Dyck, purposely refused to put Willie in the game until he showed more hustle. It was difficult for us as parents to watch him sit on the bench game after game, but we kept our mouths shut. We never believed in making a fuss, even if we didn't think our kid was getting a fair deal. I guess I had learned that approach long ago at the Cub Scout Blue and Gold dinner. Jack always said that Willie was an intelligent player but that he needed to move faster. His Aunt Laurie had expressed it best when she first watched Willie play during his junior high basketball years.

"He ain't pretty, but he gets the job done," she observed. In high school competition, however, Willie needed to move much more quickly to get the job done. After sitting on the bench for about four straight games during his senior season, he finally got the nod from Jack one night, when all was not going well in a contest against Coeur d'Alene. During that opportunity, Willie figured it out. Once on the floor, he raced all over the court, defending, dribbling or shooting. It seemed like every shot he took dropped smack dab through the hoop. The team still didn't win the game, but Willie's hustle earned him "Player of the Week" honors for the Bulldogs. He maintained a similar pace through the rest of the season to inspire his teammates' accolades.

His other passion was student government, where he often served as a class officer through his junior year. That spring, Willie decided to run for student body president. The kid had poise. Three different times he stood before classes numbering 300-plus and dressed in jeans, a white shirt and tie gave his campaign spiel devoid of notes.

The second and third times he delivered the speech, however, his address was a bit briefer than the initial speech. I was junior class adviser at the time. So, when it was time for Willie to address the eleventh-graders, I attended. As he was introduced, I beamed with maternal pride. It was hard to believe that the little boy had so quickly become such a polished young adult. He had no problem standing before the large group of classmates, outlining his goals as the school's ASB president. The next-year's seniors listened to his every word. About two-thirds of the way through his address, Willie, the comedian, decided to veer off on a different vein. Building to an intended crescendo, he began, with careful detail and vivid examples, describing how lucky the Sandpoint High students should feel with all their educational and social opportunities. This was surely leading somewhere, I thought, still beaming with parental pride.

"We *could* live in Clark Fork and have Inbreeding 101," he said.

Willie's audience immediately went nuts. So did his mother.

Instantly, as the punch line left his lips, 300 sets of eyes belonging to 300 gleeful adolescents stared not at Willie but at Willie's mother. Willie's horrified mother stared back, then shot a venomous glance across the gym at her son. The kids knew, and Willie knew that when this speech ended, he and his mother might be having a conversation.

We did.

As the junior class students were dismissed, I marched straight toward the podium, eyed my young-adult son square in the face, summoned him with an emphatic index finger, and ordered, "Follow me," leading him outside the gymnasium. Dumbfounded, Willie followed like a puppy dog. He had just let loose one of the great lines of his life; now he was headed out of Bulldog gym to the doghouse. I continued marching out the door, stopping abruptly at the dumpsters for an about-face and began the lecture.

"Whatever happens now, you deserve," I barked as Willie, all 6 feet, 3 inches of him, towered over me with an expression of shock and defensiveness. "I can't believe you said that – in front of 300 students and all those teachers. The word is bound to spread to people who definitely will not appreciate your comment, and when it does, you'd better be prepared to deal with it. How could you stoop so low?"

Willie wanted to respond, but like any incensed mother on a roll, I allowed no rebuttal.

"I think you need to apologize – and publicly," I announced. "I don't know where or when, but you'd better do it, if you know what's good for you. That's all I've got to say. You'd better do what's right and be prepared to take the consequences." I walked off and left him there. He wanted to talk back, but he knew better.

Willie had two more speeches to give. Word filtered back to me quickly that he had apologized for any inappropriate, insensitive or offensive remarks he may have made in previous speeches. That night, after I told Bill about Willie's performance, we again gathered in the kitchen, much like the time with Mrs. Sawyer's notes.

"Son," Bill began in his usual, calm manner, "there once was a secretary of agriculture named Earl Butz. He was really popular, too. But he once got carried away with some public comments. He lost his job." While penning this story, I searched the Internet to learn what Earl Butz had actually said. On an Earl Butz egg-on-the-face scale of 1 to 10, I would say Willie's comment rated a 3. Still, all things are relative. To this day, he has never visibly paid the price, except for his strange desire to crouch down on the car seat beneath the window while traveling through Clark Fork.

I don't know if it was because the comment was a hit with Willie's teen friends or if they actually thought he would be a good leader, but he got elected. Willie enjoyed his senior year, especially basketball and the months spent planning for the senior prom with his buddy Seth.

Seth had the distinction of gradually becoming Willie's best friend after a rocky beginning. Their friendship would have seemed like a natural occurrence, considering that each had a parent who grew up in the small town of Oakdale in southwest Louisiana. Not so. Both boys also shared a network of teacher lineage, and over the decades those teachers taught each other's kids. Years later, both sets of Louisiana parents discovered that the Sagle, Idaho, countryside where Katie Jane lived was fewer than 10 miles from the Sandpoint, Idaho, countryside where Bill Love lived.

Word of the shared experience spread quickly. The Noonans and the Loves got together and discovered we had two boys the same age. Similar age does not guarantee instant friendship. William E. Love III towered over Seth Noonan, but Seth was a scrapper. One day when Katie brought Seth to our house, she left with a smile, confident that this would signal the beginning of a long friendship. Within the hour after Willie, Seth and Annie went outside to play, I could hear shrieking. I stood outside the sliding glass door in time to see Willie and Annie bawling and running for cover from that mean little boy who had strong-armed them off the platform underneath their willow tree. Neither wanted anything to do with Seth ever again. So, for several years, we maintained a casual relationship with the Noonans and exchanged occasional telephone calls.

Then, when Willie and Seth were sophomores, the teacher bond continued. I would not only teach Willie, but I would keep the generational string going by also teaching Seth. In fact, the two boys sat next to each other in my fifth-period English class. Apparently, any bad feelings about the Seth attack of years before had dissipated. The boys ended up appreciating each other.

Plans for the prom dominated the springtime months of Willie and Seth's senior year. The boys surmised that the field of date prospects at Sandpoint High School failed to fit their needs. So, they set up a plan to hang out for an afternoon in Silver Lake Mall 40 miles away in Coeur d'Alene with hopes that two "Miss Rights" would come strutting along, just dying to accompany them to the prom. Apparently, that plan fizzled. Eventually, Seth asked a young lady from Sandpoint High School.

Willie remained dateless until the night of his final basketball game at the regional tournament in Post Falls. His team lost miserably. He and his buddies left the gym dejected and boarded the bus. When they later stopped at a convenience store along the way, Willie bought a bag of Doritos Nacho cheese-flavored tortilla chips and a soda to drown his sorrows. An hour later, when they climbed off the bus in the SHS parking lot, the boys noticed that the Sandpoint Junior Miss program was still going at the middle school next door. Wasting no time, the boys soon stood inside the gym where local junior girls were vying for the much-coveted title. Suddenly, the "most beautiful girl in the world" came on to give a short presentation as Rathdrum, Idaho's, outgoing Junior Miss. Her name was Tina, and her purpose was to represent her community at this competition. At the back of the auditorium, Willie stood among his friends, transfixed by this lovely young royal whom he had never seen before.

His date to the prom was determined. He knew it, but she didn't.

Knowing that Nacho breath may not cut it when asking a perfect stranger from a town 45 miles away to the Sandpoint High School Senior Prom, Willie begged a favor from his friend Rachel Honsinger, who was chewing a mouthful of gum at the time.

"Let me borrow your gum," he said.

The bond of friendship can be powerful. Not even questioning his intentions, Rachel stuck two fingers in her mouth, pulled out her wad of gum and handed it to Willie. He placed it in his mouth and began chewing away all remnants of Nachos as he moved through the crowd toward the stage, never taking his eyes off the unaware Tina.

Willie reached the side door to the stage just as Tina finished her speech and began walking down the side stairs. Suddenly a tall, blond, unfamiliar 17-year-old with big brown eyes stood before her, blocking her way.

"Would you go to the prom with me?" he asked.

Apparently, it was meant to be. After listening to the answers to questions like "Who are you?" "What prom?" and "When is this prom?" Tina said, "Yes." Apparently, Rachel Honsinger's ABC (already been chewed) gum did the trick.

Both Willie and his buddy Seth now had dates to the prom. Senior year would be complete. The 1995 prom came and went. Tina would later reconnect with Willie in classes at the University of Idaho. They would remain friends, but his true love, Deborah, would come along a few years later in Boise.

As if staying up for most of prom night was not enough, Willie and some friends took off the next day for an evening REM concert at the Gorge at the town of George in Washington along the Columbia River. I still remember the feeling of relief as they arrived home safe and sound, coming down the driveway at 4 a.m. the next morning, which was a Monday and a school day. Willie managed to make it through that long day and his regular work shift as "Arby Melt Boy" at the local roast-beef franchise.

The following week he made arrangements with teachers to take his finals the day of graduation so that we could fly off to the East Coast to attend a West Point commencement. Four years earlier I had written letters of recommendation for a young man named Jim Patton to secure a presidential nomination to the academy. When he invited me to his graduation from West Point, I was thrilled. My older brother Mike had graduated from the academy 20 years earlier, so attending this ceremony was all the more meaningful. I also viewed this trip as the perfect inspiration for the next phase of Willie's life. During the week, we had a great time visiting New York, touring the academy, walking around Philadelphia and spending a day in Washington, D.C. With the flight home landing on the day before Willie's graduation in Sandpoint, we hit a major snag upon arriving in Denver. Spokane International Airport was fogged in and not taking any flights until the next day. With no luggage, we soon boarded another flight bound for Salt Lake City. We spent a short night at the Howard Johnson's Hotel and took a taxi back to the airport for a 12:30 flight to Spokane. Again, upon our arrival, no luggage had come for either of us. After that hassle, we pulled into Sandpoint at 3:31 p.m., one minute too late for Willie to take his finals and with little time to find some dress clothes for the event just a couple of hours away. Willie borrowed slacks, a shirt and tie from his dad while I ran off to Penney's for my ensemble. His teachers allowed him to take his tests the next day, and he was officially graduated from Sandpoint High School and bound for the University of Idaho at Moscow in the fall.

After dreading this new void in our lives and crying for every day three weeks prior to taking Willie and his belongings to the University of Idaho campus, I continued my tear fest all the way back to Sandpoint. He didn't seem nearly as sad as I did. He was ready to go. The sooner Mom headed home, the better. We all adjusted to his absence but not without feelings of emptiness. I did take comfort that he had a job working weekend nights at the Pantry Restaurant as a busser. My rationale was that he couldn't get into too much trouble if he was working while everyone else on campus had time for trouble. Three weeks into the semester, when we visited the campus for a Vandal football game, it was easy to see that a quick hello to Mom, Dad and little sister, along with a free meal at any of Moscow's restaurants other than The Pantry pretty much satisfied his need to see us.

So, the year went on. He came home for the holidays, and we didn't see too much of him second semester. Shortly after Willie arrived home for the summer, so did his grades. Shortly after that, he received a letter suggesting that with such dismal grades, the folks at the University definitely questioned whether or not he should be welcomed back as a student in the fall. The letter instructed him to contact his adviser, Jean Christiansen, then the assistant dean of the College of Education.

Characteristically putting it off until the last possible moment, one August morning Willie finally made the phone call. While he sat in the kitchen on the phone, I took the portable phone and retreated to the back step outside to eavesdrop on this conversation. Willie was aware that I had intended to listen in but not comment, so he had no problem with the intrusion.

After going through the preliminaries about his present academic situation and how the university didn't like to see students wasting their money, Ms. Christiansen moved on to the guts of the conversation, an interview to determine if she should give Willie the green light to return. It was obvious from the get-go that Willie had met his match in Jeanne Christiansen; none of Willie's natural charm would soften this seasoned educator. She ran him through a litany of questions extending far beyond "yes," "no," "I promise-to-do-better" answers. On that very spot, Willie was to outline for her over the phone how he intended to improve his academic performance. Some answers were easy, like "go to class more often." This response elicited a silent chuckle from me because I had made a similar discovery a generation before while I attended the university.

When he led off with "I'll try harder," she countered with "How do you intend to try harder?"

When he promised to study, she asked what kind of schedule he had set up to improve his study habits.

"I'll spend more time at the library," he said.

"And what will you do at the library?" she inquired.

By the time the conversation ended, Willie had supplied enough specifics to convince a hard-nosed Ms. Christiansen that he had possessed a sincere (maybe scared) willingness to change his ways. She also put him on a plan. She was to see him at her office for at least five or 10 minutes each week, and he was to show up with his study schedule and specific work that he was completing for each class.

The plan worked. As a sophomore Willie struggled his way out of academic probation. Second semester he no longer had to report to Ms. Christiansen every week. He seemed to be on his way to studenthood.

That spring he decided two years of residing at Targhee Hall had been enough. He switched to Graham Hall in the Wallace Complex clear across campus. Moving into the dorm that fall, Willie quickly relished his status as one of the few upperclassmen still living in Graham. His leadership and social skills once again kicked in. Someone must show the frosh the ropes on campus. Willie decided he had take that responsibility. I don't know the details, but from what I heard from the lips of another hallmate, he took his job seriously. Once while visiting, I learned that my son had been dubbed by the admiring underclassmen as "the god of Graham Hall." I would also learn at the end of the year that Willie's godlike social responsibilities once again ate into his academic responsibilities.

This discovery came one night in May, shortly before the end of his junior year when he was home visiting. Bill was out of town, so Willie and I went to dinner at the Power House Restaurant in Sandpoint. Waiting patiently until I had had a few sips of Chardonnay and knowing full well those sips would cut Mom's hard edge, Willie initiated a discussion.

"Mom," he said, "do you suppose it would be OK if I took a year off from Idaho and worked? It would give me some time to grow up, and then I'd transfer to Boise State."

It was obvious he had thought over this scenario carefully. He had accompanied us once on a visit to Boise State where Annie had enrolled the fall before. Because of his undying loyalty to the University of Idaho Vandals, he could never bring himself to become a Bronco fan. He did figure, however, that he needed a new environment and a new start on his road to earning a degree. The words were music to my ears because I had had a feeling that not all was going well, and I was beginning to wonder how much money in student loans was essentially going down the tubes.

"I think that would be a good idea," I said. So, the god of Graham Hall moved back into the Love home for a year. While employed at Badger Building Supply just down the road, he picked up some valuable skills and maturity, working behind the counter and delivering lumber products to job sites. Over the months, though, he acquired a strong desire to get back to school as soon as possible and, this time, to do the job right. That spring he went to Seattle for a few days and accompanied his old buddy Seth to a few University of Washington classes. After that visit, Willie came home, inspired and armed with a whole new appreciation for the college education he was missing. He also realized that most of his close friends were almost finished with their degrees and ready to embark on exciting careers or to pursue even further education. Taking stock, Willie looked forward to returning to school in the fall, determined to retake some classes he had blown off at the University of Idaho, to raise his grade point and to earn his degree.

That determination, the change of atmosphere and his meeting the love of his life finally provided the ideal motivation for Willie to settle down and get serious about education. He married Deborah Williams at St. Joseph's Catholic Church in August 2001. His former nemesis, Seth, served as best man at the wedding where, as noted on the local Arby's marquee, "Arby Melt Boy Marries Polar Swirl Girl." He later graduated from Boise State with a degree in English literature on May 18, 2002. After working in Boise as a cab driver and applying unsuccessfully for several career positions, Willie and Debbie agreed that it might be wise for him to search for jobs elsewhere, even if that meant being separated while she finished her degree at Boise State. A general assignment reporter position at Newport, Washington, just 30 miles from Sandpoint came open, making it possible for him to have a handy place to stay if he landed the job. Willie applied, interviewed and was writing stories two weeks later for publisher Fred Willenbrock and the *Gem State Miner* newspaper in late October 2003. Who knows for sure why Fred decided to hire him? Maybe it was his genuinely warm and outgoing personality, his maturity, or his willing attitude toward learning about the newspaper business from the ground up.

I like to think that Fred just liked what he saw as he zeroed in on the last two words of Willie's resume. These words accurately reflected a fun-loving boy who had come of age emotionally and intellectually. So succinctly, so eloquently, these two simple words signified a young man who had arrived. No longer would he exasperate the key adults in his life. William E. Love III now appreciated and acknowledged the lessons he had learned about education and himself since that Labor of Love on April Fools' Day 1977.

Besides listing his interests as sports, music, traveling and hiking, to round out his profile, Willie added "Reborn Student."

9.

Confessions of a Reborn Student

By William Love

It's been more than a decade, but I am still scared the residents of a certain small town will get me. I lie awake at night waiting, waiting for the fine folks of Clark Fork – a community I almost didn't mention due to safety concerns for myself and my family – to get their revenge. I know these rightfully vengeful souls will finally put together the posse that will come to my home and give me – the Sandpoint boy – my due.

I have my parents, especially my mother, to thank for the paranoia.

Unlike most high school students, I was unable to separate my life at school from my life at home. I was the son of a teacher, a well-known teacher at that, and I had to keep my guard up at all times to make sure that when I was doing something I shouldn't, it wasn't happening in a public setting.

Sure, with my mother being a respected teacher at Sandpoint High School, I was lucky in the sense that I didn't have to worry about the dreaded phone calls at night from a teacher surprising my parents with the details of the devious activities I had participated in earlier that day. In fact, I don't remember having one of those calls, even though I do recall spending several class periods in the hallway when my just-having-fun antics had gone a little too far.

I had, however, learned a sly approach for such situations from my good friend Seth Noonan our sophomore year. One day I was in the classroom after school when Seth told a longtime teacher at the school who was threatening to call home that his parents were having marital problems. He warned her that a call home would probably make matters worse for them in their present situation – a situation I knew was very far from the truth as they are happily married to this day. But the veteran teacher took the bait, promised not to call and told Seth she hoped things improved at home.

Instead of the dreaded phone calls, though, I had a parent who was already at the school and who was friends with all of my teachers. So, if word got to her about something I had done that I wasn't supposed to do, she usually had ample time to think about how she would deal with the situation. Her usual strategy was to wait for backup from my dad. A two-against-son discussion then took place at our Great Northern Road home, where I would get a double-headed lecture about the importance of those noble attributes such as demonstrating initiative and not being the class clown. My parents always hoped these words of wisdom would turn their teenager into an adult.

So that fine spring day at school when my mom ordered me into sequestered privacy, far away from my friends, wanting to talk to me right then and there, I knew I was in trouble, big trouble. Both Mom in an early-afternoon conversation and Dad later that evening at home told me that the contents of my campaign speech for Sandpoint High School's Associated Student Body President would quickly spread to the residents of Clark Fork. And when the citizens of that kind little community nestled next to where the Clark Fork River flows into Lake Pend Oreille heard, it would just be a matter of time before they would seek revenge that would likely include bodily harm.

Now, my mother would like you to believe what I said was akin to a major faux pas with historic significance. I am writing to set the record straight. What I said in that campaign speech to 300 members of the class of 1995 and, at that point, one proud mother was the sort of comment that has earned Jeff Foxworthy critical praise and millions of dollars. Well, at least the millions of dollars part.

I will admit that how I characterized the upstanding citizens of that small town might have been a little crass, but, like Lenny Bruce, "I was misunderstood," and the powers that be, namely my mother that day, were just trying to end my blossoming, stand-up comedy career. You have to remember this was the mid-1990s; the president was from Arkansas; it was before PC (political correctness) was all the rage, and a person could still make jokes about the gene pool – or flaws thereof – in smaller communities.

Another misconception my mother would have you believe is that all of my classmates were looking at her when I made the now-infamous, "in-the-mind-of-a-mother" comments. But when I passionately told my peers that "we should be proud of Sandpoint High School and the education we get here because we could be going to Clark Fork where they teach Inbreeding 101," I can assure you the last thing they were doing was staring at her, waiting for a reaction. They couldn't have. They were too busy rolling in the gym bleachers, laughing.

From my two previous years of student government experience as vice president for the sophomore and junior classes, I knew what it would take to win a hard-fought campaign against my very worthy opponent, Alyssa Boeck, who had been a part of student council since junior high school. So I knew, as with any good high school election, to win, a candidate needs a lot of friends. And those voters who aren't necessarily friends, must be wooed with laughter during the five-minute campaign speech.

After what my parents told me that day, I agree I probably should have spent a little more time preparing my speech because I hadn't spent any. But with a job as important as student body president on the line, I felt it was only fair to my future constituents to speak from the heart and without a canned speech.

Looking back, I know there were kinder, subtler ways of getting my message – which actually was a positive one when taken in context of the full speech – across to a gym full of my 17-year-old electorate. It was one of the many lessons I learned growing up as the son of a teacher and, more than likely, one I will some day share with the children my wife, Debbie, and I will have. As the song goes, I just wish I knew what I know now when I was younger because it would have saved me the countless lectures from my parents that were, in reality, all lessons with love.

This book is called "Lessons with Love," but it doesn't say which Love. So I figure this is my opportunity to share some life lessons, "words of wisdom" as my Uncle Kevin refers to them, which probably have yet to be covered in the pages of this book. As I find my way into adulthood, I have fallen back on these words of wisdom, better known as "WOWs," to help guide what is now an upstanding and morally perfect life.

That said, I should probably warn you that most of these WOWs are still in the developmental stage and, as a result, are continually evolving. And although they have been good lessons for me, and they may help the adult readers out there deal with their future ASB president son or daughter, it is probably in the best interest of the kids that they not learn how I came upon these life lessons. I have already been blamed for enough in my life.

In addition, for financial reasons, I am only giving you a few WOWS, because I know I will need material for "Lessons with Love II: The Pope Gets his Revenge."

WOW No. 1: Be careful what you say in a public setting. It may eventually end up in the region's biggest newspaper.

Believe it or not, the great ASB president campaign speech was not my first foray into Secretary of Defense Donald Rumsfeld's school of shock-and-awe speech-giving that leaves the orator saying something in a public setting that perhaps would be better off left unsaid.

When I was in the eighth grade at Stidwell Junior High School, I was awakened from my sleep early one morning by my mother with the urgency that I knew, even in those days before high school, did not bode well for me. That morning began with Mom asking if I realized what I had done. Still waking up on that first day of winter vacation, sleepily unprepared for a full interrogation, I honestly did not know what type of atrocity I had committed.

"You were lucky he didn't put your name in the paper," she said of the *Spokesman-Review* reporter, Kevin Keating, who had written a story for the regional paper's "Idaho Handle" edition about the afternoon assembly my school had held at the start of the first Persian Gulf War. The assembly was an emotional situation, especially for a group of junior high students who were coming to grips with the idea of war and the possibilities for some and the realities for others of their family members going off to the desert to fight Saddam.

Now, having taken some college education classes, I understand the assembly presented an appropriate venue for junior high school students to discuss their feelings on a serious matter. But being 13 years old, I felt the situation also called for a lighter moment, and who better to give the class of eighth-graders a laugh than me?

The source for my material that day had come from an earlier visit I made to the local novelty shop All Smiles. All Smiles had shelves full of gag gifts and cards to pique the interest of any future comedian, and I could spend hours in there, devising my next comedy routine.

With the war brewing in Iraq and the American public learning that there were a number of ways to spell "Hussein," I spent what little money I had on a roll of toilet paper with some inspirational text surrounding a caricature of the now-deposed leader. The toilet paper was the type of bathroom humor that is my forte and something that was always a hit at the Love home. It had drawn laughs with my family, and I knew it would work at school.

So during the assembly, I waited to share my thoughts with my friends and teachers until most of the sad stories had been told and the tears were shed. I have to say my purchase was a hit at the assembly when I lifted the spirits of the somber crowd with the help of another classmate. With toilet paper in hand and a captive crowd, we took the moment to share the message the TP conveyed so well. It was time to "Wipe out Saddam!"

Yes, the TP got the laugh I was looking for, thereby solidifying my status as the class funny man, but what I did not notice at the time was whether or not the reporter from *The Spokesman-Review* sitting in the audience had quoted me correctly in his notebook. The next morning, during her daily devour-the-newspaper-before-anyone-else-is-allowed-to-lay-hands-on-it period, my mother found out that Mr. Keating did, indeed, quote me accurately. "The only reason he didn't put your name in the paper is that he knew who you were," my mom barked.

This event would not be the first or last time I would earn either some advantage or some notoriety because of my last name. But Mom informed me Keating's decision *not* to put my name in the paper was fortunate for me because I could have really embarrassed the family – a lesson she had to continually remind me of during my nearly three decades as the son of a teacher-woman.

That morning some of my classmates were dealing with the possibilities of their relatives going off to war, but I was trying to defend an early-morning assault of my own from a one-person army in the form of an upset mother whom even the most vicious of despots would fear to confront.

Life did go on for me after this incident, and I learned not to make jokes about world issues with a newspaper reporter around. But I am pretty sure Mom did not keep that *Spokesman-Review* article in the scrapbook.

WOW No. 2: Although you might be looking out for your family, don't let that noble ambition get in the way of your grades.

Claims of nepotism can be a painful accusation, especially for a 14- or 15-year-old who has a relative or relatives who teach in that person's school. That was my situation all four years in high school, but particularly in my freshman and sophomore years, where the honors English teachers were my Aunt Barbara and my mother.

All my classmates in those English classes knew the situation, and aside from the occasional comment about what it was like to have a relative for a teacher, my peers didn't really bother me all that much about how the grading situation worked. To keep it that way, I decided early on not to overextend myself academically in these classes. This tactic was partially designed to give the smart kids in the class the opportunity to remain the smart kids, but for the most part I implemented the plan so people wouldn't question why I got the grades I did in those classes.

Of course, with a little bit of work, I probably could have earned A's in all of those classes with my mom and Barbara, but then something like that could have opened the family up to allegations of some type of grade nepotism. I knew I couldn't allow that to happen to my relatives, so I sacrificed my academic standing, doing just enough work to get a C, maybe the occasional B, to make sure the school's administration did not have to open an ugly investigation. My conscious academic dive wasn't something I wanted to do but something I felt obligated to do for my family.

In fact, I did such a good job of maintaining my cover as an average student in the classes taught by my relatives that it was easy for me to act like a below-average student in the rest of my classes. I was always too busy with the social aspects of high school to devote much time to actual class-work. Why study or do homework when there is a good game of table tennis or basketball to play? That was my guiding mantra.

At the time, I also knew in which teachers' classes I especially had to play my role as average student. While growing up, I was familiar with names like Mr. Albertson, Ms. Davis, Mr. Marker, Mr. Iverson, Mrs. Lewis, Coach Barlow and the other legendary teachers of Sandpoint High School. I knew none of them would have a problem telling my mother that I was doing poorly academically or disrupting class.

I quickly learned, however, that the newer teachers at the high school would not necessarily tell my mom about her underachieving and misbehaving son. I like to say I challenged some of the newer teachers with my behavior sometimes, to help them remember why they had become a teacher. It was also in these classes that I seldom listened or did my homework, which I know contributed greatly to the below-average student status. I think if you took my transcripts and compared my grades in the classes taught by the older teachers to those in the classes by the newer teachers, there would be a noticeable difference.

If you take the achievement of an average student and combine that with the achievement of a below-average student, you have the picture of a student who, through his own doing or lack thereof, didn't have very good grades when he graduated. Report card days at the Love household for me were not always the festive and happy ones celebrated at a lot of my friends' homes. I always considered those times as don't-ask, don't-tell days. Unfortunately, my parents – having already learned their "lesson with Young Mr. Love" when it came to requesting certain documents sent home from school and with my mom knowing when report cards were given to students – always asked me for my report card.

Again, I don't think Mom keeps any of those old report cards in the family scrapbook.

WOW No. 3: Don't worry about report cards; they are simply an arbitrary means of grading a person that do not truly reveal that person's intelligence and ability.

At least, that is what I tell myself anyway. I was lucky that there was no such thing as "No Child Left Behind" back then; otherwise, I might still be waiting for the bus to pick me up.

I know this WOW, to some readers, may conflict somewhat with WOW No. 2, but like I said earlier, these WOWs are still in developmental stage, and for someone who did as poorly as I did in school and who may not have the higher-level thinking skills ascribed to those that do well on standardized tests, sometimes there comes the need to contradict oneself. (I guess what I am trying to say is, definitely don't tell kids about WOW No. 3 until they are done with school).

To say I wasn't interested in academics during high school and the first three years of college is an understatement. I can't really explain why, other than there were other things that were of greater interest to me back then. It is funny that people cannot really choose what their minds will retain. As I often tell Debbie, I'm cursed with expansive volumes of the most useless knowledge known to mankind.

For me, a lot of that knowledge concerns sports. My mind is full of games and statistics from the past that will never do me a lick of good but that I will remember for the rest of my life. I just picture myself when I am old and senile yelling at a caretaker that we don't have any timeouts left. (I was the biggest Fab Five fan, and that North Carolina beat Michigan in the 1993 national championship game due in part to the time-out blunder by my favorite college basketball player at the time, Chris Webber, still haunts me.)

I guess in some sense we are born with certain tools that should help us in life. That is not to say we can't improve in certain areas, but at some point I came to the realization that I would never be a top-notch scientist or a successful businessperson. I will never really understand how a salmon is able to breathe in fresh water and salt water or whether the just-in-time business method is the right way to work in the business world.

At one point I had considered majoring in business. But it was after taking an introduction to business class at the University of Idaho that I realized I probably could get a business degree, but I knew I would never be happy with it. While taking that class, I also quickly understood that I would have to work really, really hard to finish the requirements for the bachelor's degree.

In fact, I was at a crossroads as to what my college major should be. I had been learning a lot about effective study habits in my weekly meetings with Dr. Jeanne Christiansen, who later became Dean of UI's College of Education, but I also knew that I did not want to work that hard. (Some habits die hard.) With that, I fell into English.

When I started to think about the classes in which I enjoyed the most success, I realized they were always associated with English. I never really had to work hard in any of my English classes, and the only classes I really enjoyed were the introductory courses that dealt with writing and literature.

With that in mind, I changed my major to English education. I felt at home in my introduction to American literature and introduction to literary studies classes; in fact, those two courses and an advanced theory class I took at Boise State University were my favorite classes during a six-year college career.

My decision to switch to an English major at the University of Idaho was great except for my other classes. I was never really able to put it all together during my three years as a Vandal, what with my heavy social schedule and the duty to show my hallmates the ropes. The best but hardest decision I made in my life was admitting that school wasn't working for me at that time in my life, and it was time for me to leave the University of Idaho. I enjoyed the knowledge I gained during my time in Moscow and appreciate what I did learn there, although most of it was not found in the textbooks.

But to take liberally from a song by the band Tragically Hip, I had "used it up," and it was time for me to move on. I took the year off from school and spent that time throwing lumber around at Badger Building Supply. It was a job I enjoyed, but almost from the first day I was clamoring to get back to the books. My return to academia, however, would not be at the University of Idaho. I knew if I went back to Moscow, I would fall in the same routine. I am a sucker for socializing, so I made the decision that I would enroll in classes at Boise State University the next fall. The place had worked for my sister, Annie, and now I hoped it would work for me.

At this time, my parents were very understanding. I don't know if they were numb from the years of bad report cards, but they accepted my decision to take time off and welcomed me back home for the year. I will always be grateful for that, because for the first time since the first grade I was getting time to mature. Today hearing Mom's story about the concerns of Mrs. Riffle, I realize that the time-out was just what I needed.

In the late summer of 1999, I made my way to Boise State, brimming with concerns about whether or not I could succeed. I was lucky and met some amazing professors who were willing to give extra time to a student who had done poorly academically in high school and college. Although I ended up working as a journalist when I graduated, I still rely every day on the lessons I learned from Devan Cook, Helen Lojek, Steven Olsen-Smith and the other professors in BSU's English department, who helped this below-average student earn a literature degree. It only took 25 years, but thanks to some patience, prodding, caring and sharing from my wife, family, friends and instructors I became a "reborn student." Yeah, if it happened again I probably would have listened a little bit more and tried a little bit harder, but the real learning for me came from the experiences of the journey, which is something that can't be graded in a report card.

And if it wasn't buried in a cedar chest somewhere in a Boise storage unit, that piece of paper I earned on May 18, 2002, would probably be proudly kept in the family scrapbook in Sandpoint.

Bonus WOW No. 4: It is only fair that you get a bonus WOW considering the hefty sum you had to pay for this book. And let me suggest you buy a copy of this book for all your family and friends, because Mom promised me royalties, and I have a very expensive tab left from my three-year party at the University of Idaho.

But your bonus WOW deals with the useless knowledge I was talking about earlier. Sometimes that useless knowledge turns out to be not so useless.

In spring 2006, Debbie and I moved back to Boise after a short stay living in Spokane, where I worked as a general assignment reporter for *The Miner Newspapers*, a terrific pair of weekly newspapers owned by Fred and Susan Willenbrock in Newport, Wash. I actually took one journalism class during my six years of college, but Fred took a chance on a literature major who thought he could write. I spent two enjoyable years there cutting my teeth in community journalism, and I will always be indebted to Fred for the opportunity he presented me.

Soon after starting in Newport, Fred discovered my passion for sports and created a position for me as sports editor for his papers. Along the way I picked up a column called the *Sports Notebook,* where I was able to write about that useless sports knowledge on a weekly basis. The column was fun to write and surprisingly won a couple of awards in its brief stint.

It was a sad day when I left Newport, because of great coworkers I was leaving but also because I didn't have a job waiting for me in Boise. Soon after arriving, however, that useless sports knowledge came in handy when I was hired as a sports reporter at the *Idaho Press-Tribune*, a daily newspaper located a short distance from Boise in Nampa. Now I get paid to go to sporting events and write about them, and I am surrounded by a great group of guys with just as much useless knowledge as me.

Life couldn't be any better.

10.

You Are Now What You Were Then

Even though I had hardly paid attention to that stupid video, its resounding theme kept playing back in my mind on that hot summer day while mowing the lawn in front of the our red barn. For some strange reason, scenes of that long-ago curriculum day had awakened in my quirky memory. Two decades had passed since the nauseating electronic instructor with the Southern drawl had reminded us over and over again during the 90-minute video that regardless of anyone's chronological age, world travels, life experiences, our unique personal value system does not change. After each anecdotal example, the droning teacher with the slick-backed hair faced the camera in his black suit, white shirt and skinny black tie, directed his pointer at the chart and its capital letters, and slowly enunciated "You ARE NOW what YOU WERE THEN."

I had definitely not appreciated those words the first thousand times I heard them in that setting, but since that day I had found myself referring to them over and over because of the gradual realization that they are very true. Regardless of where we go, what we do for a living, how much money we make or fail to make, most of us rarely change from the person we've always been since early childhood. Our value system and our behavior is firmly based on what we were taught way back *then* during our rug-rat days. In most cases, these lessons stay with us forever. Consequently, the value system of a later generation of rug rats can often clash with the truths to which parents cling so dearly, especially when those rug rats are going through their formative years. Recognizing this fact should help us have a better understanding of why kids act like they do.

Pushing the mower over swath after swath of grass, I reminisced about the darkened classroom at Stidwell Junior High where a group of Bonner County School District 82 teachers sat, putting in their time at another dreaded in-service day. As the smug teacher droned incessantly from the television screen, some colleagues sat, eyes glued to the tube, looking down only long enough to jot down important notes. Meanwhile, a few others like me, strategically located at the back of the classroom, frittered away the 90 minutes, constantly off task. We did, however, take great care not to distract the model students among us who would surely stare indignantly if they tuned in to our lack of respect for the "important" video lesson.

"YOU ARE NOW WHAT YOU WERE THEN," the man continually intoned. Well, I guess he was right. I'm a prime example. In fact, since seeing that video, I've assessed my own behavior, and I've given that dorky messenger in black significantly more credence as I've come to fully understand his premise.

Back "*then*," I had often behaved irreverently the instant a classroom situation departed even minutely from total teacher control. For the most part, I was a pretty good kid, but at times, during my own student years, my behavior could turn naughty under certain conditions involving individuals who were employed as educators but definitely *not prepared* as educators. I can even share in the guilt of helping to cause two teachers' departures from their high-school assignments long before their contract year ended. There were accomplices in both situations, but that's no excuse for the personal choices I made during my adolescence.

In one case, my elderly sophomore English teacher, Mrs. Houghton, had come to Sandpoint High School from a girls' finishing school. Apparently, the students exhibited ideal behavior at her prior teaching assignments. We sophomores in public school, however, felt that teachers needed to earn our respect. During her time with us, Mrs. Houghton, a rather large, grandmotherly type, never quite figured that out. Fourth-period English for that first semester almost always provided a great entertainment break for our class of 30-plus honor students. Like good administrators, we students developed a continuous advance plan, complete with specific strategies, on just how we would disrupt Mrs. Houghton's day. In fact, we even made her cry once. That was the time I played ringleader in a 55-minute session of ring-around-the-rosy. After asking us politely several times to sit down, a defeated Mrs. Houghton, attired in her usual red dress and red leotards, finally just collapsed in her teacher chair in tears. Soon after that event, we no longer saw Mrs. Houghton at our school. Ann Cordes replaced her. Ann had fine-tuned her own discipline plan and kept us in our seats and relatively quiet for the rest of the year.

We also drove Mr. Hogan away. He lasted three quarters as our senior government teacher. Like poor Mrs. Houghton, Mr. Hogan was not cut out for the public school classroom. He laughed at his own jokes, and they weren't at all funny to us. He also often fell asleep in class, one time snoozing through the passing bell and remaining there, with his drooling mouth hanging open and his chin propped on one fist, until the next class arrived and seated themselves. In our sixth-period government class, he walked up and down the desk rows of Room 2, never saying a word, while we openly cheated on his Friday tests. We didn't really need to cheat; we just found it entertaining to see how brazenly we could behave without reprimand. One of the few times Mr. Hogan chose to discipline a student seriously for any indiscretion, I was the chosen. Up until that day, my friends would tally how many times Mr. Hogan uttered, "All right, Marianne, be quiet." One day, it totaled 15 times in 12 minutes. Apparently, the 16th time, he chose an uncharacteristically aggressive approach to my continuous chatter.

"OK, go to the office," he finally announced when my usual yakking out loud had really started to irritate him. Mr. Hogan had suddenly changed his approach. It caught me off guard for a second or two, but at that moment I decided, for once, to obey his orders.

"OK, I'm on my way," I chirped back sarcastically, picking up my books.

"Naw, you'd better stay here," he quickly responded, apparently concerned about what the principal might hear once Marianne Big Mouth arrived in the office.

"You said to go to the office," I reminded him. "So, I'm going, and I'm going to tell Mr. Sodorff what goes on in this class."

"Sit down," he ordered, pointing toward my desk and actually displaying mild hostility.

"Nope, I'm going," I said once more, knowing my classmates were loving it. "I *always* do what I'm told." I began walking out of the room. Mr. Hogan grabbed my wrist and implored me to sit down. Wisely and more for Mr. Hogan's sake than mine, I obliged. His discipline was pathetic; his teaching, even worse. Word of what was happening in all of his classes eventually had an impact on the powers-that-be who did him a favor by replacing him with a veteran, Mr. Anderson. We had already had Mr. Leonard Anderson for junior history, and we all held him in high regard. We also knew that our final quarter of American government would no longer be the entertaining cakewalk we had enjoyed with Mr. Hogan.

YOU ARE NOW WHAT YOU WERE THEN. Bad behavior with bad teachers continued through my college years at the University of Idaho. My sociology instructor's lack of skill rivaled Mr. Hogan. I occupied a seat in the upper row of the auditorium-style classroom. Every day we carried on conversations throughout the hour, marveling at his total lack of awareness. One day, we decided to try the ultimate test of his oblivious state of mind by bringing marshmallows and wooden stick matches to class. As he continued with his boring lecture and interjected irritating nervous giggles, we enjoyed a feast of roasted marshmallows with nary an admonishing word to us during our 15-minute cookout in the top row.

Memories like this instilled a sense of wariness in me when I became a teacher. For one thing, I knew that the ghosts of teachers like Mrs. Houghton had their fingers crossed in hopes that when I stepped into my own classroom as a teacher, I would face my share of students who behaved just like I had. I also knew that I fully deserved whatever punishment came my way. So, throughout my career, I lay in wait for the derelicts and rapscallions and usually found a way to remain one step ahead of them.

LESSON: Remaining oblivious to what's happening anywhere in the classroom is unproductive. Being nice isn't gonna turn out nice. Boring kids to death is gonna cause creativity of the kind that teachers do not appreciate.

My eagle/evil eye was always focused, and I was always ready to pounce at the first hint of indiscretion. Students learned quickly after enduring the Day One Rules that they had better behave in my classroom.

Unfortunately, that strict disciplinary approach and my alleged adulthood, however, failed to change my own behavior in situations where the shoe switched to the other foot. Put me in the role of student again, make me sit through a loser's lecture, and I immediately reverted to what I had been *then*.

Consequently, throughout the seemingly endless curriculum-day video presentation, my friend Marian and I passed snide notes to each other about the "dedicated souls" in our group. Each took care to avoid having our written observations of other class members' reactions to the presentation intercepted by the "real-life facilitator," who had labored long and hard to put that tape in the machine and find the play button.

Staring straight ahead at the screen as if we were totally enthralled, Marian and I once more demonstrated that we had both mastered the art of sophisticated subversive behavior at in-service days. We had become jaded from years of attending these gatherings where some highly paid unknown from some place we had never heard of waltzed into the room, pulled out the audio-visual gimmicks, and did his or her best to pump us up with enthusiasm for the exciting new approaches we would adopt for the next time we returned to our classroom and on each day afterward. Over the years, I swore that our school district brass looked long and hard to find these people as a means of torturing us. All too often, we had to endure real weirdos who were aware of the newest of educational trends and who had mastered the latest goofy buzzwords in educational jargon. These buzzwords, like everything else before the computer age, usually reached Bonner County School District *after* the fad had died everywhere else in the United States.

Another forgettable in-service day occurred one opening day for teachers when our district honchos brought in two men in swanky suits – one of whom proudly pointed out the gap between his two front teeth and assured us that people with such dental anomalies were truly special. That bothered me since I had thought my left-handed anomaly had been always made me special. Anyway, the two men methodically, dramatically and repetitively taught us about the "Bucket and Dipper" theory, suggesting that it is much better to *fill* people's buckets than to *dip* from them. From that point on, armed with our own symbolic, full buckets for the school year, we all tried, often but soon in vain, to refrain from dipping out of anybody else's. On another occasion, our two-day in-service instructor bored the group so badly that during the bathroom break, a teacher named John from the host school secretly flipped the breaker switch so the visiting instructor's overhead projector would not work. Then, the culprit told several of us to keep a close watch on the guy's expression when he tried to turn on the machine. We loved it, especially because the guy was helpless without his machine. We were dismissed early but remembered our manners long enough to avoid exploding into laughter until *after* we left the room. *You are now what you were then!*

Over the years, we teachers have turned into skeptics about these imported speakers from somewhere else whom the district pays and then prays will magically push our buttons, enlighten our minds, sweeten our attitudes and turn us into the world's most wonderful teachers. Sometimes, that happens. Sometimes, not. Occasionally, I dismissed my cynicism long enough to have a little empathy while considering what pressure such experiences must be for the presenters. I tried to imagine how *I* would react.

As I continued mowing my lawn that summer day, I was consumed with "You are now what you were then," and how badly I had acted toward the speakers on those many curriculum days. Then I thought *You're gonna be what that guy was, and you're gonna get what's coming to you.*

I shuddered.

I had been asked to present an in-service for the beginning of the school year at a district in Montana. Within just a week or two, I would be on the other side of the desk from other teachers. Maybe – just maybe

– there could be a few Mariannes in my audience who hated in-services and the presenters as much as I did. Then, I thought about another all too-true saying: What goes around comes around. The more I thought about that, the more I decided I had better get my act together and give these staff members something of such supreme value that no one would even think of flipping the breaker switch during the lavatory breaks. But then I thought, *Gee, I don't have to worry about that ... I don't use overhead projectors.*

Well, it's also important to know that anything is possible when attempting to communicate to other human beings – even without overhead projectors. Sadly, I overlooked that possibility before I did my presentation. Instead, I diligently prepared a lesson plan to beat all lesson plans. Dotting every "i" and crossing every "t," I compiled a small booklet of what I thought were original writing ideas. Considering the need for a creative approach, I concocted the analogy of the freeway system where the basic essay structure or story line should move smoothly like the divided highway while other minor ideas could be incorporated within this structure, much like cars entering the freeway from on-ramps. Corny, yes, but it made sense to me at the time.

The speaking day came. I felt both cocky and fortunate. Because of my invitation to do this presentation for another district, I would have to miss my own district's in-service day. I also felt sorry for the poor saps back home who would have to endure six hours of insurance pitches, contract-negotiating dilemmas and bonding exercises. Driving the 80 miles eastward, I arrived at the school just in time to scope things out and find where I would be giving my presentation, which was scheduled for right after lunch break. Since I needed no electronic aids, the administrators assigned me to the gym, which was filled with at least 300 chairs. I gulped. Soon, I learned that, like our district, the full group would listen to a keynote speaker and then head to numerous other venues around the school for their individual seminars.

The $3,000 keynote speaker, a dynamic spitfire from Texas, gave that Montana district its money's worth. She was also beautiful. Throughout her 90-minute presentation, she told compelling stories about her personal experiences with high school students and all the emotions they face while going through awkward periods in their life, dealing with family situations, facing outside temptations and even sometimes contemplating suicide. She captivated the entire audience so effectively that every eye and ear in the room remained transfixed throughout her presentation.

"What an act to follow!" I thought. However, I took comfort in the fact that I had usually kept my adult audiences pretty spellbound over the years. In fact, my experience with adults had always reinvigorated my love for teaching. I had spent one semester a few years before working with 10 adults ranging from their 20s to their 50s. Their hunger to learn what they had missed out on as teenagers was so intense that they devoured every word. During each session they treated me as if I were a goddess whose jewels of wisdom, no matter how insignificant, meant everything. Their appreciation and enthusiasm for all knowledge during those three-hour nightly classes spoiled me to the point of almost dreading the next day when I would face my less-than-motivated high school students. Thinking about those great evenings with my adult class helped ease my fears toward the upcoming afternoon session.

Surely, they'll love what I have to offer, I reasoned. Lunch hour passed. I took my time going to the gym since my materials were already in place, rationalizing that "a grand entrance will be good." After the last of half a dozen trips to the bathroom to calm my nerves, I headed toward the gym. Thirty seconds before the appointed time for the session to begin, I approached the podium. Scattered along the front row sat my class, all six people.

Hmm, guess I'm not exactly a headliner, I thought, then again rationalized, *but it will be fun to work with a small group. We can get to know each other. I can relax.* Soon after I assumed my position, three more teachers (two women and one man in their early 30s) casually waltzed in, taking the front seats directly in front of my podium.

"Welcome," I said, wasting no time introducing myself. The tardy souls immediately began eyeing each other and grinning. I avoided their faces, keeping my eyes focused on a couple of attentive older women teachers, and continued with my spiel.

"When your superintendent called last spring, he asked me to talk about creative writing," I began, hoping to appeal instantly to their innermost teaching feelings and to establish some pedagogic camaraderie. "I thought and thought and decided that if I were sitting in a session like this just before the beginning of a school year, my mind would surely be focused somewhere else: coming up with all the ways I was going to keep my kids excited this year."

The front trio continued to whisper and giggle out loud. I continued to ignore them and carried on with my characteristic storytelling.

"So, while mowing the lawn last week, I thought about writing projects during my 27 years of teaching where kids seemed to have the most fun," I explained. "From that day until last week, every time a great teaching moment resurfaced, I'd stop mowing, run to my computer, and document those activities just for you. I've added to the list a few ideas used by my sisters and another teacher who writes for a journalism publication." Two-thirds of my seminar students continued to listen attentively, while the three late amigos kept up their chatting in the front row. I began to seethe.

How dare them, I thought. *They're so rude*. Avoiding eye contact, I maintained outward composure and continued.

"And like any good teacher, I prepared handouts," I happily announced. "My hope, therefore, is that you will have something that will give your students something of value and fun for this school year." This generous gesture hardly influenced my troublemakers.

Their giggles and wiggles were starting to get under my skin. I wanted so much to look them straight in the eye and yell, "Would you just shut up!" Professionalism was essential at this moment, especially since I was a guest in this school district. Positive feedback on this presentation could mean other opportunities to escape Bonner County in-service days in the future. I had been able to deal fairly successfully with unruly students for 27 years, and today was no time to lose it in front of a group of my peers. I was just astounded that other professionals could act so badly toward one of their own. And I hadn't ever done anything to these three jerks. Hadn't ever seen them before. *Why* would they act that way?

Two revelations eventually explained everything – one embarrassingly visual, the other, a great big "duh" slowly unfolding within my own mind.

As I reached down to pick up a pile of handouts, my first clue for the bad behavior became openly apparent. Two buttons on my blouse had managed to escape from their buttonholes. My bra was showing.

"Uh-oh!" I blurted, dropping the pile and grabbing the blouse in hopes of quickly returning the buttons to where they belonged. "Excuse me! Guess such things go with the territory sometimes … blah, blah, blah … "

I don't even remember what blubbering stupidity came out of my mouth after that, but I do know that sweat came from every pore in my body, and venom spewed deep inside as the three smart alecks broke into simultaneous laughter. It was one of those moments where I knew they weren't laughing with me; they were fiendishly laughing *at* me.

All I could do was regain my composure and get through the rest of the presentation. Fortunately, the remaining dutifully attentive ladies in the small class saved my day. Focusing on their empathetic expressions and doing my best to ignore the rude trio, I distributed the handouts, said a few more words and asked for questions. When nobody seemed curious about anything I had to offer, I dismissed them, gathered up my stuff and fled from the building, never to return.

In the safety of my car while driving home, I had developed a new attitude about my escape from Bonner County's in-service day. How nice it would have been to spend the day in the company of my colleagues, complaining under my breath about the poor unfortunate souls the district hired to start our school year off with a bang. I also brooded about those awful teachers who ruined my presentation and once more, the video truth came resounding back loud and clear: *You Are Now What You Were Then.* Suddenly it dawned on me. Those three hideous souls in the front row were reincarnations of Mrs. Houghton, Mr. Hogan and the college sociology teacher.

I had gotten exactly what I deserved.

11.

Stupid Teacher Tricks

"Let's tape up our noses and go talk to Tom," I suggested as a trio of us sat in the faculty room one day during fourth-hour prep. The group had finished correcting papers and planning for our next day's lessons. We had some time to kill. My friend Pam, who taught home economics, and her enthusiastic student teacher, Jean Ann, thought my suggestion to sport a new look when dropping in on the principal sounded like a great idea. So, we rummaged around the room and found a Scotch tape dispenser. The assortment of newly created pig faces with squashed-back, exposed nasal passages cut quite a picture. A few giggles and off we headed to the office.

Once there, we stood outside the door while Tom finished a phone conversation.

"Let's go in backward so he'll have a real surprise," I suggested. We each turned so that we couldn't see each other, with our backs to his door, and waited to hear him hang up the phone. Then, bent over and restraining ourselves from bursting into laughter, we performed an unrehearsed reverse shuffle into his office. Once there, we sat down and faced him.

Tom wasn't too surprised, but I was. My two porcine comrades had gotten me good that day. When we had turned around outside the office, they secretly removed the tape from their noses. So, when we faced Tom, he eyed two somewhat normal-looking educators and one whose temporarily deformed countenance may have given him cause for concern.

We had taped up our noses on other occasions outside the school. The exercise had started at one of our social gatherings and was always a hit, especially with the help of a sip or two of wine. The nose-tapers were like-minded souls who had gradually bonded around the lunch table in Carol Pietsch's home economics classroom. One by one, Betsy, the French teacher; Dana and Pam, both home-ec majors; Marian, the Spanish and drama teacher; Cheryl, who taught math, and I had joined the SHS faculty. Maybe it was our similar ages. Maybe it was our quirky senses of humor, but we worked together for several years, somewhat like a sisterhood, always holding great respect for each other's talents. Our occasional gatherings outside of school usually seemed to gravitate toward some form of creative glee. At her beautiful country home, Betsy, her talented son, Hon, and daughter, Holly, had amassed a huge array of colorful costumes – including hats, dresses, skirts, you-name-it. At parties, the entry requirement was to sort through the garments, assemble an outfit, don the ensemble, assume the proper demeanor and then strut our stuff. Such performances usually highlighted our gatherings.

On another occasion, Pam, her friend Jim, and Marian arrived unannounced at our house one August day. I had no fresh treats to share with them, but I could not bear the thought of being inhospitable. Going to the freezer, I found a decorated tin of the past holiday season's Christmas cookies. I knew they were stale, but they were food. At least, I had *something* to offer. Apparently, Jim was hungry at the time. He gobbled a couple down, but Pam, who later graduated from San Francisco Culinary Institute, made a few critical comments. I think the term "sawdust" in reference to the well-aged treats may have been used in my midst a time or two that day. I hadn't been able to get rid of those cookies at Christmas, and knowing they might just sit in the freezer for another year, I seized a great opportunity.

"Jim, why don't you just take these cookies for the road," I suggested. "You can return the tin later. I'm in no hurry." Well, they did take their time. A year or two later, I received the round tin, wrapped as a present, still bearing the cookies, which by now set off a putrid odor if opened. Apparently, Jim hadn't been as hungry as I thought.

I can't remember the exact circumstance, but something told me that turnabout would certainly be fair and fun play. I kept the cookies in the tin. Two years later, Pam had moved to San Francisco. That year, my mother and I were headed to Mexico. Since we had a long layover in San Francisco, I invited Pam and Marian, who was visiting at the time, to come to the airport to see us. I also took the cookies with me and presented them to Pam.

As I write, the calendar has jumped ahead 20 years. The cookies have traveled back and forth to California. They even rode around in the trunk of my daughter Annie's car while she lived in Boise. The cookies now sit in my laundry room. Pam eventually met and married Alan. They have a very nice son, Kyle, who I believe is 11 years old at the time of this writing. When he graduates from high school, he shall receive a very special present from the Love house, along with a suggestion to wear a surgical mask – definitely not Scotch tape – while opening the gift.

Another time while our sisterhood all still taught together at SHS, some of the women met at my house one winter evening. My family had already gone to bed before Pam, Betsy and Marian arrived. One of the guests carried with her a large sack with a box inside. They had apparently done some intriguing homework before coming to the party, because they couldn't wait to open the box, which contained a homemade board game. In preparation for this evening visit, they had created the Sandpoint High Monopoly game. Its playing board featured a drawing of our high school, which, at the time, was laid out in the shape of a "U." Each square represented a classroom. Landing on a spot meant picking up a card from the pile of questions and answering correctly to proceed on. Though I cannot divulge the question content, it did involve salacious, never-to-be-forgotten but probably-never-to-be-discussed-publicly events in SHS history. I can guarantee readers that if anyone outside our intimate group of friends had laid eyes on any or all of the cards, four women teachers would surely have paid a large fine for libel or would have gone directly to jail. But then again, all were facts no matter how outrageous. We laughed hysterically, but, because we had to protect our futures, we ceremoniously deposited the box and all its contents into the raging flames of our woodstove.

Then, we talked some more, taped up our noses, and called it a night.

I actually thought nose-taping was such a catchy group activity that I had introduced it to my *Monticola* yearbook staff, who took it even a step further by going beyond the proboscis. Once, after completing a difficult deadline, staff members released their stress by spending half an hour artfully taping up the face and upper appendages of a willing student. Then, of course, like good yearbook staffers, they brought out their cameras and began clicking close-ups of the ghoulish-looking finished product. My colleague, Pam, occasionally joined in the fun whenever she came to visit my classroom during yearbook hour. We had even captured her on film and published her lovely, taped-up facial mug in the yearbook that year.

Until our visit to his office that day, I'm sure Tom Keough had never seen such a sight, so naturally he did take a moment to study my new look and to comment briefly. Fortunate for me that day, he reacted kindly and seemed outwardly unconcerned. After all, Tom too had a sense of humor. A sense of humor is essential in education, and over the years I have found that stupid teacher tricks, like taping up one's nose, could provide necessary comic relief at opportune moments – not only in situations with colleagues but also with students.

As my career continued, my need for occasional spontaneous diversions to classroom routines arose, and I perfected the nose-taping activity, adding Styrofoam glasses to the props. Successfully coordinating this full facial effect took some doing, especially when the element of surprise was so important. That meant having materials readily available in my desk drawer and making sure the students were focusing on anything but me during my preparation time. Once their attention was diverted, I bent over and pretended to be searching for something in my lower desk drawer. First, came the nose operation, which wasn't too hard if I could just get the tape to stick tightly to the top of my head. Never mind that glob of hair that would painfully come off with the tape once removed. Occasional oily nose skin also caused delays in the process. Next, I pulled out two small Styrofoam cups with the bottoms cut off. Precision was a must as I would quickly fit the bottom of each cup into my respective eye sockets, often dropping one on the floor while inserting the other. Once the ensemble was complete, I had to perform rapidly because Styrofoam cups do not like staying in eye sockets for extended periods of time.

So, slamming the desk drawer shut with a resounding crash usually interrupted at least a few students' concentration. Some would look my way, nudge their neighbors, and eventually the entire class would come alive with laughter as they watched their goofy teacher begin her lecture. I could always count on at least one cup falling to the floor if I so much as moved my body, but the initial impact left a permanent impression on many students.

In fact, two young women, Jillian and Stacy, liked the idea so well that they took along a supply of tape and cups for a spring break trip across the Washington desert to Seattle. Donning the props and peering out the window at cars alongside them on I-90 kept the two teens entertained for hours. Fortunately, their surprised observers kept their vehicles on the freeway after spotting the two alien-like creatures staring at them. My tape-and-cup routine was usually successful in each class once each year, and I usually waited until well into the session when my students knew me and my unpredictable ways well enough (*I think*) to feel assured that their teacher wasn't losing it.

Styrofoam cups are also readily available at teacher curriculum days along with the coffee and donuts. I do remember resorting to their creative use once during a session in our school cafeteria when the lecturer droned on so monotonously that half the teacher audience fell asleep or began to develop glazed stares.

Somebody needs to wake them from their stupors, I had reasoned after withstanding all the boredom I could stand. *Why not Marianne?* Once those white cups were firmly implanted in their sockets, friends at surrounding tables suddenly came alive and began enjoying the session or at least the sideshow of comic relief.

I spent my long career in an economically depressed North Idaho school district. If ever we forgot that we were poor, the administration always reminded us. Thus, we employed other stupid teacher tricks to survive the constant supply-shortage threats that found a spot on virtually every faculty-meeting agenda.

"Our paper supply is low," the resident principal would grimly announce. "Please limit your copies. We must conserve if we're going to make it until the end of the semester." This always seemed a bit strange to us, considering the massive number of memos churned out from the office and landing in our teachers' boxes. This hypocrisy also reminded me a bit of George Orwell's *Animal Farm* where the low-grade animals went without while the leaders enjoyed all the comforts.

After a few years of annual paper shortages, some colleagues, especially a guy named Bill, took measures into their own hands. Bill was known as one of the faculty wisecrackers. He also coached and taught biology down the hall from me. As I got to know Bill better and better over the years, he included me in his inner paper circle. During the late-August workdays, preceding the beginning of each school year, Bill somehow and very quietly "requisitioned" large supplies of copy paper, which he hid, along with the lab equipment and microscopes, in his storage cabinets. He squirreled away reams and reams of paper and then notified a small cadre of trusted rebels to "come on down and get paper any time you need it." So, whenever the faculty-meeting paper shortage threats began, we all eyed each other across the meeting room and just smiled.

Stupid teacher tricks often occurred during these interminable and repetitive staff meetings, when we knew that we would be listening to regurgitations of the same Big Three virtually every meeting:

1. You must curb your copy-machine usage – OR – get your copies two weeks in advance!
2. You need to send home progress reports at least every 24 hours for those students who suddenly flunk at the last minute and have parents who call the principal because they never had any idea their kid was thinking of flunking, let alone actually following through with it.
3. Let's find ways to make a newer, better, more efficient tardy policy.

To avoid screaming out loud, "Haven't we covered this three million times before?" we had to resort to some means of entertainment for the endless discussion where the same whiners would drone on about the same topics and report, in mind-boggling detail, all cases of the most recent individual violations of the policy in *their* classrooms as if *they're* the only teachers who ever had a kid walk in late.

So, during these gripe-and-groan marathons, some of us conjured up sneaky but creative ways to amuse ourselves. A fellow English teacher – *before he turned into an administrator* – brought a remote controlled-fart machine to one meeting in the library and set it under another English teacher's seat. He chose the most vocal, most demonstrative person on staff as his victim. As the principal attempted to make yet another serious point about the tardy policy, the machine sounded off beneath the lady's chair. Folks seated immediately around her quit looking at the principal and started eyeing her with accusing looks. Unperturbed at first, she reacted properly the second time around.

"All right, who did that?" she blurted, as the principal, oblivious to the sideshow, continued his spiel and those in the know attempted to look straight ahead. The small uproar died down, and the meeting went on. A few minutes later, the explosive sound clearly interrupted during a moment of dead air.

"OK, what's going on?" the victim barked as several snickers followed. The principal looked her way indignantly for interrupting his sacred words of wisdom, then continued down his agenda. She eventually found the device and passed it on down the table but never ever zeroed into the guilty party.

The guilty party could have won an Academy Award for his performance. This individual liked to perform in other sly ways during such gatherings, and he knew he had a willing audience with the easily distracted lady named Love. His favorite trick was to look me square in the face and extend his tongue as far up into his nose as possible, a feat seldom observed by anyone but me. Sometimes, it took a while for me to spot the contortions of his talented, wandering tongue, but once I spotted it, a spirited competition ensued. After all, as children in our North Boyer farmhouse, my family and I had practiced such tricks. My older brother often took the lead in demonstrating exactly how to move that tongue outside the mouth, then hold the base in place, stretch and curl up the tip in snake-like fashion, extending toward either nasal orifice. It was quite a disgusting sight, to say the least – even worse than taped-up noses. And to run across another talented tongue trickster within my profession, who relished such entertainment during boring staff meetings in my workplace, delighted me to no end. This sense of camaraderie with my colleague was as exciting as other occasions over my career when I would meet individuals who actually knew and enthusiastically spouted the universal response to the query, "Are you a turtle?" I refuse to divulge the secret answer. Readers will have to go on their own search mission to be initiated into the Turtle Club and learn the proper response for greeting a fellow Turtle.

Speaking of entertaining teachers' meetings, I did run across a novel idea for making agendas run more smoothly when "Simple Simon" ran our school district. We had experienced a revolving-door sequence of such superintendents. I must allude to this gentleman because on many occasions, during the brief time Simple Simon spent with us, we discovered him snoozing during group discussions. I figured it must have been a challenge for him to intelligently determine his policies on important school matters when he slumbered so much. Apparently, however, he did have an opinion or two, because he formulated a call to action when one of the SHS principals took offense at some cartoons aimed at him (the principal) in the *Cedar Post*, which I advised at the time. The principal then threatened my job.

Word spread within the school and the district almost instantly.

LESSON: If you want information widely distributed within the school and the community in a hurry, tell one person on staff or tell one student. Then, advise them not to tell a soul. This done, you can bet on the news spreading almost instantly. You can also expect it to become a bit skewed as it travels. We, on the *Cedar Post* staff, experimented with this very phenomenon one day and used our results in an editorial, cautioning readers to be a bit more discerning about spreading everything they hear on the street.

The word did, indeed, spread quickly around the school that I had received an intimidating memo from my principal one Friday afternoon in late January 1992. The memo appeared in my box just days after a school-wide assembly, designed to revive positive spirit among the student body and staff, had occurred.

The first semester that year, which had launched the opening of our new high school, had been disastrous for multiple reasons. It all began with a list of stringent, ridiculous rules issued and published in staff and student handbooks, written by the principal, when the school opened. Instead of starting off a new era in Sandpoint High School's history on an upbeat note, the main messages issued from his office focused on negative consequences for negative behavior. Most of us felt that we had entered a stalag rather than a new school. Numerous events, including frequent class schedule changes inflicted for no apparent reason, kept students and staff in constant upheaval. Adding to the confusion, the principal was rarely seen by teachers or students, for reasons still mysterious to most of us. Most students agreed that they would not have recognized him if they met him on the street.

After a few months, the atmosphere in our new building had deteriorated so much that student leaders, with help from some parents, launched a high-profile, well-organized protest to air their concerns. Instead of attending class, hundreds of students, many accompanied by their supportive teachers, gathered in the gym. Local media and Spokane television stations showed up to cover the event. With such publicity, Sandpoint community leaders became concerned about what was happening at the new school.

After the protest, with hopes of setting a new tone, a group of staff and students pinpointed the start of the new semester time as a perfect transition period to coordinate a sanctioned, school-wide unity assembly. We hoped an upbeat activity would help launch a fresh start and reverse the negative air about the school. With lots of help from staff members, parents and students, I organized the spirit assembly. After reviewing the final details point-by-point and speaker-by-speaker, the principal approved of our plan and even acted uncharacteristically excited about the possibilities that lay ahead. We invited community leaders to speak as well as the principal, and the ASB and class presidents. We also passed out copies of the school "Alma Mater" and the "Bulldog Fight Song," neither of which had been learned by many students for years.

When the much-anticipated assembly day came, everyone showed up – except the principal. No one had been notified in advance of his absence. I was astounded, as was the student body, when we all learned that he was once again a no-show. This *faux pas* served as the crowning blow since he had missed several other high-profile school events, and the kids had definitely noticed. When the announcement came that the assistant principal would speak in his place, the student body booed in disgust.

The following week a cartoon appeared in the school paper with the principal's photo. It included his name and read "MISSING from several important school assemblies and other events," sending a pointed message that students had not appreciated his absence. Apparently, *he* did not appreciate the cartoon because he retaliated within minutes of the paper's distribution by typing and delivering a nastily worded memo about "you and yours" to my staff mailbox. This stunned me because my cartoonists, Mark and Tim, had already dubbed him as "Air Sword" in prior cartoons in a not-so-subtle artistic assault on his style of administrating the staff and the student body of 1,200. Each week that the satiric artwork appeared in the paper, he had never uttered a word. I actually began to think that he must have an unusually open mind for a principal and felt a strange sense of admiration for him, in spite of his faults. I thought it was neat that he had so bravely weathered the cartoon criticism. Reading the memo, I learned why he had given so much latitude.

"I read my first *Cedar Post* ever today," the note began, "and I do not appreciate the cartoon." If we had been stunned by his behavior before, we were shell-shocked by this open admission, which explained so much while reinforcing the perception we already had – that he just hadn't cared enough, throughout an entire semester, to read the school paper!

The boys' cartoon had hit a raw nerve and had roused him from his administrative apathy. He went on the offensive. I was his target. The teachers' association reacted quickly to his threatening memo, and the snoozing superintendent, whose loyalties leaned with the principal, decided to take the lead in getting this ugly conflict between me and my immediate boss resolved. A meeting was scheduled at the Central Office, the same building that had once served as my elementary school. A lawyer from the Idaho Education Association flew up from Boise to act as my advocate during the meeting. I was told I could also bring a couple of staff members for support. The seating arrangement resulted in my location directly across the table from the principal. Everyone behaved with civility, greeting one another as if we were all friends, as we prepared to begin.

On this day, the wide-awake superintendent sat at one end of the table. As he opened the meeting, he pulled out a *fly swatter wrapped in aluminum foil.*

"We're going to use an old Indian technique," he announced, brandishing the silver swatter before us. Participants watched it wave back and forth as he spoke. "This works like the Indian peace pipe. In order to speak today, you must hold the silver fly swatter. When you are finished with what you have to say, pass the swatter to the next person and remain quiet."

Hmm, I thought to myself, avoiding eye contact with any of my colleagues at the table. *This must be big-time stuff if we have to use a prop like this to manage our way through this meeting.* Irreverently, I had already begun to minimize the seriousness of the situation. I pondered how many other meetings and other teachers in places unknown to me had exchanged the silver fly swatter to complete their weighty business on this strange man's watch.

We followed the rules and passed the swatter while airing a long list of concerns from both sides. Oddly enough, the approach to civil and productive discussion worked, because we left the meeting much calmer, shaking hands and promising to keep communication lines open. My job was intact. My students continued telling the truth with their cartoons. However, as the second semester wore on, the principal's good intentions to do better began to wane. He finally self-destructed just before graduation with his executive decision to allow seniors to camp out on the school lawn with no supervision.

LESSON: Give the go-ahead to a group of graduating seniors for an unsupervised activity, and plan for the worst.

This man must never have learned the second part of the lesson because the worst did happen. Within days of the incident, the man no longer worked for the school district. That quick action was hastened along by the sleeping superintendent's sudden resignation earlier in the spring. I'm pretty sure his replacement did not appreciate learning – by reading on the front page of the local newspaper – about the out-of-control school kegger busted by the city police on the Sandpoint High School grounds. One tantalizing detail in the article even reported that students had urinated on the side of the building – the brand-new school, no less. I doubt very seriously, that this new head man pulled out a silver fly swatter to discuss his concerns with the principal.

Most of the stupid teacher tricks I learned over the years and their consequences served me well. Although I generally followed a fairly regular, highly disciplined and predictable regimen in my classroom, occasional, sometimes-quirky spontaneity often served as a valuable tool. It kept kids off guard. It also kept me from stagnating. A constant belief – that if I was bored, my students would be bored even more – served as a guiding principle for me and inspired me always to search out a different approach to teaching the same ol' thing.

Sometimes my approaches were admittedly dumb, which, fortunate for me, I knew before using them. Take, for example, my set of posters designed with hamburger stickers to teach young writers about necessary essay ingredients. This visual tool admittedly reached "new frontiers in stupid," to coin a phrase from my colleague and our school's fine history teacher, George Marker. George was known for his colorful commentary on most subjects.

"This is really stupid," I would begin while showing the first poster, "but I think you'll understand." The poster showing the top sesame-seed bun with only a bottom bun and nothing in between illustrated to the students that successful writers couldn't just create a catchy introduction and a conclusion with no real meat in the middle. Another poster showed a burger, bottom bun and lots of condiments.

"Many people would have a tough time eating their burgers this way," I would explain, "and just as many writing masters would balk at a detailed essay with no introduction." Students had no problem agreeing with me that my poster illustrations were pretty corny, but they did get the point, while not being subjected to another dry lecture on essay construction. As long as I stayed ahead of the game with my off-the-wall tricks to induce my kids to learn, my crazy methods turned out pretty successful in the quest to teach something.

I do remember, however, initiating a couple of situations in the class-room, only to have them backfire on me.

LESSON: Know your students well. How literal is their thinking? Do they appreciate and understand satire? Do they like having attention drawn to themselves? Had they been having a bad day? These variables and many others unknown at the moment can adversely affect a teacher's most creative gimmick.

I learned the above lesson the hard way on two occasions when students broke into tears during my unpredictable approach to classroom management. For years while teaching the literary tool of dramatic irony, I had walked around the classroom, explaining the concept. While doing so, I would pick a student at random and carefully tape a small sign on the student's back. The sign read "Kick Me." Chuckles would ensue. The kid would eventually figure out; a few laughs later, the lesson of dramatic irony was clear to the class. In one case, though, my student "guinea pig" burst into tears with embarrassment. Talk about feeling rotten. I kept her after class, apologized profusely and called her parents. She normally had a great sense of humor, but this situation on this particular day had not a created a good mix for her emotions.

In another case, three young ladies sat at a front table by the window and gabbed every day. They were usually pretty good about restraining themselves while I was lecturing. One day, while in a light, playful mood, just as they started their yakkety-yak routine, I decided to have a little fun with them and direct them to the office to speak about their talkativeness with the principal. He and I had discussed this trio and their daily chatter prior to that class hour. We had even laughed about the possibility of setting them up by my sending them to the office for a talk with him. He promised to play the stern role of enforcer and then have some fun with them. Like me, he enjoyed a bit of harmless intimidation and figured this meeting with my talkative trio would provide a good opportunity to get to know them a little better.

So, on this day, I sent them on their way, figuring they would end up having some good laughs once the joke was exposed. What I didn't know was that the principal had been called away from his office. When the girls arrived, the assistant principal was in charge. A stern disciplinarian, this gentleman knew that if I *ever* sent a kid his way, it must be pretty serious. Feeling a need to support me, he went into action and sternly reprimanded them for "surely" driving Mrs. Love to the brink. Then, he sent them back to class. When they all walked through the door in tears, my heart sank. I felt like a total heel. It took me quite a while to explain myself out of that one, but they forgave me.

LESSON: If you're going to set someone up, make sure you've covered ALL the bases.

Overall, I don't know if I would have survived my teaching career had it not been for many, many stupid teacher tricks along the way. They enlivened my classroom, and they saved me from insanity through many bureaucratic dramas. My only advice is to be careful; they can sometimes come back to haunt you.

12.

Hair Hut: Marianne's Fountain of Youth

"**D**id you dye your hair?" the loud voice inquired from across the classroom. There was surely nothing subtle about this kid – or any of the other curious teens who yelled out such inquiries time and again, always the day after my Hair Hut visits. Hair Hut self-improvement experiences began for me in the '90s. Just like a teacher's need to keep current with new teaching trends, I also knew the importance of maintaining a reasonably youthful image while running my classroom. And, as the years passed by and time caught up with me, my hair was part of that image.

As a teacher of teenagers, I learned early in my career that staying hip with hair, clothes, mannerisms, music, etc. could be a definite asset. Kids keep close track of every nuance of a teacher's being. In fact, I doubt that too many other professions in the world receive the consistent, hypercritical scrutiny that teachers receive, especially in high school settings where being "cool" is essential. Teens maintain their own standards, and they appreciate teachers who maintain a *moderate* semblance of being cool.

LESSON: The trick for teachers, however, is to avoid going too far overboard in the hip department because kids can also sense and will reject any behavior that is not authentic.

I remember a great example of this truth. It occurred one day early in my career, on my return to school the day after a substitute had taken my classes.

"Who *was* that woman?" the kids asked me each hour. "She was weird." Throughout the day, I learned from reports that the rather large woman had waltzed into the room, leaned her mini-skirt-clad body against the desk and started the hour with "Well, are you all groovin' in this steam?"

The sophomores from rural Sandpoint had no clue what she was talking about. As she continued the hour with her hippy-dippy lingo, my uncool English students reasoned that they didn't want her to come back again.

Speaking of substitutes, over the years, I found that some make the fatal mistake of putting on an all-knowing, I'm-with-you persona when they enter a high school classroom. These are the same folks who usually disregard the lesson plan (which really irritates the teachers they're replacing) and get off on their own soapbox, providing worldly advice about how the young folks should live their lives. Nine times out of 10, the kids tune out and plan to tattle on them to the regular teacher the next day. And, nine times out of 10, this brand of substitute does not get asked back.

I was always amazed how astute and, at times, painfully honest teens can be while sharing their observations or perceptions of whoever happens to be standing in front of their classes. If only we teachers could channel that attention to detail toward adults' individual mannerisms, hairdos or clothing choices and inspire students to use those same tools in the day-to-day learning process. Even the most spaced-out kid can hit the nail on the head if you ask him to describe something about his teacher's appearance or personal habits. Of course, sometimes these descriptions can get a bit skewed, depending on how the teen feels about the teacher, but most are right on. The SHS faculty learned, from reading a *Cedar Post* newspaper article one year, that we teachers can hide nothing from adolescent eyes watching every move five hours a day.

The newspaper story focused on faculty idiosyncrasies. In one case, the coach who always studied the ceiling panels while talking one-on-one to a student got nailed. In another, the history teacher whose stage presence included a suggestion of obsessively applying lotion to his hands by constantly rubbing them together throughout his lectures immediately tipped off everyone in the school to his identity. The description of a husband-and-wife teaching combo, both of short, blocky stature, who showed up each day with their matching color-coded polyester ensembles left no doubt who had been pegged. Each day both spouses appeared in all brown, all navy blue, all cranberry red or all green. This was from head to toe – including socks and tenny runners. I guess they drew straws to decide what color to wear on Fridays. Even my journalism mentor, who advised the students that wrote the article, could not escape analysis. In his case, his fetish for rubbing his forehead while lecturing received attention.

As for me, any number of habits could have made the list, but the kids chose the fact that my head seemed much too heavy for my neck to support it whenever I was passionately dishing out information about direct objects, denouements or declarative sentences. The student reporters chose to expose me publicly for propping up my chin with one hand throughout all lecture times. Of course, I personally thought the habit of rocking back and forth in my chair, nearly falling over backward, topped the other bad habit. Or, even more eccentric, was my lifelong, totally subconscious predisposition toward chewing my tongue as if attacking a piece of tough round steak. This occurs any time I ever do anything with my hands, including peeling apples, taking pictures or writing. Certainly, the students must have noticed these neurotic habits, but for some reason, the reporters failed to include them in the newspaper story. I didn't mind. There's not much we can do about our personal peculiarities, and it is a bit disconcerting to be subject to such scrutiny year after year.

My worries about what others think drove me, throughout my years at Sandpoint High School, to keep moderately current with trends and to do everything possible to push back the perception of turning into an old hag. In the early '70s, when we no longer had to wear dresses, I (who have always loathed wearing dresses) was first in line to buy several polyester slacks-and-tops ensembles. One pair of pants even sported a purple herringbone pattern to match a dark purple vest.

This welcome liberation of professional women's clothing requirements meant that I would no longer have to worry about snide comments being whispered behind me in the classroom as I stretched my arm toward the top of the blackboard to write information for students' notes. Up to that point, I had remained fully aware that an ugly, fat, white bulge between my nylons and panty girdle always hung out for all to see whenever my dress hem elevated in concert with my hands as I reached toward the top of the board. I knew those kids noticed. So, the ability to wear slacks served as a welcome milestone in my teaching career.

When piercing one's ears became the "in" thing to do, I endured a session in my mobile home living room while my sister-in-law, Joyce, numbed both of my earlobes with ice cubes in readiness for her piercing kit. The tools included a potato cut in half, a bottle of rubbing alcohol, and a sharp darning needle. Holding the flat side of the potato behind the lobe, I could hear the gristle *crunch* inside as the needle pierced its core. From that day on, my earring ensemble ranged from ornate, dangly lunkers to simple, silver rings. After Joyce's surgery session, I never submitted my body to any more invasive decor, in spite of fantasizing the magnitude of the kids' subtle outburst should I ever walk into the classroom with a gold nose ring.

There was a time in the '70s when pigtails and corduroy bib overalls became the rage with the female set. I had hated having to wear denim bibs as a farm kid, but as a twentysomething, I rather liked them. The hair stayed in braids until son Willie came along and insisted on systematically scalping me with his ever-grabbing baby fingers. My earring size took a dive, too, after a couple of painful sessions with Willie grabbing hold and yanking until the bloody hoop separated from the ear.

As time went on, I remained pretty selective about jumping into fads that would show up inside my classroom – no purple or spiked hair, no platform shoes and definitely no black capes or heavy metal. Though I would not assume their tastes, I still found that most students who took on these far-out approaches to their outward appearance were pretty much the same within as their peers who dressed more conservatively. The rebels fascinated me, and I often felt driven to get to know them better as a means of enriching my own outlook on the world.

Toward the end of my career, we had moved into the new school across the parking lot from where I had taught for more than 20 years. I still don't know if they ever figured out how to regulate the central heating system or if it was just my age, but my daily ensembles assumed the layered look to withstand a cold, dank classroom one moment and a hot and stuffy one the next. We had no control over the temperature in our individual rooms. At that point in my life, comfort began to overrule image. My standard apparel from September to June included a turtleneck, a blouse, a sweater and a blazer, allowing me to discard or add items according to the thermostat. Shoes got wider and flatter, especially after the first day of school when my feet were reintroduced to the cruel, hard cement surface for six hours a day.

By the time we'd reached this new school, I was becoming acutely aware of the need for a new personal look of my own if I were to maintain some semblance of youth. This awareness intensified every time I looked into those fancy new school mirrors and noticed that my hair seemed to be turning grayer and grayer. A frank remark from a younger sister finally moved me into action.

My visits to one of Sandpoint's long-established beauty salons began one summer day shortly after I hit the half-century mark. The original Hair Hut no longer stands, but I continue to enjoy a quasi-illicit affair with the asphyxiating goop its beauticians conjured up for my specific needs. The information listing all my personal hair statistics appears on a 3 by 5 card filed away in a small, metal box lest Joyce Campbell, my regular hairdresser, decides to take full retirement. So, six times a year whenever I plop into her chair, she happily fills my hair care needs. The two-hour drill goes as follows:

In the space of a few short minutes, Joyce has wrapped a protective sheet over my clothing and tied a plastic bag to my head. Out comes the crochet needle. She digs through the plastic, hooks a swath of hair and pulls it through the hole. This fishing-for-hair procedure is repeated at regular stops along my scalp. Ten minutes later, I look like a monster who has just been plugged in to a high-powered socket. Back in those early days, I always wished they would pull the curtains so that God and all the

Laundromat patrons from next door wouldn't have to watch it all. The old Hair Hut's huge panel of picture windows facing the old Harold's Super Foods parking lot offered a great opportunity for anybody to walk by and get jolted from the scary scene inside. Traffic, however, was usually limited to the resident squirrels that didn't really care what we looked like as long as they got their daily peanut handouts from Joyce.

At her new location, Joyce no longer feeds the squirrels, but her procedure hasn't changed. Once she gets me looking really weird, she mixes up the magic potion and applies it to the exposed swaths. As she rubs it down around my scalp, I work really hard in my chair to avoid asphyxiation. Generally, this segment of the process brings all story-telling, gossiping, or complaining about all the new developments going on in Sandpoint to a lull, mainly because I have difficulty telling stories and breathing those overpowering fumes at the same time. She brings me a cup of fresh coffee and spends the next few minutes reading the "News of Record" and "Letters to the Editor" in the *Bonner County Daily Bee*.

Once the allotted time for the dye to highlight my top mop with a little fake color is up, Joyce removes the plastic scarf. Soon, I'm lying almost flat on my back, with eyes squeezed shut, as Joyce's deft, experienced fingers run through my hair and gently massage my skull with shampoo. Next, come the comb and sharp scissors.

"You've been cutting your own hair again, haven't you?" she comments while trying to even up the botch job I've done during desperate moments of cutting those bangs and whacking off the out-of-control, fast-growing side hairs. The hair-repair job complete, a blow dry transforms my hideous hair into presentability. I marvel at how good I look, give Joyce a hug and a check, and head on my way with an renewed air of confidence, eager to run into friends while my hairdo still looks nice. While I was still teaching, the only downside to this two-hour process would come soon enough the next day when the kids would notice and blurt out their comments.

I never really envisioned a day when I would stoop to coloring my hair to satisfy the hypercritical youthful masses, but sibling pressure, especially from the younger set, can have an uncanny impact on one's life plans. The impetus for My Hair Hut sessions occurred one August day a few years ago when three of my siblings and I were stacking a load of hay on a pickup truck at the folks' upper farm. Brother Kevin was flinging ropes over the bales to tie them down for a trip to his home in Missoula as our younger sister Barbara assisted him. While they figured out the best way to secure the load, Laurie, the younger of our younger sisters, and I chatted. She was in the midst of a comment when my eyes suddenly focused on a few prominent white hairs emerging from her darker strands, in her customary ponytail behind.

"Hey, what are these?" I asked, pointing out a single strand and smirking meanly. Spotting white hairs on a sister 14 years my junior gave me a certain sense of comfort. *Ah*, I thought to myself, *she's finally reaching that stage in life where the body begins to display subtle visual hints of the upcoming golden years.*

"I'm going to have to get it done before I head off to Nationals," she quickly admitted. "I usually let it go in the summertime."

Then she added a killer blow, sending my mind spinning.

"Barbara does hers too," Laurie announced.

Barbara's hair has always been striking. When she was a newborn, the almost three inches of gorgeous, dark-brown locks that complemented her huge charcoal gray eyes and olive skin fooled most admiring onlookers into thinking she certainly must be six months old. Since her birth in 1959, scissors have seldom touched Barbara's hair, which, if not hanging in a single French braid, flows freely to her waist. Never had I spotted so much as one white hair on her thirtysomething head. Now the truth was revealed that summer morning as we stood in the hillside barnyard. Laurie's hairy revelation was almost too much to bear.

Somehow the realization that *both* little sisters were doctoring their hair *before* gray follicles had started popping out all over stunned me, for these sisters – also well-established teachers – had been much smarter than I when they had secretly departed from our usual, all-natural, rural-girl policy of not fooling around with Mother Nature.

Somehow, I had always assumed that there was an unspoken, unwritten rule among us three that we would always follow the natural look in life. We lived in a land that Lady Clairol and Max Factor dared not invade. Mascara, eye shadow, rouge and Cover Girl separated us from the city girls. None of us used much makeup. My sisters didn't even wear lipstick, a habit I had started in the seventh grade. In my generation, wearing lipstick upon entering junior high and later puffing on a cigarette upon moving into a college dorm signaled a step into the next level of maturity. Madison Avenue had changed its standards by the time my sisters came along. In their era, it was no longer was cool to smoke, and clear lip gloss had taken the place of wine red, pale salmon or lurid orange.

"Marianne, it's time," my younger sister replied when I asked if she thought I ought to do something about my mop of gray hair before school started in the fall. This was the same sister who had delighted in listening to an older gentleman (who was certainly suffering from glaucoma, macular degeneration and all other forms of vision impairment) to ask me at a regional Arabian show if that was my granddaughter out there riding my horse in the warm-up ring. Laurie watched my indignant reaction as I glared at him and instantly barked back, "Not hardly. That's my sister Barbara."

The man showed no remorse for his undiplomatic mistake. I made an instant decision that I did not like this man. Laurie's gleeful reaction, however, was decidedly noticeable. When Barbara heard about the comment, she too laughed heartily. Both uncharitable sisters tucked away the episode as a legendary moment to be repeated at apt times in the future.

True, these were sisters who had come along more than a dozen years behind me. I had taught each of them for three years in English and yearbook classes while they attended high school. But there wasn't *that* much difference in our ages. I really didn't think I looked *that* old. But Laurie's firm suggestion of "It's time" created a new sense of urgency. I couldn't move quite fast enough to do something about my deteriorating youth.

Within minutes of Laurie's painfully honest comment, I stood inside the Hair Hut Beauty Salon. Virtually all activity stopped as I flung open the door and abruptly interrupted both the small talk and cutting and curling at two hair-styling stations on the far side of the room. Four sets of eyes shot my direction as I took the stage, wasting no time asking for professional comment.

"Should I dye my hair? My sister says it's time!" I asked.

"I think your hair is really pretty," a customer with thick glasses and a headful of pink curlers commented.

My self-esteem enjoyed a short-lived perk.

"Well, we could do some highlights," a young hairdresser suggested. "We wouldn't want to do anything really drastic." The staff arranged an appointment for a few days later and put me on a "plan," recording my follicle formula into their files. Walking out of the Hair Hut after that first appointment, I felt like a new woman. I knew that the hairdresser had in 90 minutes erased 10 years from my appearance. I looked forward to going to school to greet my teenage students that fall, with a new spring to my step and a confidence that this year I would no longer have to face the death-warmed-over-blah appearance of a summer suntan fading, leaving my bland, white skin to blend into my nearly white hair. No longer would anyone have the nerve to ask if I was my sisters' grandmother. Dreading the image of old and haggard, I've returned to the styling chair several times since that summer day when my virgin hair lost its innocence.

Now I'm used to the routine. During the two months between sessions, the color slowly fades from dark brown (matching my eyes and eyebrows) to a rather lovely amber tone. The Hair Hut has for me what genes could never do – from age 50 on, I've often been called a blonde and have actually found it rather flattering. The only problem, however, that I've encountered since my decision to alter my image occurred with regularity after each highlighting session. I could count on at least one student each hour coming into class, plopping down in his or her desk, visiting with a friend and then looking toward the front as I took roll and blurting out the obnoxious inquiry about what I had done with my hair. Eventually I took care of that. As the teaching career was drawing to a close, I finally resorted to President George W. Bush's fetish for making the preemptive strike.

"OK, for all who're wondering – yes, I had a hair appointment yesterday," I would announce. "So, get used to it. I *am* a human being, and I even do some of the same stuff your mother does." Once more, I would feel satisfied that I had beat them to the punch and had shut 'em up until the next time they scrutinized my appearance, when I showed up to class with a new pair of shoes or a different set of earrings.

Down to the final wire in 2002, I still clung steadfastly to that need to enhance what youthful attributes I still retained within my frame. In addition to the regular visits to Joyce's styling station, my clandestine stops for self-improvement also included the dentist's office where old friend Jim Miller once rewarded me with a complimentary teeth-whitener kit and to the Sandpoint West Athletic Club – never to exercise – but to lie down in the tanning bed.

13.

A Debt Owed

One night, about 20 years into my career, I was standing near the entryway to the high school gym, watching a basketball game and visiting with whoever walked past. A mother, who had always been very supportive while her two daughters were in school, came up to me and gave me a compliment.

"Marianne," she said, "I just want you to know how much we appreciate what you give up of your own family for the benefit of all our kids." For some reason, what was meant as a generous show of appreciation hit me like a bolt of lightning. However, I thanked her. We visited for a few minutes, and she went on her way. For the rest of the evening, I dwelled on her kind words that had made me want to sit down and cry. She was absolutely right. I did give up a lot with my own two kids for the benefit of hundreds of others. Somehow I felt numb. Time and again after that evening her words resonated, especially whenever I found myself spending weekends working away at piles of papers to be graded or devoting hours to organizing newer, better lesson plans. While advising the student newspaper in the early 1990s at the time when my two kids were about to enter high school, I found those many Saturdays, spent mostly at school, almost excruciating.

In fact, my first book sprang from my strong desire to find a way to spend more time with my family. I reasoned that if it sold well, I could cut back from my teaching load and spend more time being a decent mother and wife. Although the book sold well, it hardly provided the desired outcome. Instead of cutting back, I found myself busier than ever with the additional time spent preparing for speeches, readings and signings to promote the book.

When Willie and Annie entered the high school, I finally found a way to compensate. They could take my classes or participate in the fun activities that came along with my advising the newspaper staff. We spent some good times together on trips to national journalism conventions. Because of their exposure to the world of communication, both became involved in media-related activities after they left home, went off to college and started careers.

Still, as I look back over those years with my own children that sped by so fast, I feel a certain amount of regret for what I missed and what I failed to do and to share with Willie and Annie. I think I was able to attend only one or two parent conferences during the 14 years that they were students in our district. After all, parent conferences for teachers in all schools are generally scheduled at the same time. So, while I was involved in my marathon conferences as a high school teacher, Bill was shouldering the load of visiting with our kids' teachers. I always felt a void and a fair share of guilt for missing the conferences and for short-changing my duty as a parent – reading with my kids, helping with their homework when needed, keeping up a good line of communication with their teachers.

There was seldom a day except for Friday afternoons when I didn't come home drained. In fact, the time between Friday at 3:30 and Saturday evening was often the only opportunity I had to do anything that offered a brief escape from the steady grind of schoolwork. During the seven years I advised the school paper, even that weekend time became a memory. Consequently, my own kids seldom saw the outgoing, fun-loving, caring, devoted side of me. In fact, they had to be enrolled in my classes to witness that their mother wasn't always that worn-out, impatient, quick-to-explode grouch who was always getting ready for the next day or next week at school. Often when I wasn't working at home, I was stewing over how to fix problems that had occurred at school. I never learned how to separate my home life from my school life.

My constant, stress-directed behavior was especially hard on Annie, who, unlike her laid-back, outgoing older brother, demanded and deserved a lot more of my time than I had the energy to give. Annie was noisy, precocious, engaging, always active and especially creative. Much of her childhood activity required acknowledgement or involvement from me. Although I appreciated her needs and wanted to participate more in the life of my daughter, I felt obligated to take care of the needs at school first.

As I look back and lament my shortcomings as a parent who worked too hard as a schoolteacher, I'm lucky my kids were resilient. I'm thankful that most of the time while growing up, they understood and supported Mom's responsibilities. I'm also lucky for a husband who took up some of the gap, but more than anything, I'm especially fortunate and appreciative that a few teaching saints stepped in along the way to fill some of my parenting gaps, especially with Annie.

My sisters, Barbara and Laurie, both teachers themselves, have earned the lion's share of credit for enriching Willie's and Annie's lives. As their aunts, my younger sisters took extra time to guide them through the crucial growing-up years. During the year that our school district operated on a split-shift schedule (which quickly led to the passage of an unprecedented building levy), my teaching day ran from 6 a.m. to 12:30 p.m. Meanwhile, my sister Laurie taught at Farmin School the same time-frame as Annie and Willie attended their classes. Every day, Laurie took time to comb Annie's hair and make sure she was presentable for school. After all, I seldom saw my kids more than an hour or so each evening before crashing into bed to get up in the middle of the night for the next school day. Laurie definitely served as both savior and surrogate parent that year.

My sisters' devoted interest in and knowledge of horsemanship provided Willie and Annie with discipline, fun, a chance to compete and opportunities for recognition. The kids spent many hours on weekends and during the summers helping my sisters clean their stable, grooming horses and honing their skills for horse show competition. The rewards for their hard work often came with trips to horse shows around the region or to state and national horse judging competitions.

Barbara and Laurie also took a special interest in their Sandpoint niece and nephew in school settings. Even though Laurie still laments that Willie was not scheduled in her sixth-grade class at Farmin Elementary, she always kept track of him at school and took great pride in being his aunt.

Annie did spend a year as Laurie's student and later, most of her high school years with Barbara as a member of the yearbook staff. Barbara taught my daughter the fine points of photography, a skill in which Annie continues to excel. Annie also learned graphic design and organizational skills while working on the yearbook staff. More importantly, she gained tremendous people and leadership skills as yearbook editor her senior year.

My sisters were always there for my kids, not only as mentors but also as friends. That relationship has continued through Willie's and Annie's adulthoods.

When I think of others who've played important roles in their lives, I cannot forget how a group of teachers and their quick thinking saved a horrific day from turning worse when Annie, then an 18-month-old toddler, burned herself with sulfuric acid. Several SHS teachers and their children had gathered at our colleague Betsy's home in the country. About a month's worth of the summer vacation had elapsed, and many of us had gone on road trips soon after school had ended. We were getting together that morning to share our trip stories. While the half dozen or so adults visited, the kids went to a bedroom and began to play.

As story swapping intensified, so did the noise level. Along with each anecdote came more healthy laughs. Suddenly Betsy jumped up from her seat at the table.

"What's wrong with her?" she yelled. We all looked toward the bedroom, where Annie, wearing cut-off bib overalls, stood in the doorway, holding her hands tightly near her face. Tears were streaming down her cheeks. Her eyes were closed. Her mouth was open wide as if she was crying, but no sound was coming out. Betsy ran toward her.

"Catch her before she passes out," I yelled. "She does that quite often." We never knew why, but as a toddler Annie sometimes cried so hard that she would eventually hold her breath and pass out. I was certain that was exactly what was happening at that very moment.

As Betsy grabbed her, a collective horror took over.

"Acid!" she screamed. "She's gotten into the acid."

Always adventuresome, Annie had gone exploring into the bedroom closet and found a chemistry set. Always curious, she had opened it and found a vial of acid, which she also opened.

At that very instant, every adult in the room thought the worst: Annie must had swallowed the acid. Everything happened so fast, and I was so distraught at the thought of what was happening to Annie that the events remain a blur to me. I do remember, however, that my friends Pam and Dana took a calm leadership role. While someone called the poison hotline, Annie was whisked to the bath tub and doused in cold water.

Her skin began turning white in spots on her arm and her thigh. As the anxious moments passed, we determined that, thankfully, she had not swallowed the acid, but she was suffering excruciating pain. While some of us wailed at the horror of the situation, others continued to remain calm. Pam and Dana wrapped Annie in a cold, wet towel. We then jumped in a car and raced – as cautiously as possible – to the local hospital emergency room more than 10 miles away.

Dana's and Pam's quick thinking saved Annie from enduring major injury to her muscles and bone. The emergency room doctor told me that acid eats its way from the skin surface into deeper layers of skin, muscle and bone. I learned that the immediate dousing in cold water had stopped its action on Annie's body.

With chemical burns, at that time, the treatment was simple but agonizing. For the next six weeks of summer, Annie wore long-sleeved shirts and long pants to protect the undressed wounds from infection. Twice daily for several weeks I marched her to the bathtub and carefully peeled off her shirt. Despite my care, its sleeves always stuck to the wounds. Then, I scrubbed the wounds with Ivory soap. Each trip to the tub became more agonizing for Annie as she faced the pain of new scabs ripping away from her skin every time the shirt came off.

She's very fortunate today that both burns healed and had occurred in areas on her body that are generally covered up. Her skin has a different texture and coloration where it was burned. Telltale drip marks from that acid remain on the lower part of her arm. I hate to think of how much more severe this horrifying event could have been for Annie had my teaching friends not reacted so quickly that day.

As my daughter grew older, several other individuals enriched her life by helping her discover inner talents. I owe thanks to my teaching colleagues Ron Hunt and Mike Keough, whose love and knowledge of golf opened a new athletic door for Annie when she entered high school. Until reading this page, Annie has never known that a passing suggestion made all the difference in her high school years.

One day she had accompanied her father on a golf outing to the local Elks course. She knew very little about the sport but batted a few balls around the course. Meanwhile, my friend and colleague Ron Hunt, a longtime golfer, watched her swing and later told me that she showed great potential and that she had a natural gift. I told him we had already noticed that talent earlier and had suggested that she take some lessons. We, however, were her parents, so she had been unimpressed with our suggestion.

Leave it to Ron Hunt. With my encouragement, Ron took her aside one day and told her she ought to try out for the golf team. Annie was impressed. She turned out the spring of her freshman year for Coach Mike Keough's SHS linksters. With Mike's encouragement and guidance, she remained on the team for four years, earning her way to the state tournament twice. Once again, Ron Hunt, a teaching friend of mine, took a moment to encourage a shy young lady, adding a valuable new dimension to her life, while Mike Keough helped her enjoy a few golfing triumphs.

Other adults served as mentors or wonderful role models during Annie's childhood. My friend Raye Wilund had a son Josh whose creative sense of adventure matched Annie's. Raye spent many hours encouraging the two youngsters in their early years as they collaborated on dramatic and artistic creations while at the Wilund home. Annie's early elementary teachers, Jeanette, Ina and Lynne, also recognized and encouraged her creative curiosity during her grade school years. Their own stories of adventure planted seeds that would reap a great harvest years later when Annie set off on by herself for a six-month stay as a college exchange student in New Zealand. When Annie was in middle school, my high school teaching colleague Judy volunteered her extra time and lots of Band-Aids on Saturdays to teach our daughter how to work with stained glass and to guide her through several impressive projects, including a beautiful window depicting my sisters' Tibbs Arabians farm logo. During Annie's high school years, Nancy, owner of Meyer's Sport Tees, provided Annie with after-school employment and a special friendship that continues.

Annie is now a successful college graduate and highly respected in the work place, and I share my pride at her accomplishments with my daughter's village of teachers. These wonderful people enriched her life in areas where I fell short while spending my time working with other people's children. Annie's many mentors influenced her at key times in her young life, exposing her to infinite possibilities that have molded her both personally and professionally. I'm sure that my daughter appreciates each and every one of them as much as I do.

14.

Semester from Hell: A Learning Experience

I left Sandpoint High School in the spring of 1997, vowing never to return to a school classroom again. I had spent my entire 28-year teaching career teaching at my high school alma mater in the quiet, rural community where I was born. By 1997, Sandpoint was attracting a new breed of transplants, many of which were professionals from around the country. Our area had begun to get some positive, national notice after several years of negative publicity focusing on our so-called white supremacist influences, including the Randy Weaver standoff at Ruby Ridge and Los Angeles Police Department Detective Mark Fuhrman's (of O.J. Simpson trial notoriety) much-publicized move to Sandpoint. In reality, the White Supremacist population was minimal at best. They just managed to attract big headlines.

Over the next few years, the area's image began to change, thanks to Coldwater Creek, a fast-growing clothing and accessories catalog company that markets its goods to urban professionals around the nation. We also benefited from several favorable articles in national magazines, such as the *Reader's Digest* with a story by television personality Ben Stein, who spent much of his leisure time in Sandpoint. In addition, conveniences associated with the ever-improving home computer and the fast-growing Internet provided job flexibility to professionals who wished to escape the city woes and relocate to rural areas. Because of these and an increased local and regional effort to market the area, Sandpoint's appeal to the outside world was changing. Sandpoint's students were also changing with a wider array of influences affecting our young people. National trends, both positive and negative, that had previously remained far removed from us were beginning to seep in, bringing new challenges in our schools.

A number of negative incidents, along with an overall distaste for the disagreeable attitudes I was seeing and experiencing every day in the hallways and sometimes even in my own classroom, drove my decision to leave teaching. After enduring my share of increasing negativity and foul mouths, what's-it-to-you? nastiness and even you-owe-it-to-me expectations from several students, I gradually reasoned that any working situation had to be better than what I was experiencing during the eight hours or so that I spent at school.

Often those eight hours were extended to nearly 24 because I had never developed a technique for leaving what happened at school at the door. It all came home, and the daily problems tormented me, especially at night. Often, I would arrive at school early in the morning after managing just two or three hours of sleep. Most of my slumber period from the previous night had been spent fighting off the interminable and increasingly horrid replay of bad moments that happened during the school day. Sometimes these incidents were brief interludes, lasting just a second or two. Most didn't even seem that bad at the time they occurred, but in the midst of tossing and turning after awaking at 2 or 3 a.m., minor comments I had made in the classroom or split-second decisions affecting students often haunted me, gradually escalating over the sleepless hours into what seemed like full-fledged criminal acts on my part.

As a lifelong Roman Catholic, I've been well-acquainted with guilt since a young age. I've also discovered that guilt, like wine, grows better with age, especially in the middle of the night. For most people, such incidents would hardly merit much reason for feeling bad. For me, they were paramount. Simply put, the overall atmosphere at our school at the same time when breaking national news focused on kids bringing guns to school and blowing away their classmates contributed to this personal torment and to my eventual questioning of why I would ever want to stay in teaching.

"The inmates are running the prison" had become a favorite cliché in most faculty-room discussions as my colleagues and I agonized over situations in which brazen teenage boys and girls would spit out "F— you, b——!" with seemingly much more ease than they could ever muster up for a pleasant "Good Morning." I had gotten to the point where I knew that my own increasingly negative attitude toward such behavior was not a good thing if I were to continue teaching. I also had completed my second book *Postcards from Potato(e) Land*. My daughter, Annie, was graduating that spring, signaling an empty nest in the fall when she would go off to college.

What better time to make the break! I reasoned as we returned from a spring vacation trip to Texas to begin the fourth quarter. Previously, during April or May, I would begin to focus beyond the present and look onward toward the next school year, thinking about new and different approaches to my teaching or the excitement of taking on a new school activity to advise. Not this year. I could only envision myself somewhere else, doing anything but teaching another year. Twenty-eight years at Sandpoint High School was enough for this burned-out, bitter educator. It was time to move on and to follow my long-held dream of freelance writing.

One May morning, with resignation letter in hand, I walked into to my principal A.C. Woolnough's office, closed the door, sat down and carefully built up to announcing my decision to resign. Although empathetic about my reasons, A.C. urged me to think it over and reconsider my decision.

"I've made my decision," I announced. "It stands firm. I'm ready to do something else, and I don't think I belong in the classroom anymore." Tears began to roll down my face.

He listened and sat silent for a moment.

"Do one thing for me," he then suggested. "Apply for a year's leave of absence. You lose nothing, and if you should change your mind, you can have your job back."

"Nope," I said, "once I leave something, I want to move on." This had been true throughout my career. I never liked to look back.

"It won't take you long to write a letter to the board," he persisted. "Just write it and forget about it. But, at least, you haven't given up your chance to come back."

Only to satisfy him for the moment, I agreed to think about his suggestion and left his office. For the next few weeks, A.C. prodded me about the leave of absence, as did several other colleagues. Finally, I decided there really was nothing to lose other than the time spent writing the letter. The School Board approved my application. The school year ended. I cleared out my desk and hauled books, mementos and posters home for storage.

I had little time to think about this change because of a new book to promote and a busy lineup of freelancing assignments to complete. Northern Lights, a local power cooperative, had contacted me to design and write pages for its monthly magazine, *Ruralite*. New opportunities had also come from the *Appaloosa Journal*, a worldwide horse magazine, and *The Pacific Northwest Inlander*, a Spokane arts and culture newspaper. I also reconnected with the *Idaho Catholic Register* and the *Spokesman-Review* newspaper, for which I had written off and on over the years.

I learned quickly that life outside of Sandpoint High School meant no more summer vacations and no free weekends but more than enough pressure from multiple deadlines, which often landed at the same time. I also learned some lessons about freelancing. It provides no guarantees. Also, the hours when family members are home for dinner and relaxation often coincide with the times when story sources are also home and available for interviews. This fact was especially tough since the phone and computer in our house were located just a few feet away from the family television set. It was never pleasant asking my husband or kids to turn down the volume while I conducted my evening telephone interviews. I also learned quickly that freelancers must be assertive in regard to payment. What seems unimportant or small change to the client can be monumental to the freelancer; i.e., a $50 fee for a story might pay a regular monthly bill. Clients are not always prompt about paying freelancers. Sometimes, the writer even has to remind the client about payment and sometimes more than once. What was especially tough was knowing that the quality or number of hours devoted to a story rarely guaranteed a bonus check. If I submitted a prize-winning $50 story, it was still a $50 story, especially in our area where most wages have never been especially high.

All this aside, writing is my passion, and I rather liked the idea of now calling myself a "freelancer." So, the summer of '97 went by quickly. I did take some days off to accompany Annie and her belongings to college at Boise State. Bill and I quickly adjusted to our empty nest. I moved on with my writing projects and basked in the enjoyment of getting up any time I wished and strolling out the door to the barnyard fence to talk to the horses or to the garden to pull a few weeds. After a nice break, I would be back at work again. September came. Sitting at the computer and watching those yellow school buses go past the house in the morning, I felt little regret about my decision. Friends had assured me that when school started up in the fall, I would be missing it. Not so. The conditions under which I chose to leave my career still lingered in my psyche. Relief superseded regret.

Book sales and continued assignments led to relative financial success over the next few months. I paid all my bills, including the mortgage. I was especially proud to be able to give Annie a substantial amount of money for her first semester at BSU. My only concern about my new career path centered on the winter months of January, February and March. These months, by the best of standards, are uncertain times in North Idaho where the tourist-based economy can be affected dramatically by the weather patterns that determine Schweitzer Mountain Resort's success and create a ripple effect throughout the area. One cannot count on these months for financial security.

Thus, on December 31, 1997, two days after attending a birthday party for a colleague at which I emphatically declared once more to my teacher friends, "You'll never see me set foot inside of Sandpoint High School again," I learned the true meaning of "never say never."

Just after noon on the last day of 1997, I received a call from A.C. Woolnough.

"Marianne, how would you like to come back to Sandpoint High

School and teach English?" he asked.

"What's the deal?" I inquired, feigning ignorance but really knowing exactly what the deal was. I had heard that a husband-and-wife teaching team had turned in their resignations just before Christmas. Their decision had come from total disgust with a system that seemed to be rewarding kids for bad behavior while undermining the efforts of teachers. Both had entered the profession late in life with a committed desire to make a difference. They had been at it for about three years but had jointly decided enough was enough. Besides, they didn't need the money. Both were well-equipped financially to follow whatever path they desired. They had come to the conclusion that their teaching journey had not exactly followed the vision that had inspired them to earn their education certificates. Knowing what I know now, I would say they were victims of the times, but who could have known then? It's unfortunate they left the profession.

"We have a couple of positions to fill," A.C. explained. "You would be teaching sophomore and junior English in the portables. If you're interested, you can start in late January when the semester ends."

I could hardly contain myself. No deadlines. Several months of guaranteed salary during the uncertain winter months ahead. And, I was actually being asked to come back. A.C.'s request provided both a compliment and a timely opportunity. I was genuinely flattered that someone would want me back.

I had not tired of freelancing for a living, but I had learned its pitfalls over the past few months. By this time, I had learned that there is something *very* appealing about a guaranteed paycheck at the end of the current month and the certainty that it will even happen again the next month. Besides, this assignment would tide me through the winter, and if I didn't like it, I could quit. Somehow, though, the different schedule with no honors classes, no publication deadlines, and no clubs to advise sounded like a nice change from the pressure I had endured in the eye of the hurricane for so many years. My assignment would be what many educators refer to as "trench teaching," offering no more perks or prestige other than the occasional one-on-one small victories with individual students or classes. Best of all, I was in the driver's seat because I had not gone begging for my job back. It had come to me.

Not wanting to appear *too* eager, I told A.C. I would have to think about it and would get back to him. Lucky for me, he couldn't sense, through the telephone line, that my adrenaline was pumping. He said he would need an answer within the next couple of days. When we hung up, I went to the laundry room where Bill was working on a project.

"That was A.C. He wants me to come back and teach English," I said. "I think I'll do it." Bill seemed pleased. After waiting for what would have been an appropriate length of time to stew over this tough decision, I called A.C. and assured him he could expect me on the morning of January 28, 1998. This schedule was great because it allowed me time to wrap up the loose ends of some freelancing projects. I planned to continue writing features for the *Appaloosa Journal* but decided to notify the other editors about my decision.

I approached this return to teaching with great optimism. After all, I had only been gone a semester. Students have short attention spans, but certainly they hadn't forgotten Mrs. Love, the award-winning newspaper adviser. I had earned a fine reputation at Sandpoint High School over the years and felt confident that it would precede me and ensure an easy pathway into this renewal of my teaching vows. My visit to the portable classroom during the last Friday of the semester encouraged me, for, as I walked in, several students happily waved or said hello.

They'll love having me for a teacher, I thought, basking in the attention. Next, when I, God's gift to Sandpoint High School's portable classroom scene, marched into Portable 2 on my first morning of teaching, the orientation went well. Students sat and politely listened to *the rules* – until fifth period. The students in this class had no idea who I was. They couldn't have cared less about the great teaching experience or vast knowledge I had to offer them. All they knew was that a 50-year-old hag had shown up to disorder their day, and they were not about to cooperate. Within minutes, God's gift to Sandpoint High School's portable classroom scene knew she had met her match. Thus, began the Semester from Hell, with my recognition that my fifth-period sophomores would be my Class from Hell. The day's schedule ended fairly well with a sixth-period class of friendly, talkative juniors, some of whom I had taught the year before. The final bell rang, and I wasted no time going to the faculty room in the main building, a five-minute walk from the portables.

"Who's this Mike?" I asked. "He's the biggest jerk I've met in a long time." Mike had won the day's award for irritating me the most with his under-the-breath comments and his apparent disdain for authority. A young man, with Brad Pitt good looks, Mike had an attitude, and he wasted no time demonstrating that it might need some adjustments and soon. I determined that he and I would come to an understanding quickly, or he would be sitting in someone else's classroom. After asking around, I learned a fact that was my rare ace-in-the-hole for getting under this young man's skin. I had taught his mother. I had even known her since the day she was born. She was my sister's friend. I had bought one of my horses from his grandmother, who had been a close family friend for decades. I had also taught his aunts and uncles. Within minutes, I had enough ammunition to put a firm vise grip on Mike. That night I made a point to sort through my picture collection and found a couple I had snapped of his mother and his uncle for a special alumni newspaper we had produced a year or two before. The photos went with me the next day to school.

Before the fifth-period bell rang, Mike had already waltzed into the room and assumed a ready position by turning sideways in his front-row seat. This would provide ease in addressing the masses sitting behind him. I wasted no time walking toward him and dropping the photos on the desk.

"What are these?" he asked. "That's my mom. That's my uncle. Where did you get these?"

"I took them a year or so ago," I responded. "I've known your mother since the day she was born. Her birthday's July 6, isn't it? Your uncle's an Eagle Scout, isn't he? Your grandmother likes horses." Throughout my life, I've had a slightly bizarre ability to remember people's birthdays, lots of people's. Such details tend to be useless information in most cases except for family and close friends, but here was a time when hitting the nail on the head came in mighty handy. Instantly, Mike became painfully aware that I might know more about him than he knew about himself. This knowledge can create an uneven playing field for an undisciplined, macho sophomore male with an attitude. Teacher scores ace; kid scratches head.

LESSON: Prior personal connections between students and teachers can help or hinder in the classroom. In some situations, students may think they have a free pass because of this familiarity. With this outlook, they may suffer a few hard knocks while learning that the personal association cannot and will not affect their classroom success. Sometimes a negative situation from the past can put pressure on both student and teacher. In this case, I believe that if the teacher works more diligently to show fairness, the strained relationship may just improve with time. In other cases, a prior positive relationship between teacher and student can turn out to be very helpful for both. The latter may strive for both better behavior and better academic performance to reinforce his or her image in the eyes of the teacher or to demonstrate a sense of loyalty. During tough discipline times for teachers, these students can also serve as allies or as emotional supporters because of a positive emotional bond.

In Mike's case, my association with so many members of his family sent an immediate message: I had communicated with them frequently in the past. I could continue to do so in the future. On this second day of classes, the ball had bounced into my court, but that didn't necessarily mean an easy time ahead for either of us. Mike and I would go round and round for the next few months. I would have discussions about this troubled young man with his mother, the school counselor and even the principal, sometimes all together. Later in the year, I had to isolate him from the rest of the class, very few of whom fit the mold of model students.

The group included a mixture of athletes, drug users, spoiled, out-of-control rich kids; immature, spoiled Mama's boys with smart, often foul mouths; bullies who liked to pick on nerds, chatter boxes, and even an assortment of good students who behaved well under normal circumstances. Throughout the semester, we experienced daily dramas when Bob Posey, the parking lot attendant-turned truant officer-turned enforcer, would show up in the room, walk toward individual students and summon them to accompany him out the door. We might see that student the next day or maybe never, depending on the offense.

One student, when he did show up in class, never could get there on time. I had words with him the day he nearly pulled the door off its hinges after arriving late for approximately the 25th time. We had a tardy policy at Sandpoint High School, but most of us found that it rarely had any impact on the repeat offenders. Their reward – er – punishment was to sit out of class for a couple of days in detention. Then, our punishment was to spend extra hours preparing special assignments for them to make up their work, which they seldom did. Tardy Boy never seemed too belligerent, but he sure did know how to put on a comedy show for his peers. He apparently performed outside of school, too, when he attracted the attention of the local police as he and his buddies tried to heist a safe from a Sandpoint business. I heard he did some time in a "big house" other than his own home for that one.

Another young man in the class didn't last the semester. When I had had my fill of him and his constant antics in class and had recorded the zeroes in the grade book to prove he wasn't producing any work, I wrote up a referral slip. After checking his records, the counselors discovered he had never passed freshman English either semester, so they decided it might be nice to give him an opportunity to catch up. They transferred him to some poor ninth-grade teacher's English class. It meant one less problem for me, but that break never lasted. As soon as one troublemaker left this Peter-at-the-Dike class, another problem child's name would suddenly appear on my roster.

In one case, my new recruit was a young woman who couldn't stop talking in the sophomore classroom next door. I heard horrid reports about her from the class's male teacher and geared up for real trouble. Within minutes on her first day in Portable 2, Alicia had already found a seat near one of her friends and was yakking away at high speed when I appeared next to her desk.

"I've heard why you've been transferred into this class," I said. "Apparently, you were removed next door. If you continue the same behavior in here, you will not last long. I can be as mean and nasty as they come, or I can be your friend. You decide which."

That said, I welcomed her to class and wished her luck.

LESSON: During the '80s decade, I learned from one of my principals, Jim Wilund, to mix the good with the bad when disciplining a student.

"Always end a session on a positive note," he told me one day. That reminder reverberated and helped me work through many obstacles from that day forth. As the semester rolled on, this fidgety, high-strung young lady worked extra hard to do well academically and to remain in my class. Unlike some of the others, she actually *liked* to learn and challenged herself. Occasionally, I would have to remind her about the chatter, but for the most part, we became good friends, and she helped out as my English aide the next year.

When I first returned to teaching, my approach was to treat the students like young adults. I had gotten in the habit of greeting them as they entered the room, finding common topics to talk about before class and always accentuating the positive. I also took the high road, trying to reason with them in moderation about the importance of manners, punctuality, good study habits, decent language in the classroom, tolerance, etc. This worked in most cases, but I discovered within the first couple of weeks, as I had from experiences in earlier years, that textbook-teaching models are not always effective. In some situations, you just plain have to get down and dirty. Without compromising yourself or descending to their level, you often have to talk the talk that they understand. And, contrary to what many idealists, who have spent little or no time in the teaching trenches, tell you, many students understand and react to straight talk rather than to beating around the bush. Ultimatums rather than nicely suggesting that they would behave are sometimes very appropriate. Sometimes an occasional threat will work, but it's important that the threat is logical, legal and workable.

Having experienced ample hints early in the semester that I may need to adjust my ways, I experienced a head-on encounter in my fifth-period class on February 13, 1998. The following e-mail, written after the incident that day to one of my cyber-friends and empathizers, who lives in Florida, explains:

Good Morning,

Happy Valentine's Day to you. Do you have a big social day planned?

Part of mine will be spent preparing for and giving a speech to a teachers' honorary luncheon today. I'm going to keep it fairly low-key and talk about two aspects of my books: love and teaching. I might even point out that the two go hand in hand. And then I may point out that I'm having a difficult time finding the "love" connection right now.

This week started out on a negative note, improved day by day, then fizzled during the last eight minutes of my fifth-period class. This is the class that has the jerks, and I'm getting to the point where I'm not using such a euphemistic term of reference for them. For today's speech, I'll use the appropriate educational acronym "S-A," and I'm not referring to a written composition. My reference, instead, is more anally oriented.

In fact, when I went to my colleague's classroom after school yesterday, I walked through her door and announced, "They were S-As again!" My brief but graphic assessment was met with her marching toward me and saying, "I hate those words, but that's exactly what they are. And I'm finding myself using those words more and more."

Then we proceeded to tell each other our individual horror stories for Friday. She later called me last night and asked if I'd had a couple of beers yet. I think she had gone straight home to a bottle – and she doesn't even drink. She keeps coming up with daily plans to attack her problems. She had been a half-day teacher who picked up two math classes at semester when the husband-wife team quit.

Her experiences with her little darlings make mine look like I'm teaching a group of angelic altar boys. HER latest plan is to notify the principal on Monday of her intentions. Then she'll ask the class to take out a piece of paper and pencil. When one or any of the jerks begins to perform, she'll send them to his office, and he'll put them on detention until she has conferences with their parents.

In my case, the lads are much more subtle with their rudeness, so my strategy is going to have to be a bit more refined. We both discussed the fact that we'll have other consequences to endure when we do put the screws to them even more. We'll look forward to slashed tires or something destructive. That's the mentality we're dealing with.

Now, I know you've never met me nor her, but I need to assure you that we are known and respected for our ability to work a classroom and maintain a disciplined learning atmosphere. We're not the rookies – unfortunately. I have to keep reminding myself of that because I feel like such a failure when these incidents occur so often.

My fifth-period class self-destructed eight minutes before the end of a week that had looked halfway successful. And this was after I had handed out my customary Valentine chocolates FROM LOVE only to have one ungrateful soul whine, "You're only giving us two pieces?" In other classes, I was so pleased with how many genuine "thank yous" I had received. In this class, those who DID say "thank you," said it very quietly in fear of being mocked.

They were taking a vocabulary exam. In other classes, we had enough time to correct the test. In this one, three people were still finishing well into the hour, so I told those who were done to quietly bring their tests to my desk and staple the sheets together. Big mistake. I had not anticipated correctly. I had mistakenly and stupidly expected human-type reactions.

I don't know if on the farm you ever encountered those times when the animals are locked up and desperately want out. Before opening the gate, you're wise to find a strategic spot that would spare you bodily harm when the herd bursts through and thunders forward. Well, that's what happened. Like a human tidal wave, they pushed and shoved their way to my desk. One of the S-As grabbed the stapler while the moiling mass of bodies continued to ebb and flow in all directions.

I was so shocked I didn't react properly. Prior to this moment, I had already seen at least six sets of "wandering eyes" and had issued a stern warning to each. So I stretched my neck to look over the mass to see that the remaining test takers were not taking advantage of the diversion. Big mistake number two. I should have screamed at the human mass in front of me, much like I do my horses when they try to trample me.

Those 10 seconds had given them time to get the good ol' mean spirit back. The stapler was flying from hand to hand. Then I heard an anonymous, nasty male voice announce, "Let's piss her off!" Pissing me off consisted of five S-As grabbing the stapler and fiendishly stapling each of their papers at least a dozen times. They showed me what they thought. They were proud of their creativity, but I refused to react.

Another factor that makes life teaching in the portables miserable is the fact that they're a long ways from the main building, students have to leave early to get to the next class, and – there are no bells. So what we deal with for the last five minutes of class is clock fixation. Never mind the fact that the teacher may be trying to finish up a lesson or that someone might be trying to finish a test.

The pleas begin early and ugly.

"CAN WE GO?" usually invades the air space and my lecture. This plea usually comes from some whiny, female voice.

"No! It's not time yet," my stern voice responds.

"Everybody else is out!" somebody yells.

"NO, you don't leave until 1:57," I bark back.

They've quit paying any attention by this time. Notebooks are slapping shut. My train of thought has headed on down the tracks.

So I say, "You'll sit quietly until it's time to go."

My inclination is to let classes like the S-As go because I really don't want to look at them anymore. But I endure. You can imagine how those final five minutes went yesterday.

I wanted to yell and scream at them, but I thought about myself. A three-day weekend was coming, and I did not want to make my life any more miserable. So I kept them in their seats until one minute after it was time to leave and weakly said, "Have a nice weekend," knowing all the time that wish was intended for myself.

The beat goes on – next week brings a million new challenges. One of those will address "down-to-the-second" time management. Right now I'm hoping for a time when simply surviving the hour is no longer my number-one goal.

The following Tuesday, I approached fifth-period class, armed and ready. After taking roll, I remained silent, simply sitting back and watching for a moment or two, quietly observing as they ignored me and continued to talk, guffaw, poke, harass and cuss in varying degrees. As anything remotely resembling an educational atmosphere degenerated into yet another a mass of chaotic moiling, I calmly asked for their attention.

No reaction. The buzz continued.

"Could you please be quiet?" I announced once more.

No reaction. The buzz continued.

"ALL RIGHT, YOU JERKS! TURN AROUND! FACE THE FRONT! SHUT YOUR MOUTHS!"

The well-golly-gee amazement to my loud outburst was priceless. The room instantly went silent. Twenty-plus students suddenly stared ahead like stunned, frozen statues with a surprising revelation certainly lighting up their brains.

Hmm, she does know how to growl.

And growl I did for a good 15 minutes. After two weeks of restrained and reasoned discipline, which had worked fairly well for my other four classes but failed miserably with these thugs, I pulled out all stops. They saw the real witch or b—— within this lady named Love.

After recounting my horror at the scene from the previous Friday's test, I told them exactly what I thought of their antics, their rudeness and their animal-house behavior. I also described for them how it was going be from this day forth. Anyone so much as looking sideways would pay a price. My tolerance level had hit its peak. And for one brief, shining moment, the kids knew it. I reminded them once more that I did not have to be here. I had chosen to be here and had made a commitment, so it didn't matter to me if I stepped on a few toes in the process. In short, I would stand for no more scenes like I had witnessed the Friday before. This Tuesday afternoon explosion empowered me to rule with a strong upper hand throughout the remainder of the hour. Obedience reigned for 45 minutes. They didn't even charge for the door when they saw the herd of students from other classrooms passing by the window. Not one body moved until I had excused them.

Maybe, we had not turned just a corner, but maybe I had single-handedly in that outburst achieved a temporary 180-degree turnaround. I even entertained the thought for a while, but I had also taught long enough to know that such miracles just do not happen overnight with high school students. They usually have a way of degenerating to those old, established, comfortable ways. Nonetheless, I determined to make the most of my newfound honeymoon after this mid-afternoon divorce threat.

The semester in my painfully spartan Portable 2 classroom rolled on as a combination of occasional fun, limited progress and daily frustrations. After telling an effective sob story in the office, I finally received a class-room set of dictionaries for vocabulary lessons. Speaking of word choice, I also constantly reminded kids that "Hoover" resounded much better in my ears than "SUCK." I continued to fight battles with students over chronic tardiness but quit calling home to report the tardy infractions to parents after being reamed one evening by one indignant mother, who said her daughter needed extra time to "pee" before showing up to class after her 45-minute lunch break.

With classwork and exams, cheaters knew no subtlety. In addition to the usual "coveting of thy neighbor's answers" on tests, I witnessed more than my share of team collaboration on individual outside assignments, a practice made easier by copying research reports straight from books or the Internet. On two occasions, I nabbed red-handed two kids, who sat right in front of my desk with their crib sheets plopped in their laps during the test.

Every day was a challenge. During the nine or so minutes between classes, I'd make a mad dash to the bathroom, then spend the remaining minutes of my break time reviewing daily grammar lessons with my next-door colleague, John Search. The school experienced a few bomb scares, causing occasional and horribly organized evacuations, which sometimes neglected to include those of us off in the portable hinterland. The paperwork load turned insane, not because of assignments – in fact, the opposite. Every other weekend I filled out progress reports for more than one-third of the 140-plus students. Each week, when I posted missing assignments, the copy paper used for this update covered the entire classroom door.

Bad attitudes continued to manifest themselves in creative ways, mostly in fifth period but also occasionally in the other classes. In one particularly scary case, a student pulled a hit-and-run antic after waiting until the end of the hour to complain about the amount of extra credit I had awarded him for writing his incorrect spelling words correctly 10 times apiece. It wasn't enough, he said, adding a few inappropriate remarks, then dashed for the door. I chased after him and asked him to come back to talk about it, but he refused.

The next day he came, armed to dish out a little more verbal abuse. When I called him outside to discuss his behavior from the day before, he instantly turned angry, uttered a few expletives, went back inside to his seat and sat down. I followed him into the room and asked him to leave until we could get the problem resolved. He refused.

"You're not going to deny me my education," he defiantly announced after most of the class had entered the room. What was usually a chatty but rollicking last-hour class went instantly silent as a standoff unfolded. I remained calm on the outside but frightened within.

"Would you please take your books and go to the office?" I asked. He continued to speak defiantly, an enraged expression on his face.

"I'm not leaving," he announced once more. "I deserve my education, and you have no right to deny it to me."

"We'll talk about that later, but for now could you please go to the office?" I asked once more.

Again, he refused. Realizing there was only one other teacher in the portables that hour, and her classroom was four doors away, I went to my phone. This link between me and that faraway school office usually rang at least four times an hour in all six classrooms as the administrative workers called to give a message to one of the six of us. At this moment the receiver had no dial tone. Suddenly, this situation was beginning to seem too much like a television cop drama. I walked slowly out of the classroom and then raced to my colleague's classroom, bursting in the door where she taught math.

"Can I use your phone?" I screamed. She pointed the way. I called the office, frantically asking for an administrator. No administrator was available.

"Please get someone out here to Portable 2. I have a student who's angry, and he refuses to leave my room!" Then, I returned to my classroom where the student still sat with his triumphant bravado, hoping for me to continue pressing him. Instead, I tried to act calm as I took roll. I then recorded the absences in the grade book and bought as much time as possible before attempting to start class.

The five minutes it took for someone to arrive from the office seemed like an eternity. I wrote the "word of the day" on the white board in a desperate attempt to maintain some predictable order. Finally, my colleague, Bill Barlow, and the assistant principal, Mary Steele, walked in, asked which student, proceeded to his desk and asked him to accompany them to the office. Thankfully, he agreed.

We had a conference the next morning with his parents, and all agreed he needed to take some anger-management classes. We also concurred that, considering the circumstances, it would be wise for him to transfer to another English class. He had been a great kid in my class up until that day, when something just snapped. We learned in the conference that he worked until almost midnight every night, didn't get home until almost 1 a.m., headed for school by 7 a.m. the next morning, and repeated the process all over again every day. He felt like he could never catch up with anything, including his schoolwork. He was a capable student, but with his daily schedule, the pressure of keeping up with his grades was getting to him. Stress had been slowly destroying him. Fortunately, all worked out for everyone. This student and I were able to renew a positive relationship after what was one of the scariest episodes I had ever encountered as a teacher. My concern was probably heightened because this period was an unsettling time in many schools across the nation. Aware of news reports about horrific shooting events occurring in other schools, we teachers had quickly become programmed to expect the worst.

The incident also set off a recurring fantasy that surfaced during my many bad moments throughout the semester. My Olds Cutlass sat just a short walk from my classroom. I often considered how easy it would be to pick up my purse, walk out the door, get in the car, drive away and never come back again. I had made a commitment to A.C., though. Besides, my mother had taught me long ago that one should finish a job and never be a quitter. So, I hung in there, returning every morning, determined to do the best I could each minute, each hour and each day.

And, with each trying moment, I followed a simple strategy – be firm but kind. Slowly, I could see that it was working. For the most part, these were students who, despite their outward masks and actions of hard-core rebellion, really appreciated the fact that I gave a damn about them. Little things, like my genuine wish for them at the end of each hour to "have a good day," started catching on. I actually started liking them and feeling connected, in spite of all the grief they gave me.

As winter snows disappeared and the grass turned green, Satini Puailoa's high school football team held its spring practices every afternoon right outside our windows. They were loud. At least one hour each day, the band used that same area to practice marching. They were loud, too. The middle school youngsters enjoyed their noon hour break in the same area while we were holding class. They were not quiet. We endured each class period with a sense of foreboding. We could count on the fact that nearly every day would be chaotic and that we would never experience anything close to a normal teaching atmosphere. The plus side, however, was that we were far-removed from the main building and much of its tedious regimen. It was too far for administrators to spend much time out our way, so we enjoyed a tight-knit camaraderie of being the forgotten bunch in the hinterland.

In spite of all the problems, there were many funny episodes. Once the weather allowed Mike Keough's middle school gym students to have class outside, I observed a daily phenomenon that reminded me of my morning trips to the barn to feed my horses. There, both of our Labradors accompanied me and wait patiently as I unlatched the door. The instant it was open, even a crack, knowing there had to be a varmint in there to chase, they lunged forward, nearly knocking me down, and jumped inside to follow their noses in hot pursuit of a mouse or squirrel. In the classroom case, two young men always arrived the instant fourth period had cleared the room. After quickly plopping their books on their desks, they ran to the back window and shoved it open. Next, they would get on the desk, hang out the window and roar at the top of their lungs.

KEEEEE-OOOHHH! HEY, KEEE-OOOHH! KEEE-OOOHHH! This continued until Mr. Keough, finally distracted from his P.E. duties, would look up and acknowledge them with a wave and a smile. Once satisfied, they shut the window, returned to their desks and waited for class to start. This happened every single day.

After about two weeks of watching the routine with amazement, I commented one day.

"Ya know, you remind me of my two dogs when they accompany … ," I announced with a big smile on my face. The two guys didn't mind a bit because they were pretty happy-go-lucky souls, but my friend Mike took offense.

"How can you be so mean?" he protested from his seat in the back.

"Whaddya mean?" I asked.

"You're calling them dogs," he said. "That's pretty disrespectful."

He had put me on the defensive with what I had thought was a pretty innocent comment. I found myself in one of those situations where the explanation just digs the hole deeper. That day after school, Mike and I had one of our many conferences. I had asked him to stay after when he announced at the end of class that he wanted to be a Marine so "I can kill people." In reality, Mike's remark was not serious. It was just another of his classroom performances. Over the next few weeks, I learned that Mike's sensitivities extended far beyond what that rough and rebellious outer core would ever reveal at that age in his life. Deep down, he cared very much for people he loved and respected. Surprisingly, Mike would eventually become one of my dearest students. That took time and patience though – always key essentials for teaching.

Successful education eventually occurred as the weeks wore on. I began to see more kids actually bringing their notebooks to class and even taking notes. When I first started the semester, it was a rare student who would raise his or her hand to answer a question. As one who feeds off interaction, I finally resorted to the Pavlov's Dog theory of keeping an ample candy supply well-hidden in my desk. When a student volunteered to answer a question and answered it correctly, a piece of chocolate would be launched in his or her direction. Sometimes, when my aim wasn't so good, I would have to bring out another piece to soothe the feelings of injured parties directly in the line of fire. The candy worked. My grocery bill grew as I bought more and more sacks of the stuff to reward the increase in classroom participation. It was money well spent, because the kids got into the habit of wanting to participate. In spite of themselves, they were learning.

I thought long and hard about signing a contract for the next year of Sandpoint High School. Earlier in semester, I had indignantly announced to A.C. that I would fulfill the commitment of this semester. I doubted that I would return in the fall.

"I have a son who's majoring in education," I added. "My advice to him is to change his major." I had made similar strong statements to him before. The reversal of this policy occurred on the last day of school.

My sophomores' semester test in June was to memorize the first segment of Marc Antony's speech in Shakespeare's "Julius Caesar." With the exam schedule, the fifth-period test would end my semester. That morning I stopped by Safeway and bought two dozen assorted donuts.

In other classes, the speeches had lasted until the very end of the period. Some kids even had to stay after to complete their tests. Not so in fifth period where it was soon apparent that very little time had been spent memorizing. A couple of students managed to recite the entire text, but most were lucky to make it past "Friends, Romans, countrymen, lend me your ears." As the other students listened, some struggled to spit out all they could but gave up quickly. That meant more than enough time left over at the end of the hour, time for me to give a speech before doling out the donuts.

What could have been a funeral oration for my teaching career turned out to be a commitment to give this a try again in the fall. Having recorded grades for the exams and handing back other papers, I asked for their attention. They happily obliged, knowing that whatever Mrs. Love had to say could be pretty interesting.

"I brought ya donuts," I announced. "I don't know why."

They smiled and wiggled in their seats.

"You have made my life so miserable," I informed them with full sincerity, "but I kinda like you."

Again, they continued to wiggle and smile at me, much the way my happy Labs do.

"This has been a hard semester, but I've seen a lot of progress on your part," I explained. "You're starting to grow up, and I think there's hope for you." The speech went on with a few more compliments, but, as usual, somebody chose to interrupt me.

"Are ya coming back next fall, Mrs. Love?" a student inquired.

"Yeah, I think I might," I said after a moment's thought. Several voices chimed in at the same time.

"What do we do to get in your class?"

Those were the most powerful words I ever heard in my career. I've never forgotten that day and have never forgotten those kids. Many of them did get into my class the next year, and I taught several a third year when they were seniors.

In fact, that third year back, I created a program at Sandpoint High School called PAL Z (Peer Assistance Liai Zons). Its purpose was to improve school climate. The class included a cross section of handpicked students from all walks of life at our school.

The first person I asked to join the program was Mike; he accepted the invitation. Since high school, he has grown up and done well for himself in the construction business. Every time I see him, I can count on a big, loving hug.

I have A.C. and those students to thank for learning much about myself and where I fit as an educator. Had A.C. not insisted on my taking a leave of absence, I may have gone the rest of my life feeling bitter about education. Conditions improved in the schools, and the next five years were among the most positive I ever spent in the classroom. During my personal "Semester from Hell," those kids taught me patience, persistence and creative approaches to motivate them and to help all of us succeed. In the years before this experience, most of my students were high achievers, destined for success. My portable classroom students did not possess the same destiny. In order for me to survive and for them to achieve, I had to grow as a teacher. And for meeting that challenge, I remain forever grateful.

15.

Ya Mean SHE Taught the Pope!!!

Dorothy Keaton slouched deep in her theater seat, stifling a groan and attempting to turn invisible.

She's not gonna tell that story – is she? Dorothy thought to herself.

The proud grandmother and retired Ben Franklin five-and-dime clerk dreaded what she feared could appear next on the Panida Theater's silver screen. Curious locals had to be turned away on this November Saturday when Erik Daarstad's long-awaited Centennial film made its debut to the citizens of Sandpoint, Idaho. For nearly 90 minutes, the crowd had digested the two-hour extravaganza of interviews, wholesome people scenes and spectacular cinematography showcasing the 100-year history of our scenic little community.

Erik and his crew of interviewers, writers and historians had worked tirelessly through Sandpoint's 100th and 101st years to produce this gift to the town. Folks came, some wondering just how Sandpoint's heritage had been captured and some probably even more curious to see if their mugs had made it into the movie. After all, Erik had been ubiquitous, slinking in and out of crowds, quietly filming with his digital movie camera for the past couple of years.

A longtime Sandpoint resident, Dorothy enjoyed spotting old friends and familiar faces among the movie's vignettes, detailing how it was in the good ol' days. She watched action scenes of logging contestants falling off their perches while chopping away in Timberfest ax competitions, and old-time movie footage of Bing Crosby feigning pride while showing off a miniature Kamloops trout he had landed in the annual fishing derby. When she spotted me, the hometown teacher and one of her eldest daughter's high school chums, offering stories about Sandpoint's "discovery" during the late '60s, certainly Dorothy had to be pleased.

Yeah, she knew me all right. Dorothy's daughter Greta had shared many a funny story with me as we giggled our way through our high school years. Other connections existed. Dorothy's other daughter, Trudy, was a high school English student when I student-taught during the legendary Sandpoint Winter of '68-69 which closed schools through most of January. Dorothy's son, Kim, had missed my class when he passed through the high school in later years, but I knew that Kim had enjoyed his share of harmless devilishness during his years as a Sandpoint Bulldog. It must not have been too bad, though, because he later returned home and worked his way up the ladder to school administrator.

Kim, like his older sisters, had inherited the family's quirky humor gene; it's important for a Keaton to keep a straight face and a dry manner while telling a story guaranteed to throw any listener into hysterics. This tendency had apparently passed on, in somewhat raw form, to yet another Keaton generation, which is precisely why Dorothy was feeling squeamish as I began to discuss my classroom "Wall of Fame" during the movie interview.

Dorothy worried about what I might say about Kaleb, her grandson. Dorothy had good reason to worry because of a parent conference the preceding fall, one which taught me for the millionth time never to *assume* and ironically endeared Kaleb to me forever.

●●●

I stood before my fourth-period honors English class. Something had gotten me off the subject – a common event in my classroom. On this day, instead of discussing gerunds and participles, I had strayed to my "Wall of Fame." My hand swept across the collage of photos depicting former students in a variety of settings while I spoke of them nostalgically. Colin Moody stood in my living room making a crazy face. Courtney Ferguson and Erica Curless engaged in a mock staredown. Sarah Aavedal, in her characteristically shy manner, looked demurely through her glasses at the camera. Alana Watkins and Rachel Honsinger posed for a snapshot with my new daughter-in-law, Deborah. Steve Smith melted the hearts of many 16-year-old female students with his blue-green eyes, handsome face, curly brown hair, wholesome charm and that alluring magnetism worthy of a future as the world's sexiest male.

Meanwhile, in another photo, Cindy Wooden shook the hand of Pope John Paul II. Willie Love and his wedding groomsmen, Seth Noonan, Carson Jeffres, Matt Schultz, Dallas Spielman and Brian Trenholm leaned on the brick ramp leading to St. Joseph's Catholic Church. The only formal portrait on the wall featured Angie Rebella who had recently earned her Harvard law degree. Others from past decades remained forever young, performing antics that had passed before my camera lens during school days gone by.

"I've taught everyone on this wall," I announced to the class, "and they once sat in these uncomfortable desks just like you. They've gone out into the world and have done great things. You will too!"

Pitching my tales to inspire this class of juniors to dream big, I surveyed the classroom and could see that, as usual, I had drawn the students into the palm of my hand. All 31 appeared ready to feed off my every word about the great future that lay out there in that big world for each and every one of them. All 31 – except Kaleb Keaton.

"Kaleb, what's so funny?" I snapped.

"Nothing," he responded, attempting to muffle his obvious amusement.

"These kids were just like you," I continued on, trying to ignore the distraction. "They came from Podunk Sandpoint – some just a year ago – like Morgan Potts. She gets to work for NBC at the Winter Olympics, and she just graduated in June – Kaleb, what IS so funny?"

Kaleb's lanky, 16-year-old body was taking on the bends. His head bowed toward the desktop, hands covered his mouth as he snickered some more. Suddenly, 30 pairs of eyes stared at Kaleb, who was surely feeling the reaction from the curious minds who were wondering what had set him off this time. He was also sensing the acidic glare from the front of the room as I stopped talking and waited for him to control his insubordinate delight.

I continued on, citing Greg Parker next. This 1985 grad didn't appear on the wall, but his name *always* came up whenever I launched such pep talks. After all, when a young man leaves Sandpoint, goes off to the Naval Academy and graduates No. 1 in his class, he deserves mention.

"Greg is now on an aircraft carrier waiting to fly over Afghanistan," I informed the class. "He'll be among the first to go in when the invasion begins – Kaleb!!!!

"If it's *so* funny, why don't you share with the rest of us?"

The unruly kid was about to be bounced out the door.

"It's OK, Kaleb, tell us what's so funny." I feigned genuine appreciation for whatever had set him off. Kaleb had already demonstrated a time or two that he wasn't always going to perform according to my wishes. On several occasions, I had seen that stone face eyeing me with a contrived half-frown, his lengthy arm extending into the air, and, like a gullible sucker, had fallen for the ploy that this time Kaleb might have something genuine to contribute to our heavy-duty class discussion.

"What time is lunch today?" he would inquire. Restraint was challenging at these moments, but three decades of teaching had taught me that flying off the handle, breathing fire, glaring with my famed hate stares or threatening a kid with complete extinction aren't always the best options. Instead, I breathed deeply, as disgusted classmates groaned, and went on to the next photo. Kaleb always kept me off guard because occasionally he actually would have something significant to contribute to the discussion. Consequently, I almost always acknowledged his wish to enter into the conversation, knowing that anything was possible.

Well, on this day, he didn't want to contribute. He didn't even want to know when lunch was. He wanted to giggle for no apparent reason. I managed to complete my spiel on the wall of fame, no thanks to Kaleb. When the dismissal bell rang, he scooted out the door, allowing me no time to snatch him for an interrogation about his unilateral glee. Life moved on.

A few weeks later, parent conferences came. On this particular year, parent conferences had special meaning. They were my last ever. For years, I had loathed these two days in early November. I still believe they're the most inhumane activity school administrators ever invented. My opinion had nothing to do with meeting parents. I've always enjoyed meeting students' parents or guardians – except for those few, rare, hastily called conferences to which all teachers can relate, and because of which all teachers may question why they ever entered the profession.

Basic formula: Johnny misbehaves day after day after day. Teacher endures day after day after day and does not blow gasket but figures and prays (not aloud in school, of course) that Johnny will eventually catch on to subtle hints. Johnny doesn't. Teacher wonders silently what it must be like to live with this creature at home. Teacher learns what it's like at home within hours of incident when teacher loses the patience game, hauls off and explodes with words Johnny should have heard in response to that first indiscretion weeks earlier. Hot, steaming parents arrive at school. Teacher is called to conference. Within seconds, teacher, principal and counselor all see why Johnny acts like a bad boy. After a few accusatory remarks aimed toward the teacher or naive assertions that Johnny is incapable of error are emitted from the parents' mouths, it becomes clearly obvious that Johnny has had at least one or two good teachers. It's the negative influence at home that far exceeds any positive influence a classroom instructor could foster during a 55-minute class hour each day. With this observation, all professionals cooperate to see that damage is kept to a minimum and that the conference ends without carnage.

Often, because of the obvious personality conflict between student and this unfair teacher, the kid is transferred to another class where, within a matter of time, another similar conference will surely occur. Teacher goes home, does not sleep and rebounds the next day to try again. In my 33 years I was fortunate to encounter fewer than a handful of those experiences. In most cases, the students sadly continued along the same route they traveled in school, and sadly their after-school conferences often evolved into meetings with law enforcement officers, lawyers and judges.

Actually, the true reason I hated our annual formal parent conferences concerned their marathon nature. Beginning at 4:30 p.m. and scheduled to end four hours later and recurring on two interminable evenings, they gave me a hint of that famous "I Love Lucy" scene years ago when the pies kept coming off the assembly line much too fast for Lucy to stay on top of her job. The pies all looked the same. As fast as she would remove one, four more would be speeding by, with some actually falling off the track. This resulted in one of the classic moments of hilarity in television history as Lucy danced around like a wild woman.

Well, I never danced like a wild woman at teacher conferences, but I do distinctly remember moments when I attempted supposedly intelligent conversation while subtly crossing my legs in a desperate attempt to keep my bladder from bursting and causing me uncomfortable embarrassment in front of the endless parent lineup. Indeed, some aspects of my persona had not changed much since the notorious pocket-girdle moments of my adolescent years. I still possessed an active bladder, but the miserable girdle that led to the bladder's test of all tests in the seventh grade had long faded into the annals of Sandpoint Junior High history. Now, at parent conferences, my problem was that no bell rang at the end of 55 minutes, allowing me to race to the relief station. The parent queue kept growing, reminding me that a five-minute potty break was going to ensure at least another hour tacked on to the evening. In addition to the bladder irritant, conferences presented another problem. As most teachers know and repeat on a regular annual schedule, "parents who need to come to conferences seldom show up." This means that most parent conferences go somewhat like this:

"Hi, how are you? I'm Marianne Love, and I teach English."

"Fine, I'm Sally Jones. My son told me to be sure to come to meet you."

"Oh, yes, Donald; he's such a nice young man. Let's see, I've got a sheet of grades to share with you. Let me find it … (tongue in cheek) well, Donald could work just a little harder; he has a 97.91 average … a little more effort and he could push that up to a 99 by the end of the semester."

"I'll be sure to talk to him about that; after all, he's planning to go to

Harvard."

"Oh, that's nice."

"What does he need to do to improve his grade?"

"Uh, well, uh, encourage him to read more books – blah, blah, blah – the session goes on but not without a reminder that Donald has read a novel a day for the past five years. Donald is doing fine, he's a model student, turns his work in on time, always contributes in class ... he's guaranteed to be president some day, etc., etc.

Although my already-tired mind is currently multitasking on ear, eye and bladder control, my peripheral vision indicates that not one soul in this lineup of hyper-conscientious parents of super-conscientious students is planning to give up and go to someone else's desk. They've all locked themselves into place, and even more have joined them.

A cursory peek at my watch shows that all of 30 minutes of the evening's repetitive cycle has elapsed – at least three and one-half more hours of "praise, praise – your daughter's brilliant; she spells well – praise, praise, an Ivy League school will be a snap, praise, praise ... " After one more story about Ashley's busy, junior-year schedule, the session finally ends. One more satisfied parent heads off to see the advanced calculus teacher, I monitor my bladder capacity, reposition my legs for stronger control and extend the next upbeat greeting.

These conferences were always scheduled to end at 8:30. They did for most teachers. Invariably for me, however, 8:30 turned into 9 p.m., which turned into 9:30, and just as I would think I was visiting with my last talkative parent – eyes crossed, lips churning like thick cement, bladder locked in permanent misery mode – out of the corner of my eye, I could see that figure of a lone person walking across the empty Commons area was *not pushing a broom*. No, this was *not* the night custodian; no, this was *one more parent*.

Oh, God, I thought with what remaining brain cells I had, *will this ever end?* Fortunately for the well-intentioned individual coming my way, a lifetime of intense self-discipline kept me from screaming, "Why can't you just go home and let me outa here? Your kid's a genius – he writes like Shakespeare, speaks like Churchill, has a 239 IQ and will definitely score

1700 on the SAT – now GO HOME AND LET ME DO THE SAME!"
More often than not, this person, who had gotten my undivided attention, became so comfortable that he or she just kicked back and visited for
20 more minutes. All too often, after I finally unwound my knotted up
body, raced from the Commons and wheeled into the nearest bathroom,
I had to face the next problem.

Try going No. 1 after five and one-half hours of heavy-duty restraint.
The flood doors had gone on lock-down. Approximately two gallons of
built-up fluids remained painfully intact behind the barrier. Not even the
first toilet flush could coax one drop of pee. Mercifully, a flush or two more
and my inner mechanism eventually caught the cue. The dam broke.
Thank God for big favors. I could now tidy up, head out into the frigid
evening air, go home, hit the bed, teach the next day and get ready for one
more night of agony.

I actually preferred the spontaneous parent conferences at Yoke's grocery store where next to the pork chop display I could yell across the meat
department to my teaching friend Mona and tell her how much I enjoyed
her son, Ezra. Mona would be so busy searching for the Wood's German
sausage that she would simply respond with a delighted smile and an exuberant "Thank you" and move on with her shopping. Anywhere, almost
any time, I always loved talking to my students' parents, even on the telephone – again with a few exceptions. One of the last times I ever called a
parent during the evening from my home, the conversation went:

"Hi, I'm Marianne Love, your daughter's English teacher. I'm calling
because the school requires us to notify parents when students have four
or more tardies in our class. Your daughter has hit that mark. If she gets
any more, she'll have to take a truancy."

Silence.

"Can you remind her that she needs to come to English on time?" I
added, hoping for a cordial response, one that assured me that she would
see that the problem stops.

"Yeah," Mom said, "just a minute."

Muffled conversation was heard in the background.

"She says she has to pee. That's why she gets there late sometimes."

"Well, if you can just encourage her to plan a little better and make sure she isn't late in the future … "

Mom cut me off.

"If she has to pee, I'm not going to worry about her being late. Besides, there's always a line at the lavatories."

It was obvious this conversation was going nowhere, so with one more reminder, I concluded the conversation.

"Well, maybe she can try to get to the bathroom a little earlier. Thanks for your time. I appreciate whatever she can do to avoid having this problem turn into a truancy. "

I hung up. She hung up. Then, like so many times in my past, my slow-functioning brain reminded me that this girl had lunch hour before she had to be in my class.

"Duh!" Teachers can be so stupid at times, and, furthermore, their ability to control their bladders is much more developed than that of teenagers. That telephone conference taught me yet another lesson: Don't ruin evenings at home; instead, call during school hours when parent and child are separated. This strategy cuts out the potential of a family conference where the possibility of Mom believing little darling rather than the faceless voice at the other end puts the teacher at a definite disadvantage.

With all this in mind, Parent Conferences: November 2001, held special significance. Knowing they would be the last ever in this lifetime, I faced the two nights with the gritty optimism of a marathoner focusing on the finish line coming into view. I could endure anything or anybody – that was my thought as I stood in the faculty room exchanging small talk with colleagues before we were to march to the SHS Commons, with packets of student reports in hand, and begin the nonstop sessions with the anxious parents lined up at our tables.

All went well both nights with the exception of one conference, involving a father-daughter team. The father was impressed with his own supreme knowledge. He also appeared clearly skeptical of my ability to challenge adequately what he deemed his brilliant daughter, who must have come along to agree with him. I finally offered both him and the child prodigy the green light to make a schedule change if they felt her entire education was going down the tubes because of the moments wasted in my classroom. In a later conversation, when I repeated my suggestion, the daughter's response was that the other teacher "wasn't any better," so she would stay. As had happened in the past, I started second-guessing myself and my teaching abilities before learning from colleagues that the same parent had imparted the same message at every other teacher's table he had visited.

One other event destined to go down in my parent conference history happened immediately after the father and daughter left my table. Kaleb Keaton's parents, having patiently waited their turn, sat down with big smiles on their faces, eager to share a story with me that had made the rounds of the entire Keaton clan, delighting each listener.

"What could this be?" I thought. "Anything's possible with Kaleb. I'm going to have to be careful what I say." My instincts told me it was best to avoid offering my Kaleb insights until Kim and Julie had filled me in on their story.

Well, the story quickly offered me embarrassing insight into Kaleb's behavior during that notorious hour when his snickers had irritated me so. The tale also reinforced once more that lesson I had learned so many years before while enrolled in a U.S. Forest Service defensive-driving course and had imparted to students nearly every year since: Don't ever ASS-U-ME!

Well, I didn't really completely assume. I didn't in any way suspect that Kaleb had anything really *that* funny on his mind when he couldn't stop laughing that day. Maybe it was just a half-assumption. When Kim and Julie finally related Kaleb's version of that day, it was another bite out of the teaching apple.

"Kaleb came home and told us that he was probably in trouble with Mrs. Love," his father began. "We asked him why."

"Well, today she was telling us all about her wall of fame," Kaleb had explained to his parents that night around the Keaton family dinner table. "She pointed at the wall and then told us she had taught everybody up there. I looked at the pictures and saw Pope John Paul II, and all I could think of was 'Ya mean *she* taught the Pope?' "

Kim's explanation of his son's mysterious glee dealt me an uncomfortable jolt.

Oh, God, I thought, *I don't blame him for laughing. Who is the moron here?* Who wouldn't think it was strange that a 50-something woman had mentored an 80-something man – let alone the Pope? Of course, Kaleb had every reason to laugh that day when I had neglected to mention to the class that it was Cindy Wooden (class of 1978), whom I had taught, not the Pope. As a reporter for the Catholic News Service since 1989, Cindy had been covering Pope John Paul II's activities. For years, she had traveled with the Vatican Press Corps whenever the Pope took his world tours. If only Kaleb had shared his unique observation instead of just giggling to himself, we could have all enjoyed a good laugh. Instead, at the parent-conference with his folks weeks later, I had every reason for embarrassment.

"Oh my goodness," I said. "Why didn't he tell me that day?"

"We asked him that too," Julie responded. "He told us he just didn't think he was on quite good enough terms yet with Mrs. Love to point out her mistake to the class." We chuckled through the rest of the parent conference as Kim and Julie told me that the story about Kaleb and Mrs. Love and the Pope had turned into a Keaton-family favorite.

So, that Saturday at the Panida Theater, a year later, when Dorothy Keaton saw me discussing my Wall of Fame during the Centennial Film, she had good reason to be concerned about what came next. She worried that I might just possibly assume my well-known habit of digression and reveal to the audience her grandson's indiscreet amusement that October 2001 day in fourth-period English. A few more seconds of the video passed. I had spared Kaleb's reputation. The film moved on to a different topic. Dorothy could relax. The world doesn't need to figure out the logistics of explaining how a North Idaho English teacher in her 50s could have ever landed a job teaching Pope John Paul II.

• • •

I have often chuckled about the day Kaleb ruffled my teaching feathers. As on many other moments during my 33 years in my classroom, I had assumed incorrectly and later had learned another valuable lesson about working with kids. In most cases, a colorful, sometimes slightly "off-the-wall" story unfolded prior to the lesson learned.

Several months after my final parent conferences, on June 7, 2002, I left Sandpoint High School for the last time. My Wall of Fame came home with me. The photos now reside in a box along with dozens of other bits of memorabilia that had accumulated in my desk and file drawers throughout my teaching career. The student photos appearing in the room during that last year may have inspired a few students among the five classes of 16-year-olds who, every day for a year, observed those who had come before them, fixed in time on that wall. Who knows where the inspirations gleaned from those images will take these students in their life after Sandpoint High School? Only time will tell. For now, however, I feel very fortunate to know about many fascinating journeys taken by the students featured on the wall, as well as those taken by a host of others with whom I've kept in contact over the years.

I'm proud to brag about teaching approximately 4,500 students and being able to recognize most of them when I meet them on the street or in the canned goods aisle at Yoke's Pac n' Save grocery store. In many cases, I can remember exactly where they sat in the classroom, what hour they took English from me, and often a few spicy stories to connect with each of them. One is the tale of the blue birthday cake – with its questionable ingredients – baked by Gary Rench and Pat Perry for an in-class celebration on a day that was *not* my birthday. I could also share how much it meant to me so many years ago when Skip Harris, a brilliant young man with whom I had tangled a time or two, brought me a pair of his handcrafted earrings. I could raise a few eyebrows by sharing the lyrics to "Cocaine Kit," penned by Rob Kincaid for a Drill Team Variety Show back in the 1970s. His song satirized a radio station campaign to entice locals to tell on drug pushers. Steve Smith and Josh Moon would maybe cringe (maybe not) if I told about their decision to help themselves to four or five papers for one measly quarter from the downtown *Spokesman-Review* paper machines. I had sent them on an errand to pick up several extra copies for my Newspaper-in-Education class. Later, I sent them directly to the *Spokesman* office to pay and apologize – rather than to go to jail.

I'll never forget all the junior English classes who gave it their all while clearly enunciating Edgar Allen Poe's classic choral poem "The Bells," during inter-class competitions for the rights to donuts. Seniors competed just as diligently while writing modern-day versions of "Canterbury Tales," to be recited while on a scavenger hunt in my neighborhood. Even the neighbors got in on the act by presenting them candy as they vied for who would get a juicy steak rather than hamburgers at the barbecue that followed.

I could tell a few stories about observing human distress associated with the tiny crib sheets brought to class by a few not-so-good cheaters. My discovery of the illegal test aids led to a few life-altering moments for several scarlet-faced, unprepared, always unnamed test takers. I could never forget the helium tank hauled into the classroom by Cory Flowers for her unique parody of Marc Antony's "Friends, Romans, Countrymen" speech. Cory couldn't spit out her words quite as quickly as the other students because of a need to suck up a shot of helium from her balloon after every line. Imagine the effect, though.

Speaking of air, I could also tell of the time the new student blew in from Oklahoma and later took three days to give her oral presentation on Margaret Mitchell's "Gone with the Wind." That might take too long, though, especially if I throw in the 513 recorded "enn-a-ways" she used as transitions in her epic "summary." And that count came only after a few students had awakened from their daze and humored themselves by tallying her repetitive utterances.

Another class did sit through another book report of epic length, through most of every captivating minute of the two-day performance. Jessie Harris and I had first met when he was in the sixth grade and on a skiing outing at Schweitzer Mountain Resort. I was a novice. So was Jessie. We took the T-Bar and stood side by side while being transported to our jump-off spot. Neither of us had any previous experience at exiting a T-bar. The resulting consequence complicated our lives briefly – two bodies and two sets of skis entwined like a giant pretzel in the snow. We eventually pried ourselves apart and went our separate ways. I never forgot Jessie and knew that good times were ahead when this witty young man enrolled in my English class. Jessie's brilliant command performance came during oral book report time, when he chose "To Kill a Mockingbird" as his project. Assuming the voice and personality of each major female and male character, Jessie masterfully reenacted the portion of the trial in which Atticus Finch proves Tom Robinson's innocence. I always wished I could have captured it all on tape.

I could tell a great tale about painfully shy LaVar who, as a sophomore in the '70s, thought I ought to date – and marry – her Uncle Butch, a free spirit from the Florida Keyes. Butch did come to Sandpoint. We did go out for dinner and chuckled over his well-meaning niece's matchmaking attempt, and LaVar got over her shyness. A few years later, I married another Southerner, one named Love, whom I met after arranging dates for my drill team squad.

Because of so many endearing memories with faces to match, my teaching wall of fame could easily have extended around my classroom. No, I did not teach the Pope. But I did teach hundreds of young people from Sandpoint who provided me ample reasons to be proud of the career I began back in 1969.

16.

Love's Top 10 Teaching Memories

Faithful readers may already know that my addiction for mowing the lawn ignites my creative juices and rekindles my memory. During these frequent sessions at our former home (North Idaho grass grows green and abundantly from April through October), my mind often fires up images of isolated moments among the thousands that unfolded in my classrooms or at venues where teacherly duties took me.

A face would pop up. A name would float along with the faces in these fast-flowing streams of consciousness. At such times, I realize that an event involving this individual is tucked away within my memory, waiting for the moment when I return to ponder that person, that place or that act. Sometimes those grass-cutting reflections elicit a smile; sometimes, a frown. Often, I even caught myself chuckling out loud while pushing my mower around a tight spot between the two willow trees near the house or while cruising along atop my Sears Craftsman riding machine across our huge lawn south of the driveway.

It may sound absurd, but certain sections of this yard – that took nearly a day to mow – even elicited specific reflections. For example, while maneuvering in and around areas west of the house, bordered by the old locust tree, the adolescent grand fir, the proud tall spruce and our green metal Avista electric meter, I often thought of Josh Loveless. Josh sat in the back corner of my second-period junior English class near the end of my career. A quiet young man, who surely preferred hunting cougars with his dogs to sitting in an uncomfortable desk, Josh came alive through his writing. An enthusiastic love for outdoor pursuits, especially related to hunting, always drove his topics. In fact, he submitted some of his elk-hunting stories to a magazine called *Bugle* and got to see them published. One day, this blond, soft-spoken young man who could almost blush on command, summoned me into the school hallway to show me a plaque the magazine publishers had sent him for winning one of their writing contests.

I also taught Josh's sister Erica. As a high school student, Erica often vowed she would marry my son so her name could turn to "Love." That was not to be, as Willie found his love, Deborah, in Boise. Nonetheless, I recall good times spent with both Josh and Erica every time I nearly wiped out that Avista meter while hurrying to finish the front lawn. This association probably has something to do with the fact that their dad, Bill, an Avista employee, used to pull into our driveway once a month to read the meter, which determined how much we owed the power company. I wonder what would happen to the size of the bill if a lawnmower-meter collision ever occurred.

There was another patch of our lawn that inspired an image of Becky Marienau Hawkins' ever-present, warm-hearted smile. This vision took me back to many giggly, good times spent with her in *Monticola* yearbook class in the late 1970s. I also knew Becky outside school through our mutual 4-H involvement. In fact, a trip to southern Idaho for a horse-judging contest with Becky and 11 other females remains a classic among my numerous travels with teens. I had arranged for our group to stay in the bunkhouse of a huge cattle ranch near Dillon, Montana, on the way back. While writing a two-page newspaper photo feature about the ranch, I had gotten to know Gibbs Rehm, the manager, and his family, who were gracious hosts.

When Gibbs' wife, Jo, heard we were passing through Dillon, she offered up the house where we could throw our sleeping bags on the living room floor and spend the night. Once there, just before retiring for our hopeful night of slumber, we discovered one key problem. The toilet refused to flush. Becky's mom, Delsie, tried her best to coerce the john back into action by pouring water into the tank from a Pringle's potato chip can. No dice.

So, by the light of the full summer moon, all 13 of us trooped out and found choice spots to do our duty behind an ancient pickup parked in grass so high it looked like it surely hadn't moved from that location in several years. Lots of lighthearted squeals ensued during the midnight squat sessions. Of course, we were all ladies, so rather than employing the "drip dry" approach, we took individual supplies of toilet tissue along with us to our open-air privy in hopes of satisfying the hygiene gods.

Well, next morning, the broken-down, stationary truck had somehow found its way out of its parking spot. The vehicle was not to be seen, but the random assortment of little white wads accenting the green grass was quite a sight. I can still feel my stomach muscles working overtime from giggling and the tears streaming down my face as Becky, Delsie, Marilyn and the gang were summoned, one by one, to peer outside and behold the crop of mostly white clumps dotting the grass outside the bunkhouse window.

Nobody volunteered to go out and pick up the litter. Instead, we piled into our cars and left quickly, reluctant to look back but always wondering what the ranch hands would think when they discovered the evidence. Surely, when they saw the Pringle's can sitting next to the toilet, they would understand. Over the next couple of years and ever since that time, Becky and I have shared many a laugh about that Montana cattle-ranch commode.

Throughout lawn-mowing season, countless memories of other teaching vignettes popped up with the same regularity as springtime dandelions. Unlike the dandelions, though, these reappearances of former students and their individual stories do not bother me in the least. In fact, I view these revisits as a collection of intangible but precious gems always reminding me why I loved teaching. The day-to-day unscripted dramas, featuring a wide spectrum of characters, made for a rich bag of reflective moments to be treasured with time.

And so, after much thought, I've borrowed an idea from late-night talk-show host David Letterman. Carefully weighing and sorting through my knapsack of mental images, I've compiled Love's Top 10

Teaching Memories.

They follow:

Teaching Memory No. 10: Todd Book walking across the stage. I always loved graduation. It was a highly emotional time as families, friends and teachers gathered to celebrate a milestone in our students' lives. Todd was one of my husband's Boy Scouts, a young man who hung out in my classroom every morning with his buddies, Wayne and Stephen. He loved the outdoors and took every opportunity to hunt or fish in the mountains.

One day in the mid-'80s, he and a friend were driving down a rural road when their pickup slid off into the ditch next to some mailboxes. Todd was sitting on the passenger's side. Upon impact, a board holding a mailbox came through the window and jammed into Todd's face, knocking him unconscious. Soon after he arrived at the hospital, emergency workers discovered a blood clot on his brain, which was swelling. Todd was flown to a Spokane hospital where he remained in a coma for several weeks. The period after his awakening was followed by months of intense therapy and slow improvement. Todd returned to school in a wheelchair. Eventually, through therapy, he was able to stand on his own. Later, he took small steps. One early June evening in 1985, he took the big step of walking, slowly but determinedly, across the stage at his graduation. The entire audience stood, cried and clapped for several minutes as this quiet, young man courageously accepted his diploma from principal Jim Wilund and proudly walked to the other side.

Epilogue: Todd never completely recovered from the effects of the brain injury, but he lives on his own.

Teaching Memory No. 9, Santa Fe Scare: In April 1991, eleven of my students, another chaperone, Dwayne Sheffler, and I attended a national high school journalism conference in Albuquerque, New Mexico. As an added treat to the experience, we took a side trip to Santa Fe. While Dwayne accompanied most of the group for a late-afternoon/early-evening tour of the town, I joined the two sophomore journalism students, Erica Curless and Courtney Ferguson, and we headed west from our hotel on a mission to shop and to eat dinner at one of Santa Fe's restaurants. Along the way, I purchased a beautiful Zuni turquoise ring, while the girls picked up some souvenirs. We then found a '50s theme restaurant, ate some fat, juicy hamburgers, and headed toward the hotel to meet the rest of the group for the drive back to Albuquerque.

About a block into our return walk, a tall, slim, disheveled man, appearing extremely inebriated, began to follow us. He seemed determined to catch up with us. If we switched to the other side of the street, he crossed over. If we sped up, so did he. We tried to act calm and unconcerned. Not an easy feat, but we did our best. The hotel seemed hundreds of miles away. The man kept inching closer. We hurried our pace. With the girls ahead of me, I purposely stayed in the rear, tightly clutching my heavy purse, planning how to use it as a weapon if he caught up to us. Finally and thankfully, we recognized the back side of the hotel and broke into a run. It was strangely frustrating to walk into the lobby and find our group lounging blissfully in the couches and chairs. We tried to convince them that our lives had been in immediate danger, but we learned quickly it was a you-had-to-be-there experience. The rest of the group's so-what? response irritated us; nonetheless, our return to a secure comfort zone among friends surely made us the most relieved humans in Santa Fe that Saturday night.

Teaching Memory No. 8: Sherry Marks assisted me as an English aide in the mid-1980s. Like most of my extraordinary student helpers, she took especially good care of me. One day, in particular, she really saved my day when I returned to my first-period class of mostly senior boys, who always dared to "stone" anyone who performed well on tests. They prided themselves in maintaining low academic expectations almost as much as they loved to rehash their weekend beer parties.

On this morning, I had left just before class to visit the ladies' room (which the reader will recognize is fairly common for me). After returning, gathering my papers on my desk, and preparing to begin the day's lesson, I felt Sherry's quiet presence. Once there, with minimal fanfare, she dropped a small slip of paper near the pile of notebooks where my lesson plan lay. In an instant, she was back sitting in her chair near the window calmly correcting papers. Then, I read her note.

"Don't look now," it stated, "but your pants are unzipped." Glancing her direction, I caught a slight smile and a twinkle in her eye as she attempted to downplay the situation.

It was definitely time for me to write something on the board. Whirling around and picking up a piece of chalk, I stole the opportunity sneak a peek downward with my back to the class. Sure enough, the pants were completely unzipped. Fortunately, I wasn't wearing ragged panties that day, and lucky for me, my senior boys were too engrossed in their weekend party planning to notice.

Teaching Memory(ies) No. 7: Calling All Marc Antonys: Probably the most unpredictable day of any year in my sophomore English classes came when the students had to memorize several lines of Marc Antony's famous funeral oration in Shakespeare's "Julius Caesar." To create the proper atmosphere, the sophomores wore togas and brought oodles of edibles for a delectable Roman feast. To earn their grade, they were offered two options. They could simply memorize the passage and recite it to perfection, or they could come up with a creative way to parody the speech. More than half of each class usually chose the latter. Those famous lines are engraved in my brain, and at least a few of them remain saved in the brains of my students who learned and performed them. In fact, I wouldn't be surprised if someone stands before the mourners/revelers with his/her "heart there in the coffin with Marianne" and recites the passage at my own funeral. All I care is that whatever parody is concocted, I still remain an honorable teacher.

When reflecting on the variations of this speech that I listened to over the years, a few definitely stand out. Record players still occupied most homes when Larri Ann Smith, now a Washington physician, recited her speech in the spring of 1979. And those record players still played tunes at different speeds – some almost faster than the speed of sound, others p-a-i-n-f-u-l-l-y s-l-o-w. Sometimes the needle skipped with every revolution. Larri Ann's perfectly memorized speech exemplified all phonograph extremes. Another year, Carrie Cooper boogied atop a table while delivering her lines. Tom Rust and Toby Feuling teamed up with their *loud* electric guitars and turned the speech into a wild rock concert. Some students chose Southern accents; some wore cowboy garb; some put on a puppet show. Others parodied the *Gilligan's Island* theme song, while even others feigned drunken stupors, lying in a heap on the floor and singing Shakespeare's famous lines to the *Hee Haw* favorite, "Where Oh Where Are You Tonight?"

I'm sure that each time these scenes unfolded centuries afterward in a country yet unknown, as Antony so aptly predicted in his speech, his friend, Julius, was somewhere near Rome rolling over in his grave.

Teaching Memory No. 6: A Touching Gesture: She didn't need to do it, but her gesture showed monumental courage. I've admired her integrity since that day she summoned me aside to have a talk.

A quarter century before, she and her friends, high school seniors, had made my life at school miserable every day for nearly four months. Midway through my first year of teaching, I made a bad decision while attempting to defuse an ongoing, tense atmosphere among a group of girls in one of my classes. Within minutes of my disciplinary action, I regretted the lack of careful thought that had led to my decision. My knee-jerk discipline technique of asking the girls to leave the class solved one problem but immediately created a personal nightmare. It's not important to share the details. Let's just say it was intense. The girls retaliated continually until the end of the school year. When a situation occurred that brought the conflict to an end, I could once again resume my life, and, thankfully, I also reversed my decision to find another career.

I moved on. They moved on. Although the memory of those months still stung, I learned over the years to forgive and forget. Every new season of teaching and a more seasoned perspective on my own part reinforced the reality that most young people do grow up and especially *that we should never judge anyone solely on how they behave in high school*. So, eventually, I had developed a good relationship with the girls.

One day 25 years later, while visiting with my mother in a downtown business, I was summoned to a section of the store where one of these young women worked.

"I need to talk to you," she said.

"Sure," I said.

We walked to the back corner.

Once there, she began what had to be the most difficult moment of her life.

"I have to apologize to you," she said. "What I did to you when I was a senior was inexcusable."

"It's OK," I said, reassuring her. "I've forgotten about that long ago. Everybody grows up."

"No," she said, breaking into tears. "I need to apologize. You did not deserve to be treated that way, and I was not raised that way." She went on to explain how she had tried to avoid coming in contact with me over the years because she was so ashamed. Ironically, her actions had tormented her much longer than they ever had me.

Again, I reassured her that – yes – the semester so long ago had been a difficult time, but I had learned from it, and the emotional pain of that period had long since passed. I had all but forgotten it.

I thanked her.

She did not have to make the gesture, but her courageous act released decades of guilt for her and re-instilled a strong faith in human decency for me.

Teaching Memory No. 5: Denver Layover Laughs: As adviser of the *Cedar Post*, the SHS newspaper, I dangled an annual carrot to my students almost every fall. On the first day of class, I would announce that we would be attending the National High School Journalism convention in the spring. Besides entering our newspaper in a contest for overall quality, several staff members would compete in individual writing, design and photography contests. The event was serious business in many ways. Students were expected to attend seminars to enhance their knowledge and to pick up on new journalistic trends that we might want to try the following year.

They were also expected to follow fairly strict code of discipline while on the trip. For the most part, they did, but I would also be the first to admit that as vigilant as I was, I still tried to get some sleep at night. Overall, the trips went well. Nobody went to jail. Nobody got kicked out of the hotels. Nobody got sent home. And, thankfully, nobody faced a parent/administrative/distraught adviser tribunal to explain their behavior once home from the trip.

Somebody, however, did have to spend a day watching soap operas in his room at Super 8 in Long Beach while the other 23 students visited Beverly Hills High School and the set of *Entertainment Tonight*. Our foolproof buddy system failed in the spring of 1993 because somebody else broke the second rule ever learned in my journalism class: Never ASS-U-ME. Consequently, Matt Ginzton, the next year's editor, was still brushing his teeth when the four vans took off without him.

In addition to the high-level expectations for the student journalists' behavior and their performance at the conference, we always built in time for fun – Disneyland, the ocean beaches, the San Diego Zoo, etc. In every case, though, it was the spontaneous creativity evolving from group chemistry that left the biggest impact.

And of those many great moments, I have no problem selecting the three and one-half-hour layover in Denver airport as we returned from the aforementioned trip to Albuquerque in April 1991. That was my first year as their adviser.

We had accomplished major feats that spring, one of which was producing a 32-page special edition to say good-bye to our high school that had served SHS for 37 years. The paper turned into a monumental achievement in its scope alone – featuring stories about past school events and people spanning nearly four decades. If that wasn't enough of a challenge, this project served as the prototype for the class's major reliance on computers for layout and ad production – all accomplished with two Macintosh computers, one printer and one scanner. To achieve this, many of us came close to changing our home address to 410 South Division, where the school was located, because of several evenings a week plus every weekend spent in the *Cedar Post* room during February and March.

Needless to say, the trip to Albuquerque turned out to be a well-deserved perk for a team of kids who had dedicated so much of their time to the special edition. From the trip's start to finish, the group chemistry turned out to be an adviser's dream. Everyone seemed to enjoy anything we did, and everyone enjoyed each other – definitely not always the case when traveling with high school students.

During early shopping-for-knick-knack time, some member of our group purchased a glob of plastic feces, looking very much like a doggie deposit. Naturally, it was a hit every time we returned to our motel rooms where it would mysteriously appear on an unsuspecting student's toilet seat or in the carpet next to a lamp where one of the group decided to sprawl on the floor.

Those incidents paled, however, to the show the students put on during the layover in Denver Airport. The first hour went by fairly normally – buying snacks or playing cards. With three more hours to wait for our flight, those activities turned too mundane, so out came the fake poop and the video camera. The kids situated themselves along the aisle near a main gate where large numbers of passengers would be deplaning. Then, they strategically placed the fake poop on the carpet, where many of those passengers' feet would be passing by. A cameraperson and his eager assistants sat, waiting for the fun to begin.

From the instant the first throng of passengers came trudging through the gate, most with eyes focused on overhead flight-information monitors, our appetite for some hearty laughs was satisfied beyond expectation. Some passengers bearing briefcases were obviously so intent on rushing to that next gate without delay that they scurried past the plop, unaware of its presence. Others glanced down long enough to spot it, stare at it in disbelief as they walked by, and whisper amused comments to members of their party. Some stumbled right over it, twisted their necks to get a good look at the small obstruction, grimaced with disgust and quickly moved on. Several people, as they were deplaning, stepped smack dab in the middle of it, slightly stumbled and then quickly rubbed their shoe into the carpet to rid themselves of unwanted doggie doo – probably never taking time to think about the remote possibility of such stuff showing up inside an airport.

As time went on and more hordes of passengers hurried past, the camera kept rolling. Other waiting passengers caught on to the kids' show. Many willingly joined in on the fun, feigning disinterested expressions but with alert eyes as each plane load of passengers encountered the brown mass in the aisle. During the three hours of hilarious reactions, we watched as one person reported the obstruction to a cleaning lady with a carpet sweeper. We also watched as she went to her closet several hundred feet down the aisle way and pulled out a bucket and mop. With far less urgency than the rushing passengers, she began pushing the bucket our direction. Fortunately for the kids but not the unsuspecting lady, a large crowd of passengers temporarily obstructed her view of the reported deposit. During that few seconds, one student dashed to the aisle, picked up the brown mass and returned to his seat. The camera continued to roll as the lady and her bucket arrived on the scene – to find nothing. Apathetic and expressionless, she maneuvered the metal water bucket and its mop through the crowd, searching for the alleged soiled carpet. Finally assured that no such feces existed, she slowly headed back to her closet, pushed her mop and bucket back to their spot and went on with her carpet sweeping.

The poop pile returned to the aisle. The fun and photojournalism continued. About 30 minutes before our flight was due to leave, an elderly gentleman stood up from a chair in our section. He had been sitting among us for at least an hour. With a stern look, he walked toward the group of boys – Shawn, Vern and Colin. *Oops,* I thought while watching him stop and lean over them with the same foreboding expression, *big trouble loomed ahead.*

"I have to tell you kids that my life has not been very happy lately. I've dealt with deaths in the family and health problems over the last two years," he began. "In fact, I've been downright depressed. But I've enjoyed the last hour more than anything I can remember for a long time. You kids are a riot, and I want to thank you for brightening up my life and inspiring me to laugh again." By that time, the rest of us had gathered round the boys, worried that the gentleman was upset. Our fears quickly dissipated as he proceeded to shake the hand of every member of our group, thanking us once more as he headed off to his plane bound for Twin Falls, Idaho.

The final incident came a few minutes later when the flight crew for our jet rose from their seats in unison and headed toward the gate. As they passed by, a female attendant, appearing totally disgusted, walked directly to one of the boys, snatched the fake poop from his hands and took it with her through the gate.

"Uh-oh," I said, "I hope we don't have to deal with her." We boarded the plane, and there she stood, waiting and eyeing us with great concentration. As one of the first students walked by her, she held up the poop.

"Here, you can have it back," she said, handing it over with a smile. "I was planning to put it on one of your food trays but thought twice and decided that might not be a good idea."

We knew that with this witty lady, we had definitely met our match.

Teaching Memory No. 4: Husqvarna Hero: When Billy Mueller showed up in my fifth-period sophomore English class in 1998, he was a bit rough around the edges but likeable. I doubt that a day went by when he didn't greet me at my desk and ask, always politely, if he could go to the bathroom. This request was not uncommon for kids during that time because my classroom was in "the portables." If students happened to have a class as the south end of the main school followed by one in the portables, they knew they had better hoof it or risk being late. Some were better organized than others; some probably had bigger bladders. Billy obviously didn't fit in either category.

Actually, Billy didn't really fit into any distinct mold. He walked with a bit of a swagger. With his physique and general toughness, he could have been an outstanding athlete, but he preferred firing up his Husqvarna chain saw in the woods or putting the pedal to the metal behind the wheel of a 4-by-4 Ford pickup along muddy back roads. His academic ability lacked any hint of early nurturing. To put it kindly, Billy struggled, due to a lack of established study habits. His natural charm conflicted with his boyish dirty mind. Occasionally, I would have to remind him to refrain from wrapping his arm around me when he had come up to the desk. One day I also had to speak to him after the girl who sat behind him complained about what Billy had drawn on her spelling test when the class exchanged papers. Walking back to the desk to check out her complaint, I agreed with her that his pencil drawing of a bull elk with large antlers mounting a cow elk was inappropriate classroom art – especially in English class.

During his junior year, Billy got into some big-time trouble. He shoved a kid into a window, which shattered when the young man's head smashed into it. The disagreement focused on words exchanged because the other boy wore a black trench coat. Kids ran in their cliques and had a hard time respecting members of other groups. Feelings about the students' black trench coats or the Goths with their black capes were running bitter at the time because of symbolism associated with school shootings, such as Columbine in Colorado and Moses Lake in Washington, where the shooters wore long coats to cover up their weapons. Therefore, conflicts arose. In this case, it was physical, and Billy picked the wrong place and the wrong situation. The shattered window belonged to the vice principal's office. The incident received school-wide and regional media coverage. It also further polarized the student groups from which each young man came.

The incident resulted in Billy being expelled from school for the rest of the year. He appealed the expulsion and sought help from teachers to be reinstated. I was one of those teachers. I also had the other student in my class. Here was a case where I really liked both students, even though they represented opposite ends of the social spectrum. I also believed firmly in students accepting responsibility for their actions.

I could not, with a clear conscience, appeal on Billy's behalf. I did write a letter, however, stating that I would be more than happy to go to bat for him once he fulfilled the punishment that had resulted from his indiscretion. The letter also stressed that I believed in this young man despite his mistake. That belief was reinforced as I watched how

Billy faced up to the situation. He remained out of school and re-enrolled the following fall, having grown up considerably but still walking to his own beat.

I taught juniors that year, so once again he sat in my class while repeating the time he had lost from the expulsion. That year we worked on a project for the local history book that would be released in 2000. Billy chose to write about his great-grandfather, Jack Stevens, who had fought on Omaha Beach during World War II. His admiration for his family's beloved patriarch was clear. Class discussions often included stories about Mr. Stevens, who had also worked in the woods of the Pacific Northwest both before and after the war.

We were putting together preliminary drafts of the students' biographies for the history book when the annual Veterans Day assembly planning began. Having read and heard some of Billy's stories by then, I approached our assistant principal, Pat Valliant. When Pat came to our school, he brought with him the format for one of the most impressive Veterans programs I had ever seen – complete with a stirring slide show, patriotic songs, a haunting solo of Taps and speeches. The program included student group participation, guest speakers and special seating for the area veterans. Hardly a soul ever left Pat's assemblies without feeling moved to shed a tear. Students behaved. At times, absolute and respectful silence filled the gym occupied by more than 1,200 students and adults. The program was definitely one of highlights of the school year.

I suggested that Pat talk to Billy and encourage him to say a few words about his great-grandfather at the assembly. I told him about the fight and the expulsion and Billy's willingness to accept responsibility. His participation in the assembly might provide a great opportunity for this young man, whose public image had taken a hit. He could redeem himself in front of his peers, the public and the adults who had been involved with the disciplinary action. Pat agreed.

As Billy stepped into the spotlight, held the microphone and delivered his personal tribute to his great-grandfather, my heart pounded with pride for this rough-and-tough teen who had overcome a bad situation, taken his licks and moved forward to better himself rather than giving up. At that moment, Jack Stevens was his hero, and Billy Mueller was mine.

Teaching Memory No. 3: Naughty Dogs: We were dealing with principal parts of irregular verbs on morning when a rather irregular action not mentioned in the "How to" books for teachers occurred outside my classroom window.

Students in first-period sophomore English had been given an assignment to find the principal parts to approximately 50 verbs. In preparation for an upcoming test, I was drilling the class on troublesome verbs, such as "lie" and "lay," "rise" and "raise." While calling on several students to list off the present, past, past participle and present participles, I was becoming more aware of some mildly distracting movement and muffled giggles in the back corner of the room near the window. At first, I ignored these indiscretions, hoping they would just stop. I moved on to the next verb. The disturbance continued. I wished those boys back there would knock it off and pay attention. I called on a student to give me the principal parts of "do," but the giggling increased to such a level that I could no longer ignore it.

I shot a glance back at the two boys who were obviously concentrating on something outside the window rather than their verb's principal parts, then turned my head to see what had seized their attention. To say my concentration on the distraction was fleeting is an understatement. I swiveled my face back toward the students so quickly that I almost incurred whiplash.

Two nondescript dogs were engaging in consensual relations on the lawn right outside Room 4. Definitely an action-verb moment!

Watching my expression, the rest of the students, who *had* been paying attention, turned their heads, in perfect unison, toward the window. The entire classroom exploded into laughter.

I charged out the door.

Running down the hallway to the faculty room I flung open the door, raced in and spotted our principal, Mr. Sodorff, leaning against the wall, chatting with the staff members who had first-hour prep.

"I've got one for you," I abruptly interjected. "They *never* provided any advice on this problem in our education-methods classes at the University of Idaho. What do you do when two dogs are 'doing it' outside your classroom window?"

He stood silent for a moment, broke into a big grin and suggested a classic solution.

"Herd 'em down to the biology room," he said.

By the time I returned to the classroom, the dogs were gone, but the kids were still laughing. And 20 years later, at the Class of 1980 reunion, Jeff Sweeney, one of the two boys in the corner, was still laughing.

Teaching Memory No. 2: Nez Perce Reunion: Everyone oohed and ahhed as we looked at the tiny bundle that Linda cradled in her arms. We stood in the narrow aisle at Ross Rexall Drug Store on First and Cedar in Sandpoint. Linda and Bob had just adopted Sarah, their first child, when she was a mere two months old. A Nez Perce Indian infant from the tribe of the great Chief Joseph, Sarah was a beautiful baby with her dark skin and black hair. That was my first meeting with Sarah.

Years later, I would see her occasionally with family or friends at horse shows. Since Linda and I had been friends since my college days in the late '60s while I worked at the Schweitzer Mountain Resort ticket office, I was sure Sarah felt at home around me. She never talked much, so when I spotted her name on my sophomore honors class list one fall, I resolved to make it my special project to help her overcome her shyness.

During that year, I learned that a very bright, witty personality was hiding inside that fragile frame. Her clever perspective often came out in cartoons scrawled in her journals. Impressed with her writing skills and wanting to play a part in unveiling the talent within Sarah, I suggested that she sign up for journalism the next year. She did. As she did with every other pursuit on her high school docket, she quietly developed into a reliable, dedicated and talented high school journalist. With little fanfare, Sarah consistently demonstrated her instincts for the right questions to ask and the best details to include in every story assignment. In short, she developed quickly into an outstanding nuts-and-bolts reporter/writer. During her senior year, she served as assistant editor for our award-winning newspaper.

Sarah also participated in the school cross-country program for four years. Again, in every single meet during those four years, she remained consistent – always last. But, being last and never giving up – ever – and never complaining – ever – told a lot about Sarah's character. She served as a shining example to all who knew and loved her. She did struggle, however, as one of the few Native Americans in our school. I remember once having a conversation with her that revealed an ugly truth and nearly broke my heart.

"People treat me one of two ways," she said. "They either pretend I don't exist, or they act like they're too nervous to talk to me." Sarah's friends and family were certainly not among this group, but she felt that everyone else with whom she came in contact seemed to treat her almost as if she had a contagious disease. Indeed, it had to be a very difficult issue for a teen to deal with. Nonetheless, Sarah's friends helped form an invisible but protective ring around her. She always could count on their support, and she knew that.

After graduation, Sarah left for Linfield College in Oregon. In order to be eligible for minority scholarships, she had to register as a member of the tribe. Throughout her life, Sarah's parents knew the day would come when she would want to meet her birth family. They were aware that her birth mom worked at the tribal headquarters and took pains to see that no chance meetings took place until the time was right. The right time in Sarah's mind came when she was almost 25. She had earned a degree in biology and was working at area fisheries.

We got together for lunch one beautiful autumn day on the deck overlooking Lake Pend Oreille at the Beach House Restaurant in Sandpoint. When small talk had ended, Sarah uncharacteristically initiated a new topic. She asked me for a favor that would turn out to be one of the greatest honors of my life. One of her goals before reaching 25 was to meet her birth mother.

"I wondered if you would act as liaison," she said after explaining her intentions. From earlier visits, Sarah knew that I had already expressed a keen interest in being included in this event. I doubt, however, that she ever realized the magnitude of how thrilled I was to play such a crucial role in making it happen. This meeting would be a monumental moment in her life, and for me to be asked to witness it and actually help make the meeting happen was a special honor.

I had attended many weddings and, sadly, even helped plan funerals. One of my students went into labor in my English classroom, and I was later privileged to be among the first to see her baby boy. Taking my son with me to attend the West Point graduation of 1991 SHS grad, Jim Patton, was a special experience for a teacher. The Whitman graduation surprise honor with Angela Warren was more than special. A long day spent enjoying Los Angeles hot spots like Disneyland, Hollywood and the Comedy Store with three good friends and SHS graduates, Steve Neuder, Jeralyn Lewis and Mitzi Hawkins, had seemed like the ultimate reward at the time.

There have been many other memories. Three other local teachers and I will never forget being invited to the Giveaway Party when soccer standout Chase Mikklesen graduated from high school. When an individual like Chase reaches a transitional milestone, the custom of his Gros Ventre family calls for throwing a big party, complete with his mother Jeannie's fresh fry bread. In this case, the special guests who contributed significantly along Chase's pathway were honored with gifts of Native American crafted star quilts, sweet-grass braids and handmade earrings. I was so touched and speechless by Chase's gesture that I gave him my coveted teaching pin, a small brass apple with a red stone in the middle.

Like Chase, Sarah was facing a significant milestone. My humble words cannot express the thrill of seeing this young lady, who had grown up in a happy, comfortable home with wonderful parents and two younger siblings, cross the bridge from her white existence – which had included a Lutheran background and a lifelong involvement in the sport of skiing – and begin the journey into her own Native American heritage. She had already learned about her Nez Perce family through the books and information her parents had gathered over the years. She attended her first powwow as a young adult when our mutual friend, Betty Fredricksen, a teacher and Chippewa Indian herself, asked her to accompany us to an annual Northwest Indian gathering on the banks of the Spokane River. So, when Sarah and I parted company after that fall lunch date, she loosely organized a plan leading up to the rendezvous. The first step would be to write a letter to her birth mother, Bennie. After that contact, we would address more specific details for the meeting. The process took most of the winter, part of the delay because several of Sarah's drafts ended up in the wastebasket. Finally, after assembling what she thought were the right words, Sarah next had to bring herself to mail the letter.

Eventually, one day in February, I received a letter from Bennie, who had wasted no time contacting me after receiving Sarah's letter. At the time, Sarah was working for the Nez Perce Tribal Hatchery near McCall in southern Idaho. It took awhile for us to coordinate a date when both of us could to drive to Lewiston. That finally occurred in mid-April – the 15th to be exact. During the interim, Bennie wrote me several letters, telling me how excited she and Sarah's siblings were about the upcoming meeting. She also told me that one of the famous tribal elders, Horace Axtell, author of "A Little Bit of Wisdom," was Sarah's great-uncle and that the legendary Chief Joseph was the brother of her great-grandfather, the Nez Perce warrior Olecott. Each time I received a letter, I relayed its contents to both Sarah and Linda. The revelations all contributed to the excitement of this long-awaited meeting.

When April 15 came, Linda and Bob chose to stay in Sandpoint. I met Sarah at their house early that morning for the four-hour drive to Lewiston, and Linda handed me their cell phone, requesting that I call with all news. She would be doing projects around the house, eagerly listening for the phone to ring. Bob would be at their downtown store, the Alpine Shop, but never too far from a phone. Sarah drove her bright red Jeep convertible. We began in darkness, but by the time we reached the rolling grain fields of the Palouse south of Coeur d'Alene, the sun began casting its rays on the hillsides, suggesting a beautiful day ahead.

The trip went fairly quickly as we chatted all along the way. Shortly before 9 a.m., we reached the top of the gently winding 8-mile hill overlooking the twin cities of Lewiston, Idaho, and Clarkston, Washington, where the Clearwater and the Snake Rivers meet to form a passageway toward the Columbia and on to the ocean. I could not help but think of the history of this area Lewis and Clark had passed through nearly 200 years earlier, finding comfort and aid through their relationship with the Nez Perce, who inhabited what is now Idaho, southeastern Washington and northeastern Oregon. Such a big story in Northwest history, and today would signal the unfolding of such a huge story in the life of one of the tribe's descendants.

The Helm Restaurant, where Bill and I had dined on our wedding night back in the '70s, served as the meeting place. We expected to meet Bennie between 9 and 9:30 a.m. As we got closer to the restaurant, my sensitive stomach went into action. In between several restroom visits for me, Sarah and I sat in the booth, drinking water, watching the door – and waiting. Outwardly, she remained characteristically calm. I, on the other hand, turned into a hopeless nervous wreck as I thought of all the times the young lady across the table from me had suffered the turmoil of feeling like an outsider. In spite of her fiercely protective family and friends, Sarah had experienced situations of cruel rejection, sometimes unwittingly but painful nonetheless. As the minutes ticked by, I prayed that this would not happen again on this morning. Still no Bennie. As 9:30 turned into 9:35, then 9:40, and the waitress kept coming to see if we wanted to order breakfast, a feeling of dread consumed me, but I made every attempt to maintain a positive outlook.

Finally, I spotted a small Native American woman with long, flowing hair accompanied by a young Indian man. A young white woman, holding a little boy with big brown eyes and tiny braids in his hair, walked with them into the restaurant. I jumped from the booth and walked over to greet them. Holding two photo albums, the older woman greeted me calmly as we walked toward the booth where her 24-year-old daughter, whom she had last seen as a newborn, sat. The meeting was surprisingly quiet and unemotional. Bennie looked at Sarah. Sarah looked at her. Bennie introduced Sarah to her son Dennis – Sarah's biological brother. Bennie also introduced Natalie, her daughter-in-law who was married to another one of her sons, and Natalie's child, who was nicknamed Booger.

Sarah and Bennie sat side by side. Bennie immediately began to show family pictures from the album. Dennis, Natalie and Booger squeezed into the booth next to me. Booger wiggled like a typical 3-year-old as Dennis and Natalie sat silently, watching the mother-and-daughter pair get acquainted across the table. With each page of the album, Bennie would point to individual pictures, quietly naming each person and explaining how they were related to Sarah. I watched Dennis' expressions and wondered what must going through his mind as he kept a close eye on this new-found sister.

Soon, our group grew, as another member of the family, Bennie's sister Alfreda, arrived. While she greeted Sarah with a healthy hug, tears rolled down her face. I asked the waitress if we could move somewhere more private. Once she obliged and had us seated at a big table in the back, I excused myself, then went to the bathroom and called Linda to report that the reunion of mother, daughter, sibling and aunt had begun. Linda eagerly listened to my every word. Other Nez Perce family members joined us for breakfast. The group talked quietly as little Booger kept up a lively show of his own.

When breakfast ended, I took a few pictures, and we said good-byes to some of the group in the parking lot and prepared to follow Bennie to Lapwai where she lived. The plan was to stop first for a few minutes at the Nez Perce National Museum at Spalding about 4 miles from Lewiston.

The time spent at the museum turned out to be most poignant part of the day. We entered a dimly lit room of huge, lighted displays with benches along the walkway. As soothing Indian flute music wafted through the room, we each sat on a separate bench while Bennie told stories of her childhood. We learned that she had been shipped off to a boarding school in Oklahoma and that her mother had died fairly young, leaving older siblings to care for younger ones. She had been raised Presbyterian. In her adult life, she had also suffered from painful arthritis, clearly evident in the fingers on both hands. The condition was corrected by surgery a few months after our visit with her. As Bennie told her story, I watched half a dozen other museum visitors who had no idea of the significance of this scene as they strolled past us, studying the individual displays.

If only they knew, I thought, *what is occurring here – at this very moment – a descendant of the Chief Joseph family coming from another culture, meeting her mother for the first time and learning through this conversation the challenges of growing up as a modern-day Nez Perce on the reservation.*

We spent most of that Saturday with Bennie, visiting one of the stately white homes where cavalry officers had lived in the mid-1800s and then went to Bennie's house to look at more family pictures. Later, we joined other cousins and visited over hamburgers at Donald's, a local roadside restaurant. We also visited the facility in Lapwai where dozens of the Nez Perce breed of colorful Appaloosa horses are stabled. As often as the opportunity presented itself, I kept my distance so that Sarah and her mother could have their private moments of sharing. During these times, I would call Linda and provide updates.

About 3:30 p.m., we said good-bye. Both women assured each other that this was just the beginning. There would, indeed, be many visits ahead as Sarah drove Highway 95 between Sandpoint and Yellow Pine during extended weekends from her job of keeping track of the salmon hatch. As we climbed into the jeep and left Lapwai, I counted up four rolls of film and suggested we get them developed at the Lewiston Wal-Mart before returning to Sandpoint.

While waiting for the pictures, we topped off the day with what would turn out to be another emotional visit. I called the Crocketts who had lived on Lake Street in Sandpoint during my entire childhood. Helen had accompanied my mother to the hospital the night I was born. From that day forth, she took a special interest in my life and had seemed like a second mother to me. Helen's health had been steadily declining for the past few years. When we arrived at the house, I knew on first glance that she would not be alive much longer. In fact, she died about two weeks later, so our spur-of-the-moment visit had both special meaning and irony. I had accompanied Sarah to see her birth mother for the first time; Helen had accompanied my mother when a first daughter was born. This would be the first of many visits between Sarah and her mother; this would be my last visit with my mother's best friend. After taking a few pictures of

Helen and her family members, Sarah and I said good-bye and headed off to Wal-Mart to pick up the pictures and a small photo album for preserving memories. When we arrived at the Aavedal residence four hours later, Bob and Linda met us at the door and invited me for fresh-made pie and coffee. As we sat around the table, thumbing through the black velvet photo album and recounting the day's highlights, I watched as Bob, quietly listening to every word, teared up at the obvious joy this day brought to his daughter. On that day, Sarah had gained extra dividends in her life – two families that loved her and two cultures to enrich her.

Since April 15, 2000, Bennie and I have kept in touch through e-mail and Christmas cards. When Sarah's Aunt Alfreda died, Bennie sent me the memorial program. Sarah attended a few Nez Perce family events and made occasional stops in Lapwai on her way to and from Yellow Pine until she took a new job at a fishery in Alaska. One sunny, autumn afternoon following that first meeting, Sarah and Linda showed up at my house with a big, beautifully wrapped package. Once inside, Linda announced, "Here's a little something Sarah and I wanted you to have. Open it."

I carefully opened the box. Inside was a huge quilt crafted in warm fall colors and adorned with images of running horses, fish and faces of Indian children. Embroidered on its back side were the words:

A friend is a person with whom you dare to be yourself
–Frank Crane

"Seasons of Life"
For a good friend,
Marianne Love

Thanks for everything
Made by
Linda and Sarah Aavedal

Teaching Memory No. 1: Supreme Lesson: It was a Thursday, two days before Christmas vacation started in 1984. We had experienced a wintry week with temperatures going below zero, roadways posing hazards because of solid ice surfaces, and snow blowing in from the north. Bill had gone to Louisiana. His father had died the previous weekend and had been buried in Oakdale the day before. On this December 20, I had taken my time picking up the kids from Patti Howell's Day Care center. After all, we had an abbreviated class schedule the next day, so I could afford some extra time to go to the post office and mail cards. While there, I even enjoyed the luxury of yakking with Pam Parks, one of my colleagues. Stopping at Patti's, I chatted with my kids' babysitters, Bernetta Young and Carol Blessington, before summoning Willie and Annie to load up in the pickup, which I had driven that day because of the scary roads. We headed north on Boyer and broke into a lively chorus of "Jingle Bells." Turning on to Baldy Road, we continued our merriment.

Days before vacations – especially those of the two-week variety – always brought on a sense of euphoria for me as I thought about the good times ahead. Once the Christmas craziness ended and company had headed home, we could enjoy the silence of winter and a temporary break from the down-to-the-minute time management of school. There would be lots of lazy hours, lying on the couch watching TV. I also looked forward to cross-country skiing and pulling the kids on their sleds around the fields, quiet afternoons reading – definitely a time to savor. Bill would be home soon from Louisiana. All would be well for the Love family within the next couple of days.

While these festive thoughts resounded through my mind, our voices continued to celebrate "one-horse open sleigh." Suddenly, I caught a glimpse of something unusual off to the north, toward Greenhorn Mountain. A dramatic, orange conflagration reached skyward, lighting up the night sky. In front of the giant flame, I could see the silhouette of our majestic, classic red barn. Within an instant, joy turned to horror. Our house was burning up across the open fields less than a mile away. The driving route at that moment stretched a bit farther. We would have to continue down Baldy for half a mile, turn off on Great Northern Road and proceed another three-quarters of a mile to our driveway. We all instantly began to shriek, sob or wail, as I composed myself enough to control the pickup from sliding off the icy road. The remaining drive home lasted seemingly forever as we finally turned north.

I have no clear memory of the next few minutes – just fragmented images of myself screaming hysterically while standing before the giant flames as they shot into the night air. Neighbors like Pat Gooby and Eddie Nordgaarden tried to comfort me. Fire trucks with flashing red lights and wild sirens maneuvered their way from out of the darkness up the snowed-in driveway. I do remember a sheriff's deputy interviewing me, asking my name – did I know how the fire started? I knew nothing at that moment. All I had to offer anyone was uncontrollable emotion.

In seconds, I realized that our possessions amounted to the clothes we had worn that day, a sweater left in the back seat of the station wagon, and ironically, a freezer full of meat miraculously lugged outside by adrenaline-filled neighbors from inside the laundry room. In the light of the next day, we would discover another item ironically rescued from that room just off the kitchen – a lone, green plastic bag filled with garbage.

As the minutes passed, my family members – my dad, my mother and my siblings came down the driveway. All had spotted the flames at almost the same moment from different locations in the neighborhood. Seeing my condition, Mother immediately insisted that we go with her to the family home about a mile away. Annie, then just six years old, stood just a few feet away from us, but we could not find Willie. We frantically looked among the crowd of people and still no sign. As I walked over to our Ford Escort station wagon, parked near the huge willow tree, thinking he might be sitting inside, my eyes were drawn upward toward the expansive tree trunk. The kids played in a partially completed tree house, calling it their apartment. That's where Willie was crouched with an expression reflecting the horror of the moment – his huge, fearful brown eyes transfixed on the leaping flames that cast an orange tint on his face. He was silent, but his statue-like pose spoke far more eloquently of the depth of this catastrophe than any words I was able to speak.

In less than one week's time, Bill had lost his father, and we had lost our home. We faced a daunting situation, especially five days before Christmas. A lifetime's worth of philosophical sayings would be uttered or would drift through my mind over the next few days. This event would demonstrate their truth firsthand in so many ways. Material possessions are fleeting, but life is precious. Possessions can be replaced, but lives cannot.

After convincing Willie to come down from his perch in that giant willow, we accompanied Mother to her house. In the kitchen, my sister Barbara had been tutoring Rod Berget, also one of my students. His mother, Judy, another teacher, had come to pick him up. She teamed up with Mother to try to calm me down as I, still blubbering like a baby, headed to the telephone to call Bill in Louisiana. The two women immediately urged me to calm down before making the call. Knowing that words would not quite do the trick, my mother held out a small bottle of whiskey, a souvenir from an airline flight she had taken to Spain that summer. Judy held a glass.

"Drink this; it will help you," Mother announced.

"No," I said. "I'll be all right."

"No, Marianne, this will help calm you down," she insisted.

"I'm *not* going to drink it," I shot back just as Mother began pouring the whiskey into the glass in Judy's hand. It was obvious these two women were on a mission. In that split second, however, the "calmers" stood over the "calmee" and accidentally proceeded to pour the entire bottle of hooch into my crotch.

Although I did not imbibe a drop, the whiskey did jerk me to my senses. If ever there were a need for comic relief, this was it. I had to laugh. Looking down at my Jim Beam-soaked khaki slacks, I reacted calmly as the two women who hovered over me immediately broke into apologetic laughter.

"Thank you so much! The only clothes I own in the world are the ones on my body," I announced, taking great pains to enunciate each and every word. "And now you've spilled whiskey all over my crotch!" The incident served as a turning point. Humor does help in the depths of despair.

The momentary levity put me back on course for the obstacles that would lie ahead. I called Bill, who had ironically been having dinner with the Oakdale, Louisiana, fire chief. His location 2,500 miles away spared him the horror that all of us in Idaho had just witnessed. It was shocking, yes, but in his usual fashion, he remained calm, knowing that he would have to concentrate on a pretty big obstacle of his own – getting home earlier than planned in the midst of hectic Christmas airline traffic. We had a lot on our plate that night, but we would soon learn that we also had a lot of guardian angels looking over us.

As soon as I hung up, Mother's phone started ringing. It rang steadily that night. In every case, the caller had heard about the fire and wanted to offer help – a temporary home, clothes, money, food. The gestures seemed endless and continued the next day when cars started streaming into Mother's driveway with bundles and baskets with envelopes, containing cash or checks. A student in my first-period class, Robbie Hubbard, brought a plate of cookies, a hug and a simple "I'm sorry for your loss."

School lasted until noon, and soon thereafter, my sister Barbara came home from the high school where she also taught. She carried her books and a heavy cloth bag, which she set in the middle of the kitchen table. We all stood, wondering what it was for a second. Then she explained.

"This is from the high school staff and students," she said. "There's over $1,000 cash in that bag. They collected it this morning. You are also to go to the counseling office at the school when you have time to pick up the other items." A later trip to the school revealed a huge room filled with dozens of piles of items stacked to the ceiling, all brought to school by students and colleagues that morning. Overcome with the magnitude of such widespread generosity, I broke into tears after Barbara finished telling me about the efforts that had transpired overnight and during the morning hours at school.

"How can I ever repay all these people?" I asked, feeling overwhelmed. "There's no way possible."

"You have a gift," my mother suggested. "You have the gift of writing. You can write something for the paper, and they'll know that you appreciate what they've done."

Later that day, my brother Jim and I drove into Spokane to pick up Bill, only to learn that his flight had been delayed until the next morning. After a few hours sleep, I sat in the motel restaurant with a yellow legal pad and penned my thoughts, which later appeared in the local paper.

The fire and its aftermath involved a tapestry of giving, caring people representing every age and every interest in our community. It changed my outlook forever. I couldn't repay each person individually, but since that time, I've followed the simple suggestion of one of my favorite folk hymns "Pass It On."

For several years afterward, whenever it came time for the school-wide food/toy drive, I looked forward to galvanizing my students into action by telling my Christmas story of 1984 when our family became recipients of that very drive. I told them about the sack of money gathered in less than three hours, the room filled with boxes, the dozens of visitors to my parents' driveway. "You never know when a split-second incident can put you on the receiving end," I said. "And when you are, I know from experience that you're overwhelmed with gratitude for living in such a caring community."

After telling the story, I would challenge them to do their best and to have a good time attempting to unseat the "master of all food-drive organizers," my colleague, Rick Gehring, who taught math at Sandpoint High School. Every year a plaque went to the classroom that topped the charts for items collected. We always exchanged friendly banter between our classes to inspire enthusiasm. Although always competitive, we never did win first place because Rick, never showing his hand until the last day, had calculated a foolproof strategy for getting his troops to comb the town for donations. I believe his homeroom held an undefeated record for more than a decade – regardless of what method was used to determine who was the best. One year my students chose not to compete in the drive.

"Let's pick just one family and put together something really special for them," Christine Bauer, then a senior, suggested to her fellow photography students. So, we followed her lead and gathered money, food and clothing. We also extended our fun by meeting at my house one Saturday and baking Christmas goodies. The satisfied pride among those students when their collection was ready to be delivered rivaled the thrill experienced by athletic teams capturing the state championship. Whether they won or lost the annual food drive title, each year wonderful stories emerged about students sacrificing for others as homeroom classes gathered thousands of pounds of food and welcomed items for families in need.

Because of these annual holiday food drives and thanks to one life-changing catastrophe, I learned the ultimate "Lesson with Love."

17.

Epilogue

I finished the manuscript for this book at 6:16 a.m. on January 9, 2005. Three hours later, I maneuvered my way down our drifting driveway en-route to Spokane Airport for a flight to Boise. This trip would reunite me with a former student whom I hadn't seen in 10 years. Her name is Sue Self Scully. A few weeks earlier, Sue had sent me the following e-mail.

Hello,

It is great to hear from you! Actually we must be telepathic as I have been thinking about you.

I wonder what you are going to be doing on Monday, January 10 as I would like to invite you to a luncheon in Boise. I am going to receive an award from the Idaho Association of School Administrators for Outstanding Idaho Assistant Principal of the Year – how about that!

We were told we could invite a special person and/or educator who influenced our lives, and, of course I instantly thought of you! I would be glad to pay for your hotel room at the Double Tree on Sunday night. I understand that that time of year and weather conditions could make things difficult, but if you could swing it, I would love to have you there. The luncheon is part of our annual Idaho School Administrator's conference.

Last year we were supposed to fill out a card about our most influential teacher, and I took a picture out of your book and put it on the card and posted it. Your ears were probably ringing. I have to go now.

Could I have your phone number so I can call you later? I will e-mail or call you soon.

I gladly accepted her invitation, adding that even if I had to crawl, I would be there. The wrath of a North Idaho winter threatened my trip. Driving the trusty, old Ford tractor, though, Bill cleared the blowing, growing drifts from the driveway, allowing me a straight shot to the road. I figured that once I reached the highway and headed south, the wind and snow would settle down. Not so. Usually a speed demon, that morning I seldom surpassed 50 mph until I reached Interstate 90 near Post Falls. The remainder of the drive was fairly smooth sailing until I started up the hill to the airport. I tapped the button signaling the Jimmy to go back into 4-wheel drive and again slowed down to 45 mph.

There was no hurry, though. The bad weather had caused my first flight to Seattle to be delayed an hour. That unplanned wait gave me time to sit and reflect about what a monumental and meaningful gesture Sue's invitation had been for me. I could also think about that day nearly 30 years earlier when she and I had walked down the streets of Wenatchee, Washington, after the town's annual Apple Blossom Festival Parade. It was the first time our Ponderettes Drill Team had ever marched in the parade during my advisership. Sue's leadership contributed a major part toward our participation. For three years, I had been very impressed with her as a pint-sized, natural leader whose influence was giant among her peers; therefore, I was saddened when I heard through the grapevine that, in spite of her academic success and leadership, she might not go on to college. So, seizing this few minutes of our visit while we headed back to the bus, I shared with Sue my thoughts about her potential, strongly encouraging her to continue on to college and to become a teacher.

She took my advice. I could not help but smile with satisfaction while waiting for my flight. What a coincidence to finish my memoirs of my 33-year teaching career on the same day I would be honoring a student whom I had encouraged to become an educator. The timing seemed appropriate.

I will forever cherish the short time I spent in Boise reconnecting with Sue and watching her accept the huge plaque in front of 250 professional educators, including Idaho State Superintendent of Public Instruction, Dr. Marilyn Howard. The experience reinforced another of my oft repeated "Lessons with Love": Often, teachers may never know how a few seconds of their time spent with a student will lead to a life-altering, positive and lasting difference for that individual.

Because of Sue's belief in thanking the people who helped her along the way, I am fortunate to know that one isolated conversation along a sidewalk in Wenatchee many years ago made all the difference.

For that, I am grateful.

I have been fortunate to experience other situations where students have extended their appreciation for time spent with them. Whether it's been an enthusiastic wave along a country road, a package of Vermont moose seeds, a personalized parody of a speech memorized in sophomore English, a certificate of appreciation from the University of Chicago – each gesture has conveyed a student's gratitude. But, I am the one who feels most grateful for all these students who have contributed to my life.

I thank God for giving me the gift of teaching.

About the Author

The author of three books and a retired high school teacher, Marianne Love wouldn't have lasted long in North Idaho if she didn't have a sense of humor.

Her 33-year teaching career began in 1969 and lasted until retirement in 2002, all at her alma mater, Sandpoint High School, in the rural community where she was born in 1947 and still lives. She taught English and journalism, as well as performed stints advising the student council, newspaper, yearbook and drill team, among others.

Though she remained in her hometown to teach young people, Love says she feels fortunate to have hundreds of students who have provided her a "window to the world." Her greatest joy is keeping in touch with former students and trumpeting their life journeys through her writing.

Her work with high school journalists earned regional acclaim and the Dow Jones Newspaper Fund's national award as "Special Recognized High School Journalism Teacher," among other honors. In 2004, she was inducted into the Sandpoint High School Academic Teaching Hall of Fame.

A graduate of the University of Idaho, Love has written for many newspapers and magazines regionally and nationally. Her work currently appears regularly in the *Appaloosa Journal*, *Spokesman-Review*, *The River Journal* and *Sandpoint Magazine*. Her first two books, "Pocket Girdles" and "Postcards from Potato(e) Land," humorous memoirs from her childhood in Sandpoint, have been through multiple printings. She also maintains a Web site at www.mariannelove.com and a daily blog at www.slightdetour.blogspot.com.

A local horse show announcer, emcee, horse fanatic and dog owner, Love lives with her patient husband, Bill, and a menagerie of resident and visiting critters at the "Lovestead" north of Sandpoint. Their son, William, and his wife, Deborah, live in Boise, Idaho, while their daughter, Annie, resides in Seattle.

Photo by "Just Joe" Gere, SHS '92

Author Marianne Love appears with former students Jeff "JT" Bock (SHS '92) and Jenny Jacobson Meyer (SHS '92) at the showing of "Jenny's Journal" in 2006 at the Panida Theater in Sandpoint, Idaho. The trio collaborated for three years on the award-winning documentary chronicling Jenny's inspirational battle with inflammatory breast cancer.

Pocket Girdles

And Other Confessions of a Northwest Farm Girl
Pocket Girdles is Marianne Love's first book, a collection of
laugh-out-loud autobiographical stories that captures the
phenomenon of growing up in rural Idaho in the 1950s
and early '60s – a peek into a different era that anyone
who grew up in the country will recognize.
214 pages • $9.95

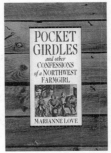

Postcards from Potato(e)Land

The portrait of life begun in *Pocket Girdles* gains more
brushstrokes in this second collection of autobiographical
stories by Marianne Love, as she deftly captures the humor
in ordinary events and the richness of everyday life in
Sandpoint, Idaho. If you can't be living in a small town –
or, if you can – *Postcards* will make you feel at home, complete with a grin on your face.
194 pages • $11.95

All three of Marianne Love's books, including *Lessons with Love*, are available
at bookstores, by phone at 1-800-880-3573, or online from Marianne's
hometown, at:

www.SandpointGeneralStore.com